ROMMEL'S INTELLIGENCE IN THE DESERT CAMPAIGN

ROMMEL'S INTELLIGENCE
IN THE
DESERT CAMPAIGN
1941-1943

HANS-OTTO BEHRENDT

WILLIAM KIMBER · LONDON

First published in Britain in 1985 by
WILLIAM KIMBER & CO. LIMITED
100 Jermyn Street, London, SW1Y 6EE

© Rombach & Co GmbH, 1980
© English translation, Hans-Otto Behrendt, 1985
ISBN 0-7183-0515-9

This book was first published in Germany
in 1980 by Rombach & Co GmbH, Druck
und Verlagshaus, Freiburg im Breisgau.

Typeset by Tellgate Ltd., London WC1
and printed and bound in Great Britain by
The Garden City Press Limited,
Letchworth, Hertfordshire, SG6 1JS

Contents

List of Illustrations

The author and publishers would like to thank
Mr David Irving for his help in supplying photographs
for inclusion in this book.

List of Maps

A key to the symbols used will be found on page 236

Foreword
by
Colonel (GS) Othmar Hackl, Ph.D.,
Chief, Research Office of Military History,
West Germany

The author of this book was for exactly two years – from the spring of 1941 until 1943 – an intelligence officer in the German Afrika Korps and the higher commands to which it gave birth – first as lieutenant, then as captain and assistant staff officer (G-3) and for a short period G-2 (Intelligence). He writes as an authority, somebody who not only acquired military experience and the knowledge arising from that experience, but also somebody thoroughly familiar with the theatre of operations about which is is writing.

His military career furnished him with an insight into the peculiarities of intelligence operations during the African campaign. Thus his narrative provides valuable information about signals intelligence (now known as Sigint), a subject which has recently aroused particular interest, as well as touching upon other aspects of intelligence. While the author has made a close study of the surviving records, and these have enabled him to amplify his own recollections, the emphasis of the book is on his own experience.

It does not dwell on the better known events of the campaign in North Africa, but it does reflect the ever-changing battle scene from the viewpoint of an officer responsible for providing appreciations of the enemy situation, and of a signals intelligence unit that gained particularly high marks because of the effectiveness of its work.

Hans-Otto Behrendt's informative book entailed several years of research at home and abroad. Military historians everywhere will be greatly in his debt.

Othmar Hackl

Author's Introduction

Thucydides remarked that those who take part in a campaign know the least about it. Yet it seems justifiable to write of my own experiences of intelligence operations through the two years of the African campaign if only in order that the general knowledge of that campaign might be widened. Given that so much has already been written about that campaign, I had to ask myself what value this book on its intelligence aspects might still have for historical research. The answer is that most publications have dealt with the work of intelligence (the *Ic-Dienst*) only superficially, and have romantically overestimated the effects of espionage. Therefore I considered that the working methods of and the daily influx of material available to intelligence officers should be explained. In this way I hope to contribute from personal experience to the history of World War II.

If after reading this book the more interested reader finds he desires to revise his opinions of some of the hitherto accepted versions of historical episodes, that has been the purpose of this book. It is not another resumé of operations and tactics in North Africa, though it does not of course dispense entirely with the historical framework within which the intelligence activities described were conducted.

A brief history of this theatre and a discussion of the special conditions prevailing there seemed necessary. The basis of the narrative was broadened to include a detailed study of the war diaries of the German Africa Korps and the higher commands of which it formed the embryo – Panzergruppe Afrika, later renamed Panzerarmee Afrika; and Army Group Afrika. Evaluation of these records – particularly the bulky appendices to these war diaries – was supplemented by personal papers and memory, refreshed as necessary by conversations with participants on both sides of the battle front.

Being versed in foreign languages including English, I was able to interrogate British and Empire prisoners of war and to study captured British documents from the outset of my service in Africa in the spring of 1941. Initially I was based on Tripoli, and then actively operated with a combat group under Lieutenant-Colonel Count Gerd von Schwerin. In March 1941 this unit advanced as far as the southern frontier of the Fezzan; at the beginning of April it participated in the advance through Cyrenaica, on which occasion the German expeditionary's force's commander, Lieutenant-General Erwin Rommel, ordered me to proceed with a small combat team to block the Mechili-Derna road. There I reinforced the Ponath group. Only at the end of April did I become G-3 (the third *Ordonnanzoffizier*) of the Afrika Korps's Intelligence service. From this time onwards therefore I write from personal experience of intelligence operations.

To what extent did daily intelligence reports influence the decisions taken by Rommel and his chief of staff? There can be no finite answer to this question. It is up to the reader to form his own view in the light of this narrative of the operations of the radio monitoring service and the other branches of intelligence.

Supplementary research for witnesses of particular events and the relevant records in Italy, Britain, the United States and especially Australia often opened up new paths of inquiry, but took longer than expected. I felt it necessary to describe how the German officers and men adapted to the new battlefield and its unfamiliar conditions as well as the problems encountered in co-operating with the Italians. Finally I also had to consider the work of British intelligence and their achievements in reporting on the German command and combat troops.

According to Carl von Clausewitz, the word intelligence (*Nachrichten*) signifies all that is known about the enemy and his territory; it becomes the basis of strategy and operations in war. Measured by this yardstick, rarely has one general known as little as Rommel did when he set foot on African soil in mid-February 1941.

The basis of all daily activities in the German intelligence service should have been the secret army manual (*Heeresdruckvorschift*) No 89, dated 1st March 1941. Its essential tenet was that as much information as possible should be collected about the enemy's striking power in peacetime. This was impossible in Africa. Apart from anything else coalition warfare in this distant theatre brought rules of its own. The German, Italian, and British Commands did not differ on the necessity of gaining full insight into the enemy Order of Battle, intentions and plans. But the technical means of achieving this differed vastly: the Italians had no armoured cars for long range reconnaissance; the Germans were numerically inferior to the British in armoured cars. The Italian airforce was equipped with obsolete aircraft, so their air reconnaissance ran into difficulties against British fighter planes. True, the German airforce possessed more modern aircraft but given the increasing British air superiority they found themselves fighting against ever-increasing odds.

The monitoring of enemy radio transmissions (*Horchaufklärung* or Y-service) in World War II has rightly attracted increased attention from both journalists and historians, although some of the newly revealed facts have been treated with undue sensationalism. In the North African theatre of war, for a long while the Germans enjoyed superiority in radio interception. We owed this to the activities of Captain Alfred Seebohm's 3rd Radio Intercept Company, a unit of the 56th Signals Battalion. Its achievements are best described by citing specific examples and assessing its special importance in the decision-making of the German Command. German superiority in this field ended on 10th July 1942 when virtually the whole company was killed or captured in action. To shed light on the events of that day, and on the fate of Seebohm himself and his unit, seemed to me legitimate within the scope of this book's inquiry. Many of the veterans involved in that episode have contributed to this clarification.

After over thirty years of Allied silence about their interception of the top secret German messages enciphered by the Enigma family of cypher machines during World War II, Group Captain F.W. Winterbotham made the first authoritative British revelations in his book *The Ultra Secret* in 1974. While this was based on memory rather than documentary records, it gave the first indication of the Allied successes in deciphering German radio traffic. This book takes those relevations into account. In 1978 after the completion of this book Mr Ronald Lewin's *Ultra Goes to War* was published. It affords a further insight into the origins of, and the great technical and human achievement involved in. If there was any doubt about the role of Ultra and about the crucial part played by Poland's prewar deciphering section, *Ultra Goes to War* has dispelled it. It is now clear that, by smuggling the documents and Enigma code-machines to Great Britain via France, Poland rendered an invaluable service to

---

* German *Nachrichtenabteilung. Abteilung* has no exact counterpart in English, and is here translated as Battalion when applying to German formations and assessment of Allied battle order.

the Allied cause. From Mr Lewin's investigations it is absolutely certain that Enigma-enciphered, top secret radio signals between the German Supreme Command (OKW) and lower echelons, especially headquarters in the Mediterranean and North Africa, were deciphered by Ultra. The question might well then arise, as to why it took so long to overwhelm Rommel's Panzer Army in Africa: the answer is quite obvious – even if the most efficient deciphering of the most important enemy messages provides a clear advance picture of the enemy's intentions, it is no substitute either for modern armaments like tanks, artillery and aircraft, or for operational skill and soldiers with battlefield experience.

Effective cryptanalysis presupposes that the deciphered orders are actually obeyed by their recipient. Rommel's first offensive in March and April 1941 evidently succeeded mainly because he did *not* heed the limiting orders which the Supreme Command had issued to him to halt at El Agheila on the eastern border of Tripolitania. The British High Command accordingly assumed that they would be temporarily able to hold onto the nearby position they had reached with only small forces, while they sent the desert-experienced 7th Armoured Division off to Greece. The British holding forces were aware of their weakness and withdrew quickly (Rommel even considered *too* quickly) before the first Italian-German thrust. He followed through with a dynamic push right across Cyrenaica and to his own surprise his momentum carried him on to the Egyptian frontier. The second German offensive in January 1942 succeeded because there was no radio communication at all, and the Supreme Command did not intervene with the vulnerable Enigma messages.

In the case of Rommel's May 1942 offensive, the plans were known to the enemy in advance through Ultra; but he still triumphed because of faults by the British Command, and thanks to his own tactical skill. After serious reverses at the beginning he reached the position later known as El Alamein.

Here, Ultra played a major part in the defeat of the last Italian-German offensive at Alam Halfa at the end of August 1942. General Sir Bernard Montgomery, the new British commander facing him, was fully prepared; he let us advance and then repelled the attack using the desert airforce to particular effect in bombing and strafing the attacking forces. While Ultra played a crucial part in the sinking of Rommel's oil tankers and supply convoys, perhaps it was not so relevant in the fighting that led to his defeat in the Alamein position at the beginning of November 1942. The decisive factor now was quite simply the sheer British superiority in tanks, artillery and aircraft for which no amount of tactical skill and self-sacrifice could compensate. During this battle Ultra served only in the role of a chronicler.

After the manuscript of this book was finished, the first volume (of three in all) of the official history of British Intelligence was published.* It deals with the history and the first months of the German expedition to the North African threats. While this has little that is new to add to Ronald Lewin's book published a year earlier, it is written from the official archives of the military and civilian authorities involved. And it does depict the trials and tribulations of British Intelligence in more detail and colour than hitherto.

I wish to thank Manfred Rommel, now mayor of Stuttgart, for permission to use his illustrious father's documents on the North African campaign; Professor Berndt Wischmann for his frank letter about his experiences on 10th July 1942; Professor Charles Burdick of the University of San Jose, California, for providing assistance and documents; Herr Wolfgang Hagemann, who put me in touch with the Ufficio Storico in Rome and Colonel Gruccu, Chief of the Ufficio Storico, who provided access to the military records of the Italian General Staff relating to North Africa; and Colonel Adalbert von Taysen, himself a veteran of these exploits, for his valuable advice. I have also to thank Major Werner Hundt for his comments and Oberamtsrat Hässler for valuable oral information. I am is particularly grateful to Herr Heinrich Habel, the last CO of 621 Radio Intercept Company for constant helpfulness over the many questions that arose. Mrs Erika Liss and Sir Kenneth Strong of the Cabinet Office Historical Section gave kind attention to my queries. I am especially indebted to the Australian War Memorial at Canberra for their unfailing assistance: in addition to their director N.J. Flanagan; I am grateful to Mr A.J. Sweeting MBE, assistant director, for establishing contacts with former Australian combatants. For permission to make use of the maps in *Tobruk and El Alamein* by Barton Maugham I am indebted to the copyright owners, the Australian War Memorial. Mr Cox of the Public Record Office kindly provided documents about the fate of 621 Company.

* F.H. Hinsley, E.E. Thomas, C.F.G. Ransom and R.C. Knight, *British Intelligence in the Second World War*, (HMSO, London, 1979). See especially chap 6, 'The Mediterranean and Middle East to November 1940'; and chap 12, 'North Africa and the Mediterranean, November 1940 to June 1941.'

Research was aided by the West German federal military archives in Freiburg, who obligingly gave access to the necessary records; many thanks are owed to its director, Dr Stahl, as well as to Lieutenant-Colonel Bottler, Lieutenant-Colonel Forwick, and Amtsrat Meyer for their friendly advice and help. The editorial director of the Research Office of Military History, Dr Ursula von Gersdorff, gave encouragement and assistance, and both to her and her successor Baron Hiller von Gaertringen, and to Dr Manfred Klink cordial thanks are due.

HANS-OTTO BEHRENDT
Hanover

Acknowledgements to the
English edition

I must first thank Colonel (GS) Dr Othmar Hackl, Amts-Chef of the West German Ministry of Defence's Militärgeschichtliches Forschungsamt, Freiburg, whose unbureaucratic decision to grant rights on behalf of the Amt to the publishers permitted the publication of this edition. I am grateful also to Dr Hiller von Gaertringen, the Amt's editor, for his help in clearing the formalities involved. I acknowledge with my grateful thanks the valuable assistance and friendly interest I received from Mr Edward E. Thomas while the English edition was being prepared. To Mrs Katharine Sim I owe thanks for her initiative in bringing about an edition of what is in any case a 'half-British' book. My grateful thanks go also to Mr David Irving who was kind enough to supervise and check the English text. I wish also to thank William Kimber for the patience he showed when this project was first mooted and throughout the publication of this volume and Mrs Amy Myers for her help in editing the English text.

Finally I thank my wife Ingeborg for her help and patience during the years needed to complete this book.

H-O. B.

CHAPTER ONE

Background to the German Intervention in North Africa

After the Italians attacked Abyssinia in 1935 and conquered it in May 1936, the English built up their forces in Egypt considerably. They motorised these formations and transformed the cavalry into armoured troops. The Egyptian western desert became their training area, with the consequence that units stationed there soon felt at home in the desert. In 1937 the German Military Attaché in London, Colonel Baron Geyr von Schweppenburg, visited the British garrison in Egypt on his tour of the Near East. German army relations with England were good at that time, and he was allowed an excellent insight into their methods; he came away with a high impression of their training.

After Italy declared war on Great Britain in June 1940, Egypt was in a paradoxical military and diplomatic situation. An Italian victory would release the Egyptians from the British alliance, a possibility which greatly troubled the British Foreign Office. Yet despite that alliance Egypt was not at war with Italy, even after Italian forces had partly occupied its territory, from Sollum to Sidi Barrani!*

Reorganizing the danger that faced them in the possible loss of Egypt, the British Government reacted politically and militarily: the Secretary of State for War, Mr Anthony Eden, visited Egypt in mid-October 1940, and offered concessions to Arab countries. Meanwhile Mr Churchill further strengthened his position in Egypt by bringing up troops and materials from the Dominions east of Suez and by sending reinforcements, including half Britain's available tanks, from the homeland.

At this time the western frontier of Egypt was protected by the 'Western Desert Force', the main constituents being 7th Armoured Division, composed of armoured and mechanised troops, and the partly mechanized 4th Indian Division. For the time being the British adopted a wait-and-see attitude: when the Italians pushed

---

* To avoid air attacks on Alexandria and Cairo, the British asked Egypt not to declare war on the Axis powers.

eastwards and occupied Sidi Barrani on 13th September 1940, they would withdraw their reconnaissance screen. Mersa Matruh, eighty miles further to the east and railhead of the Alexandria railway, became the focal point of British defence with reconnaissance extending far to the west.

The Italian Offensive

The Italians were also making plans for an offensive, reported in detail to Berlin by the German Military Attaché in Rome, General Enno von Rintelen. He knew Libya well and pointed out that what mattered for an offensive against Egypt were aircraft, tanks, artillery and ammunition as well as their safe passage, and that these factors were more important than numerical superiority in men. He reported that Marshal Rodolfo Graziani realised this and was making careful preparations. (Marshal Balbo had been shot down by his own AA guns in June and succeeded by Graziani as Supreme Commander in Libya.) On 5th August he had reported on the situation in Libya to Mussolini in Rome's Palazzo Venezia in the presence of Marshal Pietro Badoglio and General Soddu. He briefed them on his planned offensive into Egypt. He pointed out the difficulty of operating in the desert at this, the hottest time of year, and dwelt on the general supply problems. He indicated moreover that his troops were numerically scarcely sufficient and the degree of mechanisation wholly inadequate. While he was prepared to accept inferiority in medium tanks and artillery he did ask for air superiority and, in addition, time for further training. 'It is after all a colonial war of supreme importance,' he pointed out and concluded with the ominous remark that it was not for him to point out the dangers of a defeat which would be all the more annihilating and irreversible if suffered in the desert.

In retrospect it is clear that in view of its railhead and airfields Graziani should have pushed on to Mersa Matruh. But he would not be hurried, and finally Mussolini ordered the operations to begin on 9th September. His forces advanced eastwards – to no great surprise of the British – crossing the Egyptian frontier on 13th September and after about fifty miles they occupied Sidi Barrani three days later, the British garrison having withdrawn. There Graziani halted, and neither cajolement, admonition nor bluster from the Duce would persuade him to move on. He answered all of them, with a threat of resignation. On 1st November he won the Duce's confidence again 'to work for a new African victory'.

The British Response

In mid-October 1940 General Sir Archibald Wavell, Commander in Chief Middle East since July 1939, began to consider the advisability of a counter-attack with limited objectives. He ordered Lt-General Maitland Wilson, the field commander of the British troops in Egypt, to appraise the possibility of such an attack on both flanks of the Italian position. In April 1941, German troops would capture a British Intelligence survey issued at this time, analysing the strength and morale of the Italian troops in North Africa. Its author came to the conclusion that in spite of all general re-equipment and better arms, and although the morale of the troops had been raised by Mussolini, the seeming strength of the Italians might well be an illusion. Its last sentence read: 'Behind all this remains Caporetto'.* At Caporetto, in October 1917, the main failure was that of the Italian High Command.

Generals Wavell, Wilson and Richard O'Connor (Commander of the Western Desert Force), after long deliberations, decided to direct their main attack against the centre of the Italian disposition south of Sidi Barrani, and to employ only minor forces for the attack on the flanks, near Bir Sofafi in the south and at the coast in the north. The offensive was scheduled for the last week of November, but after Italy's invasion of Greece at the end of October; it was postponed till the first week in December.

The British appreciated that they were facing seven weak Italian divisions. These they would attack with two strong divisions: 7th Armoured Division with 4th and 7th Armoured Brigades and 7th Support Group; and 4th Indian Division, supported by 7th Royal Tank Regiment with 48 Infantry Tanks MkII (Matildas), and in addition the Selby Force (1800 men strong), operating on the coast.

In October the Italian Military Information Service (SIM) had obtained information about a planned British offensive; the Duce was right in his criticism that the long halt at Sidi Barrani was more to the advantage of the English.

One example illuminates the Italian attitude. On 27th November Graziani requested the Tenth Army to examine the possibility of closing the twenty mile wide gap between the Maletti Group and the Cyrene Division in order to prevent any penetration by enemy mechanised troops. 'It seems that this aim is attainable if the area

1. Author's recollections. This sentence was written in capital letters; it engraved itself on the author's memory by its very terseness.

around hill 192 west of Bir Enba is occupied'. But General Italo Gariboldi, the interim C-in-C of Tenth Army, remarked that, all things being equal, if Bir Enba were fortified the enemy would think an attack imminent and defend himself there with all vigour. In his opinion it was a question of time: if the intention was to hold the present position for a long time, it would indeed be advantageous to fortify Bir Enba, as this would weld the Italian line together. But if this were only a temporary halt it would be preferable to forgo fortification, at least for the moment, and to act decisively at the right moment. Hence nothing happened.

On 30th November SIM delivered a voluminous analysis of the political and military situation. This concluded that there was a significant reinforcement of the British troops in Egypt, there now being in all 300,000 men, including Dominion and Egyptian troops; and that there had been an influx of mechanised troops, and the formation of new tank units for the desert. GHQ Italian Tenth Army completed this picture with information provided by air reconnaissance. This had revealed *inter alia*: Troop movements that suggested the relief of armoured troops or reinforcement of the front; frequent visits of front line units by senior commanders; the appearance of new battalions in the advanced zone; and reinforcement of the artillery. On this basis Tenth Army did not rule out the possibility of an enemy attack with limited objectives against an Italian strongpoint.

On 6th December SIM telegraphed to the Italian Supreme Command, Africa:

> Increased enemy activity and especially patrol reconnaissance in front of Cyrene Division together with unconfirmed but currently incoming news about a British offensive against Italian positions in North Africa could be indications of approaching operations in the Western Desert. But extensive demolition of coastal highway roads and news from Cairo about our own approaching offensive against Mersa Matruh would speak against this hypothesis.

The Historical Branch of the Italian War Department later commented:

> Nobody could fail to notice the steady augmentation of enemy troops and tanks in the area west of Matruh, almost up to our front line units. The threat of an imminent British offensive grew more and more real, particularly on 7th December after information was obtained from prisoners-of-war that the British would launch their attack within ten days.

From the intelligence they then had the Italian information service overestimated the total enemy forces stationed in Egypt in December 1940, putting them at 16 or 17 Divisions; on the other hand they assessed the forces facing them in the Sidi Barrani-Matruh area (not including the British garrison in Egypt and west of Alexandria) somewhat more correctly as the following table shows:

Italians
(excluding forces in the Marmarica/Cyrenaica):

    Libyan Division Group:
        3 Infantry Divisions
    XXI Army Corps:
        3 Infantry Divisions and
        1 Armoured Brigade with
        2 Battalions

British
        7th Armoured Division
        6th Armoured Division*
        4th Infantry Division*
        4th Indian Infantry Division
        supported by 7th Royal Tank Regiment
        with 48 'I'-Tanks, and
        1 battalion heavy tanks.

On the basis of these figures the Italians put the British superiority in tanks at four to one – 226 British medium and heavy tanks against 55 Italian tanks; (in addition 220 Italian light tanks were matched against 74 British armoured scout cars and 195 British light tanks, in all 269 British armoured vehicles).

The Italian light tanks were considered comparable to the British light tanks and armoured scout cars – unjustly, as became apparent. The Italians estimated their superiority in infantry to be 2:1;† expected a numerical superiority in field artillery of all calibres, although only the 10·5 cm guns (of which there were only eleven batteries) were truly equal to the British field guns in penetrating power and range; and a British superiority in anti-tank guns of two to one. Even if only two British divisions attacked, it was assumed that the all-important British superiority in tanks would remain at four to one.

* Not present in fact. Orders of battle given in this narrative are as reconstructed by German or Italian intelligence and include units that were not present, or are incorrectly designated.

† Italian troops numbered 80,000 in the battle area. The British troops less than a half of that.

On 8th December two Italian columns advanced from their positions near Sidi Barrani to the south-east in order to reconnoitre against the enemy. As there was no reaction from the British, the raiders shot up some abandoned positions and withdrew again.

The British Offensive of December 1940

On the night of 8/9th December 1940 – at one-thirty A.M. – the commander of 2nd Libyan Division reported unusually deep penetrations by Royal Air Force planes over the strongpoint of Nibeiwa (some fifteen miles to the south of Sidi Barrani), which seemed to be designed to camouflage movements by mechanised units: he presumed that the enemy intended to attack Alam Nibeiwa, the southernmost Italian position. (General O'Connor on the contrary reported that the Italians had detected nothing and that the aircraft sounds had drowned the tank engines.) Marshal Graziani also had presentiments. At three A.M. he advised that Tenth Army should be put on full alert and ordered the commander of 5th Air Group to fly massed attacks alongside the east-west line Bir Enba (twenty-five miles south of Sidi Barrani) to Ganawaiyat (forty miles east of Bir Enba), the probable line of the British advance. At five-forty A.M. the British tank and artillery attack began in full strength against Alam Nibeiwa. Resistance ceased at 11.45 A.M. There General Maletti was killed in action at a machine-gun position.

At 11.25 A.M. the British artillery fired the first rounds at the strongpoint of Alam el Tummar. After a desperate counter-attack by the Libyans at 18.00 hrs, resistance ceased here as well. The capture of these two Italian positions had been the British objective for 9th December. There followed the attack on the positions around Sidi Barrani, and this was taken at mid-day two days later, but only after stubborn resistance: one (English) radio message intercepted by the Fascist 3rd January Division said, 'Our attack beaten off, everywhere strong resistance, renew attack at 14.00 hrs'. Another was later heard saying: 'Resistance still tough, attack 16.00 hrs'.

The Italians had fought fiercely in places, but given their inferiority in arms and equipment they had no real chance. It had been shown that in battle the stronger tanks would win, just as the German Panzer divisions would later find out at El Alamein.

How decisive tanks can be when opposing an enemy weak in tanks and without adequate anti-tank guns! In those three December days in 1940 the Western Desert Force (7th Armoured Division, 4th Indian Division and Selby Force) under General O'Connor annihilated two Italian corps, taking 38,000 prisoners and capturing 73 tanks and 237 guns, for only 624 British losses – dead, wounded and missing. The Italian army as a whole fought well, but hamstrung by its inferior weapons, defective motor vehicle equipment, tools and tanks, its defeat was inevitable. General Graziani was right when he told Mussolini in a report on the military situation of 17th December: 'In this theatre of war, one armoured division is stronger than a whole army.' As for the British view of the Italian strategic deployment: General Wavell said in a report of February 1941 that it seemed to him totally wrong; the Italian forces were dispersed on a broad front in a series of entrenched camps unable to provide mutual support, and separated by great distance from each other.

The British had pursued active reconnaissance on the ground and in the air, and had detected that the northern group of strongpoints was separated from the southern group (around Bir Sofafi near the escarpment) by the twenty mile wide gap. This was the gap which General O'Connor used to break through between the two groups of strongpoints. After that there was no stopping him. Bardia fell on 5th January 1941, Tobruk on 23rd January; and at the beginning of February Benghazi itself had been captured by the British.

When the advancing British armoured and motorised formations had regained the Via Balbia, the coastal highway, about sixty miles south of Benghazi and so cut off the retreat of the rest of the Italian troops sweeping back across the Cyrenaica, the Italians could not force a breakthrough despite a desperate fight. Only 7,000 Italians and 1,300 Libyans managed to break through and escape, taking with them some tanks and seventy-nine guns. The Italian Tenth Army had ceased to exist. At first the British Middle East Command put the number of prisoners at 130,000, but later they reduced the figure to 115,000: In addition they claimed the destruction of four hundred tanks and 1,200 guns.

Understandably, the Italian High Command tried to attribute their defeat to the matériel and numerical superiority of the enemy. In February 1941 they were further mesmerized by a captured enemy map that appeared to reveal a disturbing situation facing Tripolitania. The departure of 7th Armoured Division for Greece and its relief by the weak and inexperienced 2nd Armoured Division, newly arrived and insufficiently equipped, had as yet escaped notice by both the SIM and the German counter-espionage service (Abwehr). This map was for the time being the only document on which the German Command could base its estimate of the enemy situation. The Italian Command was extremely reticent with advice and help, having suffered a defeat from which they never fully recovered. They counselled the utmost caution, and yielded only with reluctance to Rommel's aggressive spirit. This would change as time went on, but only after the Sollum battle ('Battleaxe') from 15th to 17th June was Rommel's authority undisputed.

Considerations and preparations for the German intervention
The German interest in the Mediterranean went back some years; since the Spanish Civil War there had been close Italo-German co-operation in the military field. In 1937, some years before the possibility of German soldiers fighting in Africa was contemplated, the Military Attaché in London Geyr von Schweppenburg had made the journey to Egypt and Palestine already mentioned. Excerpts from his report show his unerring judgment:

> The defence of Egypt from the West is favoured by the natural conditions of the Libyan Desert. Advance is possible only by motorised troops and only a few routes are practicable. Therefore the Italians could bring only limited forces into action. This military factor is as important as the defence possibilities behind the Nile which affords a strong natural barrier.
>
> The British supply routes, round the Cape to Suez and via Palestine and Iraq from the Persian Gulf and India, are fully adequate for a successful defence of Egypt.
>
> For Egypt's defence, secure protection on the right flank is necessary, i.e. supremacy in the Eastern Mediterranean. It can be assumed that the British naval forces are fully equal to this task. By the way, the sea routes for Italian supplies are in British hands.

He concludes: 'Any offensive from the west must come to a halt on the Nile if not before.' This is certainly the earliest German opinion about the strategic realities of an attack on Egypt from the west. It was confirmed during the war.

The strategy of active intervention in the Near East in order to neutralise Britain, was repeatedly discussed on the German side in the summer of 1940. The Italian Military Attaché in Berlin reported one such conference on 3rd September with General Alfred Jodl, chief of the OKW operations staff. Jodl informed him in broad outline of a plan to send German armour to Libya, but remarked that the start of Graziani's offensive in Egypt should not depend on that. Meanwhile General von Rintelen reported from Rome on 24th September on the efficiency of Italian armoured forces in war, and

Rommel (in shadow) with General Gambara, and to Gambara's right Major F.W. von Mellenthin, Rommel's G-2. Mersa-el-Brega, Christmas 1941.

Rommel, General Gause, Lt Col Westphal, and Major von Mellenthin outside the operations staff omnibus. To the rear rights, Lt Schmitz, ADC. Mersa-el-Brega, Christmas, 1941.

Erwin Rommel.

added a clear warning that Germany could not leave them to fend for themselves until their back was broken.

To clarify the situation, the Chief of General Staff General Franz Halder sent Major-General Wilhelm Ritter von Thoma to Libya for consultations. For operations there the German Army (OKH) had earmarked von Thoma's 3rd Panzer Division; but only on 4th November the OKW war diary records that after taking the reports by Field Marshal Walther von Brauchitsch as C-in-C of the Army and Major-General Ritter von Thoma, Hitler decided to refrain from sending an armoured formation to Libya for the time being.

What was more crucial for the Italians, was the fact that, encouraged by their initial success in occupying Sidi Barrani, they had declined German aid. They wanted to launch the attack on Egypt alone. At that time, mid-September 1940, everything seemed to be favouring the Italians, and their next objective, Mersa Matruh, was within easy reach. On 29th September Marshal Graziani was invited to a high level conference in Rome on the situation in the Libyan theatre of operations. Mussolini was convinced they should advance in mid-October, Badoglio thought it impossible before November. Graziani now reserved any final decision until he had had a chance to examine all the factors on the spot. In an appreciation issued a few days later, on 5th October, Mussolini again underlined the importance of capturing Mersa Matruh and emphasised that this delay was of greater advantage to the British than to the Italians. Once they had taken Mersa Matruh they could see whether to destroy the Greek or the Egyptian pillar of British resistance in the Mediterranean. At the same time as Badoglio conveyed this appreciation to Graziani he informed him that the Duce had declined the offer of German aid, since he considered the Italian forces strong enough to capture Matruh. They could always seek German aid in the form of tanks, Stukas, and motor vehicles for the attack beyond Matruh on Egypt proper (Alexandria) later.

The deterioration of the situation in North Africa after the loss of Sidi Barrani in December revived the discussions on German aid. This time it was at the request of the Italians. On 18th December Marshal Ugo Cavallero, who had succeeded Badoglio as Chief of General Staff on the sixth, notified von Rintelen that Germany would be invited to send an armoured division. This request was further endorsed in remarks by his deputy General Alfredo Guzzoni on the 20th, that any aid must be provided quickly and that the despatch of *two* divisions would be welcome. On 10th January the German Military Mission in Rome informed the Italians that Hitler had decreed the assembly of a German Panzer formation for the defence of Tripolitania (Directive No 22). This was important, because if the Italians lost Libya completely it would release British forces in Egypt for service elsewhere. Even more important would be the psychological effect on the Italian population and the threat that airfields in North Africa could then present.

Alarmed by the continuing Italian retreat, on 17th January 1941 the OKW asked the Italian General Staff to provide a revised assessment of the situation in North Africa in order to decide whether the despatch of German troops was still possible. On the next day the Italian General Staff stated that the situation in Libya while not yet desperate was surely grave, as the loss of Cyrenaica and subsequently also of Tripolitania could not be ruled out; and that the Germans should provide for and assemble one Panzer Korps. Its despatch should however depend on how the situation developed in a month's time or so.

On 18th and 19th January Mussolini met Hitler at Berchtesgaden and approved the plan to send a German blocking force (*Sperrverband*), to Libya, an operation codenamed 'Sunflower'. On the 19th General Guzzoni, Deputy Chief of General Staff, met with Field Marshal Keitel and General Jodl of the OKW, reported on the situation in North Africa, and told them that the reinforcement of the three Tripolitanian divisions was under way – that the despatch of the Ariete Armoured Division and the Trento Division had begun. He maintained that the transport of the German troops could be co-ordinated with these two Italian divisions. General Jodl replied that the formation chosen by the Germans was 5th Light Division (with 9,300 men, 2,000 motor vehicles, and 111 anti-tank guns); this could be re-equipped later in accordance with any suggestions that its commander, von Thoma, presently on reconnaissance in Libya, might make. The division would be ready for embarkation about 15th February and for its transport about forty-five days would be needed. In accordance with the Führer's wishes, it was to be committed in action immediately, wherever Marshal Graziani deemed necessary.

On 22nd January OKW commented on Guzzoni's appreciation as follows: 'Provided that the situation does not basically change the loss of Tripolitania becomes unlikely, and it will become even less of a threat from May onwards, as owing to heat large-scale operations are no longer feasible in Libya.' This was a remarkable statement in view of the battles that would rage in the summers of 1941 and 1942.

The Italians warmly welcomed the despatch of 5th Light Division to Libya. It would begin crossing to Tripoli in mid-February and some material could be shipped across even before then. But General Hans von Funck, the new commander designated for the 'Blocking Force', took the view in a report to Hitler and senior officers that the planned blocking force would no longer be sufficient and that a Panzer formation should be sent over, capable of taking the offensive, together with a Corps HQ. Since they were faced by the probable loss of at least Cyrenaica, a Panzer division should be transferred. It was already too late, he added, as no Panzer division could be combat-ready in Tripolitania until the end of April.

On 3rd February Hitler ordered the transport of the *Sperrverband* to be accelerated; it was to be reinforced by a Panzer regiment; and the subsequent transfer of a Panzer division should be arranged. Furthermore, it should be proposed to the Italian High Command that all motorised formations should come jointly under German command. An order for the intervention of German troops in an Italian theatre of war, Operation Sunflower, was issued by the OKW High Command on 5th February:

1. German troops in Libya will come tactically under the orders of the Italian Supreme Commander; in addition they are subordinate to the Commander-in-Chief of the Army, through whom a liaison officer will liaise with the Italian Supreme Commander.

2. They should be sent into action only as a complete unit (of at least divisional strength), unless they are directly threatened or in the event of a crisis.

3. The formation must be completely under the control of the German Commander.

4. If in his view the commission of his troops might lead to defeat, the German Commander has the right and the duty, after duly notifying the German General with the Italian Supreme Command in Rome (von Rintelen), to ask for the Führer's decision through the Supreme Commander of the Army.

5. The X Air Corps (*Flieger Korps*) remains under the orders of the Supreme Commander of the Air Force (Göring), on whose instructions it will execute its tasks in close connection with Italian headquarters.

Reporting back in Berlin, von Rintelen was informed that the *Sperrverband* would be reinforced by a Panzer regiment and an

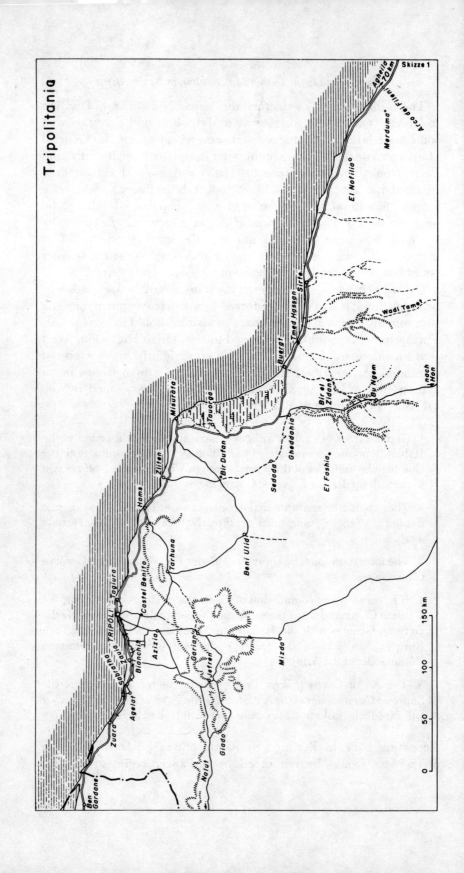

Tripolitania

Skizze 1

Field-Marshal Erwin Rommel stands astride the Via Balbia road built by Italians all the way along the North African coast. From a captured roll of German film.

Constantin von Neurath in front of his tent.

Rommel with General Italo Gariboldi, Italian commander in North Africa, in the spring of 1941.

artillery battalion, and that a Corps HQ under Major-General Erwin Rommel would be transferred to Libya. The Italians would be asked to agree to subordinate Italian armoured formations to this Corps Command. It was also planned to transfer a second full Panzer division to North Africa.

Rommel and von Rintelen were briefed in Berlin for their conference with the Italian Supreme Command and Marshal Graziani: Tripolitania was to be defended not near Tripoli itself, but on the Sirte bend, with infantry in the north, and with German and Italian mechanized formations on the south flank, in order to act if and when the enemy attacked.

The Duce agreed to these propositions on 9th February. General Graziani tendered his resignation and it was granted. The first transport echelon for Operation Sunflower reached the port of Tripoli on 10th February, the second four days later. On the 12th Rommel arrived, in the meantime promoted to lieutenant-general, with Hitler's aide-de-camp, Colonel (GS) Rudolf Schmundt, and his chief of staff, Lieutenant-Colonel von dem Borne. Later that same day the remaining 'Reconnaissance Staff Rommel' landed.

Thus for Rommel and his staff the African campaign began on 12th February 1941. From this day onwards Rommel's restless energy acted as a stimulating elixir on Italians and Germans alike, in his attempt to protect Tripolitania and deny the enemy the briefest respite. For the Germans he was a source of energy; while for the Italians his self-confidence and determination dispelled the apathy caused by their previously hopeless situation and by their drop in morale after the defeat at Sidi Barrani.

Rommel's staff at that time consisted of: Lieutenant-Colonel (GS) von dem Borne as Chief of Staff; Major (GS) Grunow as Air Force Liaison Officer, Lieutenant von Görne as Panzer Officer; Lieutenant Hundt as Engineer Officer; and Lieutenant Hans-Otto Behrendt in command of his personal staff. Detailed from the Staff of the Military Attaché in Rome to act as G-2 Intelligence was Captain August von Plehwe, and Rome also supplied the first staff interpreters, Dr Hagemann and Dr Schulz. This 'Reconnaissance Staff Rommel' was in a way the advance party of the Corps HQ foreseen; this was activated on 16th February with the official designation of Corps HQ 'Commander, German Troops Libya'. OKW further decreed on the 19th that the planned Panzer Korps should bear the name 'Deutsches Afrika Korps'. Initially, the Corps headquarters – a hotel in Tripoli – lacked any kind of technical equipment needed for command functions: messengers took the place of telephones; typewriters were made available only by courtesy of the Italians; the very paper and writing materials still had to be procured, before orders could be written and situation maps drawn up. Everything had to be improvised.

To those members of his staff not already familiar with Rommel through his book *Infanterie greift an* (Infantry Attacks) his energetic manner and his approval on each and every task soon showed them that this was a truly dynamic commander. There was no hesitation, no resignation – for which they had criticised the Italians: he radiated drive and enterprise. In a series of low level flights to the front line area he secured for himself a clear idea of the desert terrain and of the kind of measures to adopt. Rommel anticipated that the British would resume their offensive after they had mopped up in Cyrenaica; he felt that when it was resumed he should try to halt it as far to the east of Tripolitania as possible. Therefore he did his utmost to disembark the German troops arriving at Tripoli as quickly as possible and to rush them as far to the east of the position originally planned at Sirte as possible. Typical of Rommel's speed was that on 14th February at six-thirty P.M. the 3rd Reconnaissance Battalion and 39th Anti-Tank Battalion arrived at Tripoli harbour; they were unloaded by night under searchlight, and finished disembarcation within twelve hours; on 15th February both formations were already at Misurata; on the next day at three P.M. the leading groups of the 3rd Reconnaissance Battalion had already arrived at Sirte. In other words, just forty-eight hours after their arrival in harbour German troops were three hundred miles east of Tripoli – and operational.

CHAPTER TWO

The Theatre of War

Geography and Climate

The German troops who came to defend Libya during that spring of 1941 found a land that except for its towns and the settlement areas in Tripolitania and Cyrenaica to the east of the colony that was different from anything they had seen before. The desert astonished them at first by its sheer vastness; but they grew accustomed to it. The Italian colony of Libya extended about one thousand miles from west to east and, on average, seven hundred miles inland, from north to south; in surface area, about 800,000 square miles, it is about three and a half times the size of the German Reich of 1937.

The distances to be travelled were considerable. From Tripoli to Sirte which would initially be the main line of defence was a distance of about three hundred miles; from there on to Agheila, southernmost point of the Gulf of Sirte bend, was over two hundred miles more; Benghazi, the capital of Cyrenaica, was nearly two hundred miles beyond that. From Tripoli to the Egyptian frontier was well over one thousand miles. The only road was the tarmac surfaced but narrow Via Balbia, that snaked along the Libyan coast line and established a link between Egypt and Tunisia. Apart from this one highway local road networks existed only in the neighbourhood of Tripoli and in Cyrenaica.

For all that, the German soldier who landed at the airport or, as most did, at the port of Tripoli, might initially be forgiven for assuming that Africa was not so very different – that perhaps he was in some southern Italian town instead. True, the people looked strange in their oriental clothing and there was the Moorish architecture, but the dwellings erected by the Italians, the streets, the irrigated fields and the olive groves would remind him somewhat of the Southern Italy through which all Africa-bound soldiers had come on their way southwards; only the sunshine was fiercer and bathed everything in a more merciless glare.

But once he headed out of the town eastwards the picture changed: the settlements through which he travelled still looked like agricultural colonies and allotments. After about sixty miles of the

ride to the front line, the settlements and plantations, the palm tree
groves and fields ceased to break up the countryside. The earth's
naked crust now dominated the landscape; gravel and stone desert
occasionally dotted with grey vegetation – mostly camel-thorn –
formed a semi-desert alongside the coast. From now on, after leaving
the agricultural regions, the landscape did not change until south of
Benghazi and even then it was interrupted only by the Jebel Akhdar,
the 'green mountain' of Cyrenaica, from its eastern border until near
Alexandria in Egypt!

The Cyrenaican peninsula in the north, in whose valleys
abandoned Italian settler houses and new, but uncultivated,
plantations demonstrated what might have been achieved there, was
only a transit or recreation area in this desert war. At any rate it was
no battleground, for it could too easily be outflanked on the desert
tracks to the south. In fact, after the British used this outflanking
manoeuvre in January 1941 to cut off the remainder of Graziani's
army as it streamed back across Cyrenaica, this southern desert
would be navigated four times by the respective victors of the battles
in the east and south-west of Cyrenaica.

The flat desert landscape in the south of Cyrenaica reaches in the
east as far as the Egyptian frontier; it offers little obstacle for long-
range movements. It borders on the Egyptian western desert which
is bounded in the north by a three hundred mile stretch of
Mediterranean coastline, from Sollum in the west to Alexandria in
the east.

The frontier between Libya and Egypt was for a long time
indeterminate and only after the Italians occupied Libya in 1911 did
this question become critical. It had not really mattered so long as
both countries were part of the Ottoman Empire. Lord Kitchener,
acting with great foresight, tried to claim Tobruk for Egypt at that
time, but he was frustrated by the Foreign Office in London, who
declined to support the claim (which was without any legal title.)
Only in 1927 was the frontier provisionally delineated and it was
settled between Egypt and Italy by a treaty in 1938. At the beginning
of the thirties the Italians had hermetically sealed the frontier along
its whole length by a wire fence reaching from Sollum in the north to
the Sand Sea near Siwa, in order to cut off the Senussis from Egypt.
This 'frontier-fence' would in its northern reaches play an important
role as an orientation line during the battles in the Egyptian frontier
area.

The Egyptian western desert (the eastern end of the Libyan

desert), which hosted the later battles for the northern area, consists of a plateau some six hundred feet high, which drops to lower levels in an escarpment east of Sollum. This escarpment in the north-west was to prove militarily of great consequence insofar as it narrows the coastal plain from south-east to north-west, with the result that for about thirty miles to the east of the Egyptian frontier only two ascents are possible. One is by the serpentine roads of the Halfaya Pass: these allow a descent five miles east of Sollum, onto a flat tongue of the steep escarpment. And the other is at Sollum itself, where the declining slope of the plateau reaches the coast and a steep coast runs to the north. If both ascents are blocked a vast detour has to be made by any one wanting to advance into the Marmarica from the east.

This plateau, which in the west is adjacent to the plains south of the Marmarica, slowly flattens out to the east and north up to the Nile Delta, but drops steeply in the south into the great depressions of Siwa and Qattara. These depressions running from Siwa (two hundred miles south of Sollum) roughly to the north-east with sheer drops of three hundred to a thousand feet, form the southern boundary of the Libyan plateau. It shrinks from a width of two hundred miles (the part between Siwa and Sollum) 250 miles east of Sollum to only forty miles distance between the difficult western ascent from the Qattara depression and El Alamein, the one and only place to build a defensive position against an enemy attacking from the west.

From British Regulations

The conditions of a particular theatre of war, in this case the desert war, could not be better described than in the British regulations on operations by motorised troops in the North-Western Desert, a copy of which was captured in September 1941. Among the points made were the following:

Firstly, the general comment that even if the principles of military operations in the western desert did not differ from those for any other theatre of war, their application was influenced by its special conditions. These were: the great distances involved; the lack of precise landmarks; the almost total absence of accurately mapped roads; the scarcity of tactically or strategically valuable ground; the complete lack of air cover; the scarcity of water, fuel or avenues for food supply.

The huge distances involved limited military operations to the employment of motorised forces. Only on coastal roads was the employment of other arms possible. An important factor when considering each operation was the distance and time that the unit would be left to its own resources.

From the military viewpoint, the lack of accurately mapped landmarks over a wide area was a serious handicap. It meant in effect that a formation operating in such an area could not use the normal methods of framing and issuing orders. Often the only course was to issue an order consisting of little more than the route and distance up to contact with the enemy and thereafter to give verbal orders on the spot.

Dust and sandstorms were an almost everyday occurrence at certain times of the year and even if they were absent, vehicles were constantly moving in a self-created cloud of dust. This often diminished visibility to a few metres, injured the eyes, increased wear and tear on the matériel and led to jams or blocks in weapons. In order to counter this, certain precautionary measures had to be considered: everyone to be equipped with goggles for protection against the dazzling light as well as the dust; all machinery to be equipped with effective air purifiers and great care given to its maintenance; weapons to be supplied with dust-proof covers; whenever circumstances allowed, distances between vehicles to be substantially increased; and never to trust to eyesight alone.

Strategically or tactically significant desert regions were those where food supplies including water were obtainable, or those that controlled the supply lines or dispositions of the enemy forces, or any obstacles or narrow roads connecting such places. Usually it was possible to inspect such regions beforehand, and so far as time allowed make officers acquainted with them. Land reconnaissance outside these areas rarely turned out to be of any use, until the enemy forces were located by the RAF. Thus the value of effective cooperation with the airforce in North-Western Desert operations was great.

There was no cover against air raids in the desert. If the enemy had a powerful airforce, surprise could only be obtained by night movements or by wide dispersal of forces. The latter needed a commander with very good judgement and quick in his reactions.

Troops in motorised transport got thoroughly shaken about in the desert, which combined with the dust and heat, diminished their fighting capability. Troops were as exhausted after a 70 to 100-mile journey as if they had walked fifteen miles on a hot day.

Motorcycles were of little use, being difficult and dangerous to handle in the desert. They could not keep up with wheeled and track-laying vehicles, and had frequent breakdowns and punctures. If used at all, they must be in pairs to avoid the danger of men being left alone in the desert.

So far as desert orientation was concerned, the shortage of mapped roads necessitated movement being based on navigation of course and distance, for which a reliable compass and mileage indicator were necessary. Preferably the compass should be a nautical one or a gyro-compass that could be used inside the vehicle. If this were not feasible, sun-compasses had to be procured. Leaders of units and sub-units should also have a prismatic compass in case of need, and mileage indicators had to be tested accurately on a measured distance.

Every formation had to have a specially appointed navigation officer, supplied with instruments that would enable him if necessary to fix his position by the stars.

Vehicle tracks in the desert remained for a considerable time. Therefore attention had to be given by all ranks to the dangers of relying on such tracks if they seemed to run in the right direction. It was better to resist the temptation of following them and keep instead to the course ordered. Native guides unless specially trained were of little use over long distances.

In its next section, on reconnaissance, the rules pointed out that although thorough ground reconnaissance was always necessary, this was particularly so for motorised vehicles, partly because of the diversity of the ground encountered and partly because of the presence of vast wadis that sometimes remained invisible even from a short distance away. It was a wise rule never to enter a wadi with a motorised vehicle without knowing the exit, for it was always easier to get down than to get up again.

The difficulties of reconnaissance were increased by the frequency of mirage, exaggerating heights and distorting outlines. Experience would diminish the danger to a certain degree but could never rule it out. Considerable caution should be exercised in drawing conclusions from the sight of objects in the distance.

The whole ground had to be explored carefully, and sometimes a route marked out. Ground scouts in light cars were important. Obstacles most frequently met with were: regions of windborne sands, normally on the leeside of elevations; crusts of pebbles under which soft sand would be found; pieces of rock; hillocks of sand covered with round bushes; wadis with steep precipices and soft sandy bottoms, where the crossing places had to be carefully marked.

References to obstacles in Egypt itself, such as canals, railway embankments etc, ended the reconnaissance section. The document also includes rules for driving in the desert, and a wealth of technical advice. Each driver was responsible for ensuring that the following driver was still behind him. He was to keep his vehicle's tyres inflated to the prescribed pressure: the importance of this could not be overstated. He was advised not to follow the tracks of the vehicle in front, and if at all possible to steer straight and avoid turning suddenly. He was to make any gear changes necessary *before* reaching the obstacle – like soft sand or a steep decline – because changing gear when actually in soft sand could be fatal. Similarly, he was to apply his brakes as smoothly as possible; if his wheels started to dig in, he was to declutch immediately.

The British guidelines also identified the different types of going to be expected in the desert: hard gravel, called *serir* by the Bedouins; stony, rock-littered *hammada*; sand dunes; and mud. Drivers were warned to be on guard against salt pans, particularly after rain. As for breakdowns in the desert the following ground rules were laid down: However short the stop, a driver must never leave his vehicle. A vehicle can be detected from the air, but it is difficult to spot a man.

Experiences in and with the Desert

Hostile though the desert might seem to the novice sitting safe and sound in his motor car, this plethora of good advice, summarised above, shows it was possible to become familiar with it and to face its horrors with equanimity.

True, the soldiers of all those armies that clashed in Africa never attained the adaptability of the Bedouin: for him the desert 'lives', he can read its tracks like a daily newspaper. He can track his straying animals from Mersa Matruh to Upper Egypt and the Nile Valley and find them; he can withstand the desert perils of heat, sandstorms and thirst: In 1874, Gerhard Rolfs found one old pilgrim with his ten-year-old boy somewhere between Sitra and Siwa; they had taken a water-bottle and breadbag and were crossing the desert from oasis to oasis on foot. But the soldiers who had just arrived in the desert also learned little by little to size it up and face up to its dangers. They too learned in time to 'read' the tracks of vehicles – to distinguish enemy tracks from their own, and to estimate how old they were: the less fine sand in the tracks, the older they were. And they learned how to protect themselves against heat and to use their water sparingly.

One of our medical officers proved that Europeans too could survive the rigours of trekking across the desert. Major von Lutterotti of 580th Recce Company (later Battalion), was taken prisoner by a troop from the British Long Range Desert Group. He managed to escape with a little water after being told by a New Zealander, 'You haven't a chance'. He trekked about sixty miles across the desert despite its blazing summer heat: probably the only man to have survived such an ordeal. Admiration for his achievement was unstinted, since most such treks by Europeans stranded in the desert ended with death from dehydration.

North Africa enjoys a clear subtropical climate with fresh and humid winds from the Mediterranean in the summer and occasional rain, at least on the coast, in the winter, borne in on the west winds. In Tripoli and Benghazi the mean temperature hovers around 13 degrees C in January and 27 in July and August so the climate is not exactly bad. But the sandstorms – in Arabic *ghiblis* or 'South' storms – which occur particularly in the spring, are very disagreeable. They are triggered by depressions over the Mediterranean and burst out of the interior northwards to the coast. Besides temperatures of over 45 degrees C they bring with them immense quantities of dust. This very fine sand penetrates everywhere; it is very annoying and inflicts great damage on weapons and equipment as well as often causing eye diseases. The average temperatures measured in the battle areas were 20 degrees C between July and September, rising to a maximum of about 30 degrees C and 8 degrees C between December and February, but these do not reflect the more extreme temperatures which occasionally had to be endured in tents or desert positions.

As one guide book said: 'In the summer months one should avoid the desert'; this was a wise counsel which, unfortunately, the soldiers could not heed.

Although operations in the desert were considered impossible from May onwards, this was belied in 1941 and 1942 – although those particular operations were to inflict almost unbearable strains on the troops. As the battlefields were mostly near the coast, in addition to the temperatures troops also had to contend with relatively high humidity; when the humidity was 80-95% temperatures of 30 degrees became all but unbearable. Occasional winter rainfalls rendered easy desert tracks totally impassable even for tracked vehicles. In short, this subtropical climate was completely alien to Command and troops alike.

Although medical care was good the food supply was often totally unsuitable. Italian food, easy to digest, was refused; instead the soldiers got Wittler's long-life bread, 'AM' brand tinned meat from the *Amministrazione Militare*, which the Italians called *Arabo morto* and the Germans *Alter Mann* and one particular species of sausage, only occasionally enlivened by vitamin-enriched food. A lively barter trade ensued; one tin of Malta potatoes had the value of several bottles of Derna water. In 'inter-enemy-trade' captured tins of British biscuits and corned beef, not much prized by the British soldiers, were eagerly accepted.

The drinking water, bored for and pumped by teams of geologists, was very often salty, for near the coast the lighter fresh underground water lies on the heavier salty ground water. As the fresh water supply was often insufficient, it was pumped together with salt water rich in magnesium; this became the 'drinking water' of the troops. The consequential stomach upsets were a real hardship for soldiers of all ranks. The rising sick rate induced by these chronic and debilitating diseases of the stomach and intestines, as well as those caused by infections from sand flies, diminished the fighting strength of formations which were in any case seldom up to full combat strength.

The truth was that the German soldiers, although they had been medically examined for tropical fitness, arrived in the North African desert comparatively unprepared. They had to learn everything: with no roads except the Via Balbia to guide them, following tracks that frequent use had converted into torrents miles wide; driving became a kind of torture. They searched in vain for the 'roads' they expected to tally with the red lines on the maps – roads which were marked only by half obscured tracks, and heaps of camel bones, and with stone cairns for orientation. They had to endure sandstorms and bear the sand-blowing noonday winds, and flies that irritated their eyes and buzzed around with such obstinacy that this alone was a torture on the nerves. The heat might soar to 40 degrees, the humidity made their skin sticky, and they cursed the relentless sun. In summer, from seven in the morning to six at night the sun was a merciless enemy that could not be fought off, even inside tents or in the shade. In the exposed stone desert the sun beat down even more cruelly. Then came the winter: now, while the sun certainly brought daytime warmth, after it set the ice-cold damp nights threatened the health of the soldiers. Not until their second year did German soldiers become accustomed to this environment and its eccentricities. How envious the Germans were of the British prisoners-of-war who appeared to be so desert-trained and healthy!

Although Libya was an Italian colony and had been well developed for tourism before the war, the German army had many misconceptions about the country. Typical of these were suggestions, based on colonial experiences in German South-West and East Africa, that camels should be procured for transport. Yet we had only just witnessed the Italians defeated by a modern motorised and armoured enemy despite all their experience in colonial wars.

Compounding this ignorance and the false concept of what awaited our troops in Libya – basic errors which our Italian allies did nothing to correct quickly, perhaps because they could not – was the shortage of maps of the first battlefields. In our first attack on Tobruk in April 1941 it became apparent that because of this lack of data we Germans were completely unaware of the layout and nature of the Tobruk defences. These were called 'bunkers' but had nothing in common with the bunkers of our 'Westwall'. They were concrete dugouts blasted deep into the desert ground with well camouflaged shelters that melted into their surroundings so that they were virtually invisible and the first wave of attackers overlooked them. The bunker crews could then engage any German tanks and infantry that had broken through with anti tank guns and machine guns from behind.

That the first attack on Tobruk, executed by 8th Machine Gun Battalion and units of the 5th Panzer Regiment failed was mainly the consequence of our complete ignorance on the German side of the British defensive positions.

In the barren desert battlefields, which were virtually bare of vegetation even in the semi-desert along the coast, camouflage against aircraft was almost impossible. The only protection lay in dispersing the vehicles and positions around the billet or emplacement areas. The lesson of keeping three, four or five hundred yards between each vehicle was quickly learned. The German tanks and other vehicles, being painted in field-grey, were clearly visible; but the soldiers soon found ways and means of 'painting' their vehicles temporarily: one method was to strew sand on 'oiled' vehicles.

The Deutsches Afrika Korps (DAK) adapted rapidly to Africa without formal training between February and May 1941, and was combat-ready in the subtropical desert of North Africa as quickly as if it were on its home ground. It is worth mentioning this fact that it adapted itself so quickly because it proves that the German soldier could improvise. Liddell Hart says about this phenomenon:*

'The ordinary soldiers showed more initiative, and used their heads better in this war than they did in the last – especially when fighting on their own or in small parties.' On this score Elfeldt's opinion corresponded with the judgement of British commanders, who often remarked how the German soldiers excelled their opponents when operating alone or in pairs – a verdict that was in surprising contrast to the experience of 1914-18, as well as to the continuing popular view that the Germans were no good as individualists.'

The speedy adaptation to the exigencies of terrain and climate as well as to an enemy who had superior knowledge of this theatre and knew how to exploit it to the full, makes the DAK an excellent example of the German soldier's flexibility. How could he do otherwise, since no sooner had he arrived than he had to follow Rommel eastwards in his aggressive advance, from southern Cyrenaica to Derna in the north-east, despite enemy resistance, incorrect maps and a total lack of familiar landmarks in the flat monotony of an uncharted desert. All this could only be learned from experience. Very few knew what awaited them. For nearly all it was something new, an adventure in an unknown continent. So the German soldier, bursting with optimism and self-confidence, set forth into the bright light of the desert and became a part of history.

Population
Libya and Egypt belong to the very thinly populated regions of Africa: before World War II Libya had according to the census of 30th June 1939 for its vast area of 679,358 square miles (more than six times that of West Germany or Great Britain) only about 918,000 inhabitants including 770,000 Moslems. In the western Egyptian battle zone, the Western Desert, besides the semi-nomadic tribal groups of wandering Bedouins, there were only the 5,000 inhabitants of the Siwa Oasis. The main coastal town was Mersa Matruh, seat of the Governor of Egypt's Western Desert Province and at that time westernmost terminus of the railway from Alexandria.

* B.H. Liddell Hart, *The Other Side of the Hill*, Cassell, 1948.

It is worth mentioning here that this town had been largely developed by a German officer, André von Dumreicher, from Württemberg. In the Egyptian service he had become Director of the Desert Directorate in 1905, as well as commander of the Coast Guard Camel Corps which consisted of five hundred selected soldiers, mostly Sudanese; as such he was responsible for the Libyan, Arabian, Nubian and Sinai deserts. The extension of the harbour at Mersa Matruh, the drilling of wells, the planning of streets, the construction of a mosque and housing for the first colonists were all the work of Dumreicher. The Egyptians promoted him to colonel and made him a Bey, but some time after the war broke out in 1914 he was removed from his post when the British found out that the defence of Egypt's frontiers was entrusted, of all people, to a German.

Even Dumreicher had not been in a position to ascertain exactly how many Bedouin nomads lived in the Libyan desert between Alexandria and Sollum, three hundred miles to the west. Until the Italians constructed the frontier fence it was impossible to gather statistics in the desert, and even then, after it became impossible to pass back and forth through the frontier it was still not possible to do more than guess. Dumreicher may well be close to the mark with his estimate that before the war about thirty thousand Bedouin all told lived in coastal Western Egypt; of these the major part were evacuated in 1940.

Except in towns, and that was seldom, the soldiers of the DAK had contact neither with the population of Libya nor with the nomads of the desert. The indigenous population of the battle areas had mostly been evacuated, insofar as they had not already elected – as in the case of the settlers in Cyrenaica – to flee to the towns or return to Italy. In Western Egypt, besides the inhabitants of the oases of Siwa and Gara, only a few nomads still remained in tents. The author remembers having met Bedouin in the battle area only once. These were from Sawani Samalus (some forty miles west of El Alamein). They visited the headquarters of Panzerarmee Afrika near Sidi Abd el Rahman to thank us for help which we had given one of their supply caravans; when negotiating their way out of the Moghara Depression and up to the escarpment south of the Alamein front, the caravan had run into minefields near Naqh Abu Dweis. Empty motor transport returning from 90th Light Division had conveyed the wounded Bedouin, camels, and salvaged merchandise back to their encampment.

Communications

As already mentioned, only along the coast and near the larger settlements in Tripolitania and Cyrenaica did asphalt-surfaced roads exist. In the other regions there were some metalled 'roads' and so-called *pistes* – tracks with marks for motor cars – and caravan-routes, mostly very ancient. They were obscured by sand-drifts and ran only in general directions, establishing vague connections between the coast and various desert oases. The coastal spine on which the other roads in the colony depended was the Grande Strada Littoranea called the 'Via Balbia' after Marshal Italo Balbo. This highway followed the coast from the Tunisian frontier along Sirtica via Cyrenaica – where it ran doubly, from Lamluda to Barce – and then onward to the Egyptian frontier near Fort Capuzzo to the south-west of Sollum. The 'roads' over which much of the campaign would be fought, were usually unsurfaced, running from Benghazi to Mechili and Derna; from Zuetina through Mechili to Tmimi, with other 'spokes' radiating from Mechili to Tobruk and Capuzzo. There were also minor railway lines around Tripoli, about 130 miles long; and between Benghazi and Barce, about sixty miles long. These were only of local importance.

CHAPTER THREE

The Intelligence Service and its Sources

The Enemy Picture

Some of the German troops arriving in Africa had already found in the 1940 French campaign that the British were hard fighters; they did not underrate them. Moreover, the British units against which the Germans knew they were about to come up in Africa had just achieved notable victories, and they had had time to familiarize themselves with the desert war theatre. The Germans awaited them with keen anticipation.

The Germans had no way of knowing at that time that their first engagement would not be with the British troops who had become accustomed to winning – 7th Armoured Division and 4th Indian Division; instead they were faced by green troops in newly assembled formations, barely used to desert conditions, the occupying troops in Cyrenaica.

The Germans had expected the victors of Sidi Barrani. Nevertheless, invigorated by their own successes against British troops in France, and confident of flexible command and superior equipment the Germans at every level were sure that they could master the situation here in North Africa as well. At this time the German General Staff's intelligence branch Foreign Armies West assessed the British as follows:

1. It is scarcely to be expected that the higher commands have overcome their reluctance to make swift decisions, their operational ineptness, or the laborious methods of issuing orders . . . or that lower echelons have surmounted their lack of independence and inflexible methods in the interim. In particular, they seem not to have mastered flexible command of mechanised troops. One cannot escape the conclusion that an over-rigid 'Block'-system is incapable of adjusting to changes in a given situation. The press is openly critical of this. The bold command tactics of Generals Wavell and Wilson* in decisively and skilfully exploiting the opportunities of the situation are still an isolated phenomenon. Command tactics in the withdrawal from Greece were far-sighted and

---

* And, in this author's opinion, Richard O'Connor.

correct under the circumstances.

2. Those older officers with war service and experience constitute the best part of the officer-corps. . . As a field commander the British officer has fought gallantly and devotedly in Belgium, Northern France, Libya, Greece and Crete.

It is the duty of intelligence to evaluate the enemy realistically. In our case we had to depict the British as imaginative and brave fighters, if the German soldier was not to be taken unawares through having underestimated them.

For the time being the enemy situation appreciation issued by SIM remained the basis used by 'Reconnaissance Staff Rommel' for its information and decisions. Thus the SIM report dated 15th February 1941 covered the Italian retreat after the battle of Sidi Barrani, that is from about January 1941. SIM was as yet unaware that the British 7th Armoured Division had left Cyrenaica for Greece; so was the German Abwehr. Thus the formations that the Italians already knew of were still mostly shown as being in the line. It was understandable that the Italians exaggerated the enemy forces in North Africa in the spring of 1941: in fact they nearly doubled them, as became apparent after our first sweep through Cyrenaica. The Italians had ascribed their defeat to an enemy superiority that did not in reality exist except in the enemy's more modern weapons. But after the German troops first advanced beyond Sirte and got almost to Agheila before coming into contact with reconnaissance units, the first doubts arose as to the real strength of the British; for if two enemy corps had really been left on the western front of Cyrenaica in February 1941, the enemy pressure would have been considerably stronger than reported by this German spearhead.

The OKW had noted in its War Diary of 7th February: 'The repeated Italian reports about the presence of a second British armoured division on the Libyan front gain more and more probability.' This was now shown to be wrong. Units of the British 2nd Armoured Division were engaged in Cyrenaica; but this was not a second division, i.e., in addition to 7th Armoured Division.

For their part the British put the strength of the German advance against their own forces in Cyrenaica far higher than was the case. The author remembers well being asked by a British officer taken prisoner at the beginning of April: 'Isn't it right that you have an

Rommel's Storch light aircraft reviewing his scattered troops.

Rommel in North Africa

Rommel sits in the roof hatch of his armoured command truck Mammut, as it rolls eastwards along the Via Balbia.

The Via Balbia

A Panzer III and other German vehicles roll eastward along the Via Balbia, April 1941.

armoured corps here?' Yet only 5th Light Division was engaged in this advance.

The British order of battle will be dealt with later, as it emerged only after the advance when captured documents were analysed. It will suffice to state here that the British had retained in Cyrenaica 2nd Armoured Division with 3rd Armoured Brigade and a support group; and 9th Australian Division with only two brigades and 3rd Indian Motor Brigade. This was of course rather less than 'two army corps'.

All this clearly demonstrated the importance of reliable reconnaissance. It made the difference between whether or not a force could survive under given conditions of terrain and climate.

Ground and Air Reconnaissance

Ground reconnaissance and observation of the enemy before, during and after operations are fundamental. On the ground, the soldier who keeps his eyes open and a cool, steady gaze is less easy to take by surprise than the complacent dunderhead. In the air, the principles of reconnaissance are similar. Reconnaissance flights took place on most days and required great courage; they met with harassment by enemy fighters, but brought knowledge of enemy dispositions indispensable to the higher command. Even they could not provide the last word, since extensive troop movements could still take place in one night. But despite this shortcoming it will be seen how irreplaceable their results were in due course, and this became increasingly the case.

Wireless Reconnaissance

The former Chief of the General Staff's Foreign Armies West, Major-General Ulrich Liss, has stated that in time of war wireless reconnaissance (known in Britain as the Y-service) is the one source of information that surpasses all others. This means of reconnaissance is – and his experience was broadly confirmed in Africa – by far the best. One invaluable advantage is that the transmission and reception of its data are simultaneous. When properly exploited, this yields a decisive time advantage as compared with all other reconnaissance sources: because the value of other sources often suffers from the lapse of time until the point when the data is useless to the higher command.

In the African Campaign, too, the Y-service was the best source of enemy intelligence. When enemy unit strengths were clearly given together with their deployment areas, 'Y' came into its own. Even without possessing the enemy's codebooks or ciphers, our skilled radio operators were able to 'recognise' individual enemy wireless stations: could identify each W/T operator's idiosyncrasies when transmitting – his 'fist' – or speaking. Soon after the start of wireless traffic each morning the structure of the enemy wireless net became clear. An especially rich field was the chatter between some British radio operators whose pompousness impelled them to drop valuable hints that they knew more than the others and even to hint at what it was. Communications on rear wireless nets frequently abandoned any pretext of wireless discipline. Guarded language and code words were initially employed only rarely and irregularly by the British; one British report on this observed piteously that there were even some officers who thought that 'London' was sufficiently camouflaged by the phrase 'capital of England'.

When the fronts stabilised, the 'Y' unit could locate by simple direction-finding the position of each enemy headquarters; when they were shifted, this enabled valuable conclusions to be drawn as to enemy intentions. When our own troops advanced the situation became too fluid for direction finding. But then wireless reconnaissance could make a considerable contribution to victory by rapidly transmitting important enemy signals to the commander. Rommel often received these messages before the enemy commander. If British attacks or offensives were imminent, the Y-service paid off dramatically since any prior change, even radio silence, was a small piece in the mosaic which gave the overall picture of coming events. If the British were on the attack, these intercepted wireless communications might establish where their main effort was coming, or even the tactical intentions of the British command in time for the German troops to make preparations for defence.

Even so wireless reconnaissance alone, detached from all other intelligence, could not furnish infallible results. It was able to provide a detailed insight, but it often had to be supplemented by captured documents, by the interrogation of prisoners of war, and by ground and air reconnaissance; the latter became increasingly important in the course of events in Africa.

Radio monitoring was of value not only for the information it provided about the opponent, but also as a means of checking the effectiveness of one's own weapons. When the British were heard to report for instance that they had been under attack by Stukas but had suffered little or no damage, this was a measure of control of our own air attacks. Of course these reports had to be judged with caution, because after our air and artillery strikes the British kept their nerve and transmitted cool and sometimes even dismissive reports on them.

The British Y-service for its part monitored our wireless communications very closely as could be seen from the results. British Intelligence summaries identified the German divisions confronting them not merely listing their ration strengths and equipment, but just like a German status report – giving exact numbers of officers, NCOs and other ranks, together with our tank and artillery establishments. They can only have extracted these figures from the corresponding statistics which we sent to Supercomando Libia in Tripoli and which the Italians sent on to Rome in their own cipher.

Seaborne supplies from Italy to the North African theatre suffered particularly from Britain's close surveillance of our wireless nets. One report by Panzergruppe Afrika dated 1st September 1941 highlights this: this report found it particularly noteworthy that the British always executed the air attacks at the time of day for which the Italian signals had announced the arrival of cargo-carrying submarines. Thus on the very evening of the planned arrival of submarine *Zoea*, 10th August, the British delivered an air attack. In fact this submarine had been unloaded early by local arrangement and so no harm came of it. Then the submarine *Coridoni* announced its arrival over the wireless, and put into port late on 12th August. Continuous British air attacks began at once and these impeded its unloading. Submarine *Atropo* was due to arrive on the evening of 15th August, but this had to be postponed; nevertheless a violent air attack took place at the scheduled time. Arriving without prior warning the next morning, it was able to unload without incident. The next episode followed a wireless signal from the Italian Navy to the effect that the steamship *Belona* would arrive at Bardia on 24th August at three A.M. At four A.M. that day a heavy British air raid hit the port, and the sea area offshore was systematically swept with flares.

Rommel did not under estimate Britain's proficiency in the field of monitoring and deciphering Italian and German wireless communications.

Once he asked how much time it took our German cryptoanalysts to break an Italian wireless signal, and the reply was, 'About three days'.

'Then,' he answered, 'the English manage it in two!'

This mutual wireless monitoring went on without pause or respite. Consider this special case of human kindness: A seriously wounded English lieutenant had fallen into German hands: held in a German field hospital, he asked to send a message to his fiancée who was in Cairo at Shepheard's hotel, so she would know that he was all right. We fulfilled his wish: A radio message was sent in German by wireless. Thereafter it moved in ghostly fashion through the ether – first as an English translation that we overheard, and then the other way around. It echoed back and forth several times, so it can be presumed that the girl got the message in due course – an event surely impossible in any other theatre of this war.

The Radio Monitoring Platoon (*Horchzug*) Afrika arrived on 25th February 1941: At the beginning of our operations in Africa it was transferred on 6th March to the operational area in eastern Tripolitania, where it came under the command of Lieutenant Gerisch of 3rd Company, 56th Signals Battalion (*3./ Nachrichtenabteilung 56*). The rest of the 3rd Company, which had been withdrawn from the radio surveillance of Great Britain, arrived in Tripoli on 24th April and by the end of the month was already in its operational sites near Tobruk and on the Egyptian frontier. Thus the German Afrika Korps (DAK) now had an efficient and well-equipped 'Y'-company.

Its commanding officer was Lieutenant Alfred Seebohm, an officer of high calibre. His evaluation work would be greatly praised not only by the G-2 at Rommel's Korps headquarters but also by superior echelons; in time his work attracted Rommel's personal attention and that of his operations staff officer. In a fashion that was truly exemplary for intelligence staffs, Seebohm set up channels for rapid communication links to channel the most important intercepts direct to the C-in-C, his operations staff and the troops concerned. After separating the wheat from the chaff Seebohm reported his interpretation in advance by phone; whenever possible, he visited the intelligence officer (G-2) in the evening with the selected messages to discuss and assess with him and if necessary pass on. How highly the work of this company commander was esteemed is shown by an order issued by the G-2 and operations staffs of Panzergruppe Afrika in January 1942, to supplement a corresponding order already issued in August 1941:

1. Radio monitoring will be carried out by German and Italian intercept troops.
2. The assignment of German intercept troops is to be organised by Lieutenant Seebohm, CO of 3./N56.
3. The assignment of Italian intercept troops is to be organised by the Information Office (SIM) of Supercomando of the Italian Forces in North Africa.
4. The assignment of German intercept section and platoons as well as the evaluation of their results is to be controlled by Lieutenant Seebohm only.
5. The use of the [regular] Italian and German Signals Units to intercept enemy messages is to be confined to enemy combat reports.
6. All ciphers and wireless documents captured from the enemy are of the utmost importance and are to be handed over as quickly as possible to headquarters, Panzergruppe Afrika. . . .

> For the Command of the Panzergruppe
> The Chief of General Staff
> signed Westphal.

Alfred Seebohm, later promoted to captain, commanded a company that was not only proficient in wireless technique but able to stand up in combat too if need be, as the following record shows: On 24th December 1941 Seebohm reported:

Radio Direction Finders 3rd Section was overrun by enemy tanks and taken prisoner. Thanks to prudent action by the commanding officer of DF Section 3 this section escaped from captivity. The section salvaged its equipment, which is being taken to Company for repair.

And on 24th January 1942:

DF 4th Section was surprised by the enemy on its way to the new assignment area. The commanding officer was captured with the wireless documents but freed himself by cool action and personally took seventeen prisoners.

Seebohm's coverage of events in other theatres was equally instructive. The battle of Crete which began on 20th May 1941 was expertly covered by his radio monitors. On the basis of British wireless reports the situation of the German invaders at first seemed hopeless: one batch of paratroopers after another was reported annihilated by the New Zealanders, so that it appeared at first as if the airborne landings had been a failure. Only when the airborne troops went into action and forced the New Zealanders to retreat did the battle of Crete come to an end and with it the tension and tragedy. One New Zealander, who had saved himself by boat but had steered too far to the west and fallen into German hands, stated later that the German paratroopers jumped heedless of the colossal anti-aircraft fire and that he and his comrades felt only the greatest respect for them.

We cannot discuss the work of the British intercept service without mentioning the deciphering of German wireless signals at Bletchley Park, home of the British Government Code and Cipher School, under the code-name 'Ultra.' The GC and CS had been breaking German airforce signals of the highest security classifications since 1940. Advance warning was sent to General Freyberg, the Commander of 2nd New Zealand Division and British C-in-C in Crete, about the German plans to attack the island. But he made no immediate counter-attack before the Germans were reinforced and his forces had to evacuate Crete. That Freyberg failed to save Crete despite being told the enemy plans was frustrating, from the standpoint of an intelligence officer and one can understand his feelings.

Some claims about Ultra's role at the outset of our African campaign cannot be accepted without reservation. Group Captain Winterbotham has suggested that thanks to Ultra Wavell and O'Connor were fully informed about the battle order of the German troops intervening in Africa, and that therefore the retreat of the British from Cyrenaica avoided turning into a debacle. The truth is that both generals knew that there was only one German division and it had only recently arrived; but in spite of this accurate intelligence the retreat was chaotic with heavy losses. Rommel's deception tactics, including dummy tanks mounted on Volkswagens, and tents which contained only one man instead of the six assumed by the British, were not without effect, as was shown by the English officer taken prisoner near Derna who asked us about the presence of a German 'armoured corps.'

Exploitation of Captured Documents and the Press

A secondary but important source of intelligence is captured enemy documents; their disadvantage is the time it takes to bring them to the attention of headquarters in comparison with the much greater speed of wireless intelligence. In most cases captured papers yielded good results, mostly by way of confirmation of dubious information. Orders, maps, dispositions and regulations gave valuable indications supplementing our knowledge of the British order of battle, intentions and command tactics. Captured ciphers and call sign tables facilitated one's own wireless intelligence.

In particular distribution lists on documents provided solid information on command structures. Captured private diaries, which were not allowed in the German forces, could bear out otherwise unconfirmed information. Thus in one diary we discovered a note, buried amongst other pedantic comments, that a friend was 'now with 10th Armoured Division (former Cav Div)'. It enabled us to cross one armoured division off our list, previously two divisions had been supposed to exist. The same diarist had been in Greece where he had evidently only seldom glimpsed the RAF, because he called it the 'Royal Absent Force' – a jibe that certainly could not be levelled at it later in Africa.

As prisoners (regrettably) had to hand over all correspondence, their personal letters gave good insight into prevailing feelings at home or the status of the addressee. In the to and fro of desert combat important command cars with their contents were often mislaid on both sides. During the great British offensives, Crusader in November 1941 and at El Alamein in October 1942, captured maps were useful for establishing British dispositions and intentions.

To show the consequences one captured order can have, let us quote the following case: The communiqué issued by the German High Command on 15th June 1942 brought the following information:

> During the fighting in North Africa an order from the 4th Armoured Brigade has been captured, instructing that prisoners should get neither food nor sleep, nor water, accommodation or comforts (smoking) of any kind until they have been interrogated by the responsible authorities.
>
> The High Command has therefore issued orders that as from 1200 hrs on June 6 officers and men captured during the current fighting in North Africa and in German hands are to receive neither food nor drinking water until this disgraceful and inhuman order is cancelled and this is notified in an official British declaration.

The War Diary of High Command had referred to the Panzerarmee Afrika report about this captured order on 2 June. 6 June it added:

In a statement broadcast by the BBC in London, the British War office has stated that it did not issue the order about treatment of German POWs and, if such order has been issued by subordinate commands, cancel it immediately. Thereupon the retaliatory measures ordered against British POWs are cancelled with immediate effect. This is announced over German Radio on 6th June at 8 P.M. Panzerarmee Afrika has been ordered to forward the original of the captured order with a view to publishing it in facsimile.

This author had the captured order from the 4th Armoured Brigade in his own hands and clearly remembers that a 'War Office Number' was entered at the top right. The episode in fact took a different course than appears from the published statements. Shortly after finding it, the Panzerarmee ordered formations under its command by a wireless message transmitted in clear that this British order, cited with its War Office number and given in a German translation closely following the English original, should be followed for the treatment of British prisoners until it was withdrawn. As in those days British far outnumbered German POWs it took only one day for the British – also in clear, and also citing a War Office number – to retract their order. It had obviously been issued by London bureaucrats. It did not lead – thanks to immediate reaction – to an escalation of retaliation. Similar episodes occurred in other occasions, concluding favourably thanks to Rommel's gallantry and his sense of fairness.

The Intelligence Summary of the British 10th Armoured Division of 30th October 1942 captured a few days later is an example of British staff work on intelligence. It tallies broadly with German concepts and approaches. In particular it pays close attention to the construction of field fortifications and minefields on the Italo-German defence front. Nor does it exclude political matters where necessary to round off the picture of the German soldier.

Enemy press and radio broadcasts are also found, although to a lesser extent, to be a source of information about the enemy. How the other side describes battles and their outcome often gives good indication of future intentions as well as of the enemy's weak points; the latter can be deduced from the way the public is kept informed. The war in North Africa certainly lent itself to melodramatic representation, but here too the BBC described the situation as it really was and, so far as the author knows, somewhat more correctly than the communiqués issued by the German High Command which was still putting out relatively unvarnished news reports at that time and only seldom lapsed into propaganda.

Prisoner of War Statements

Soldiers who become prisoners of war mostly come directly from the battlefield. They have been taking part 'on the other side'. They have still to get over the shock of being captured by the time they are interrogated about details interesting to us. Intelligence officers then put together the results like pieces in a jigsaw puzzle, even though they may seem unimportant to the prisoner. Thus these interrogations provide a fertile source of intelligence.

Uniform badges are mute proof of what unit the prisoner belongs to, particularly valuable when – as was normally the case with British prisoners – the statements were more than scanty. The British had in fact briefed their troops meticulously on what to expect when taken prisoner, whereas in the German Army it was not customary to dwell on the possibility of being captured. The British POW knew what interrogations they would be subjected to and what questions they would be asked. An excellent British guide with poignant title *The Answer to this is Silence* was therefore translated and made available as an instructional leaflet to each member of the forces engaged in Africa to keep with his paybook on 14th May 1942: It instructed him that even as a prisoner of war he should endeavour to do his duty. When interrogated all he had to state according to the international convention was his name, rank, date and place of birth, and place of residence. To any other question he should simply reply: 'I cannot answer that.' The enemy would respect this stance. A free tongue could mean death to his comrades. He should also beware of agents in German or Italian uniforms pretending to be fellow prisoners, and also of hidden microphones.

Given the fluid situation in the African campaign our G-2, Major Zolling, thought it indispensable for such a leaflet to be issued; until then no guidelines had been given on how to behave if captured – a fate that could befall anybody.

Not only did the insignia of the armoured units, artillery or infantry give quite good hints as to enemy dispositions and sometimes clues as to his intentions, but the place of capture also allowed deductions as to enemy intentions: the deployment of particular elite units could be readily associated with preparations for an attack.

It might here be mentioned that the German forces in Africa did not control their own prison camps – to the great regret of British prisoners. All prisoners that fell into German hands were transferred through German collecting points to Italian custody and interned exclusively in Italy. In September 1943, after Italy's surrender to the Allies, a considerable number of British prisoners escaped from prison camps (with tacit Italian permission). This was deplorable from the German point of view because a large number reached the front and regained their units in Southern Italy or took part in partisan warfare in Northern Italy.

The author believes there was a fundamental difference of outlook between Germans and British as to the importance of prisoners of war as former enemy soldiers, i.e. as casualties for the enemy. Whereas the British jealously guarded every prisoner the Germans were more liberal in guarding theirs, as though it were not so vital to bring every single British soldier into the cage.

Some interrogation results will serve to show kind of the data that they yield, how important they can be, and how the data is obtained. Only reports subsequent to autumn 1942 are available, because it was only then that German cages for POW were organised and interrogating officers attached to them.

At a discussion on 7th September 1942, between a German Sonderführer of El Daba POW cage with a captured officer, a lively conversation developed: 'Right away the officer freely confirmed my report of yesterday that the 132nd Brigade of the 44th Division has been subordinated to the New Zealand division for the time being; replacement of any New Zealand battalions is not contemplated at present.'

'The officer mentioned with some emphasis the introduction of the considerably improved anti-tank ammunition; great hopes are attached to this because of its better penetration.

'He says that Prime Minister Churchill was back in Egypt again eleven days ago, after his return from the Moscow conference, visiting an area between Alam el Halfa and Deir el Agram. After a conference there was a banquet which was attended by General Freyberg and other top officers and fifty highly decorated guests. To the evident amusement of the guests Churchill uttered some very moody remarks about the great Match Problem, which is a well known problem, to use the officer's words, for the British too. Churchill subsequently departed by plane for London. The new Commander-in-Chief Middle East, General Alexander, also left

London by plane in the evening, he says, and arrived in Cairo at dawn. The former Commander-in-Chief Middle East, General Auchinleck, received a new and bigger command after his return to London.

'Speaking of the major British convoy attacked by Axis forces about a fortnight ago the officer claimed that if there are no further German sinkings Malta could hold out on the supplies that arrived for at least six months. This fact which is being withheld from the British public for obvious reasons is not in his view to be regarded as an exaggeration.

'With regard to the reinforcements in manpower sent out to the Middle East in recent months there could be no disputing, in the officer's words, that these are qualitatively greatly inferior to the troops already here, which is partly because the old guard in the Middle East is primarily made up of Regulars or first class Territorials. The fresh troops arriving from Britain had no front line experience at all.

'The employment of German paratroops was recognized by the British Intelligence Service two days before their arrival in Africa. The appreciation of the Intelligence Service that the German paratroops would be used initially as infantry was confirmed by the capture of a paratroop soldier five days after he arrived at the front.

'While the British Intelligence Service in the Middle East is open to more or less justified criticism, the radio monitoring service is in the officer's opinion brilliant in every respect and has come up with first class results again and again. The officer mentioned in the course of the conversation that American tank crews are also standing by in Egypt, but he did not want to enlarge on that. How far his remarks are trustworthy in this respect I can not assess. . . .

'Finally the officer remarked at length on the Axis prospects in this theatre. He considers it totally out of the question on account of military circumstances intravening during about the last two weeks – about which he could not say anything – that the Axis powers would ever be able to reach Alexandria or Cairo. They had had the chance of doing so until not too long ago, but surprisingly the Axis powers had not taken advantage of it.'

The same Sonderführer also reported – though inaccurately – on 7th September 1942: 'Correcting an earlier report, the details of the death of General Gott can now be clarified by the testimony of an officer. General Gott was killed by a bomb during a sneak German air raid on an airfield. His ADC lost his right leg. The original rumour that circulated in British circles was that General Gott was the victim of a motor accident, but this was not true.'*

Brigadier H.S.K. Mainwaring later reported in his memoirs† the true story of how General Gott actually lost his life. At the beginning of August when Churchill was visiting Egypt, Mainwaring was a staff officer in the western desert, little knowing the great command upheaval that was about to take place in the Middle East. He learned that he was to attend a conference in Cairo. At the time he was the Eighth Army staff officer responsible for allocating seats in the evening plane from Alexandria to Cairo. At mid-day on 7th August, he had allotted all the seats including one for himself, but then General Gott's ADC demanded one for his general; the general had his way because Mainwaring offered to drive to Cairo overnight instead. The next morning he learned of his own good fortune – the plane had been shot down killing the general and most of the passengers.

The following results were obtained from a conversation with soldiers of the 'Composed Household Cavalry' taken prisoner at Himeimat.

The 'Composed Household Cavalry' consists according to them of six companies, four in the front line and two in reserve. The prisoner belonged to D Coy. When captured he was proceeding from B Coy with three armoured cars. The unit has Humber and Daimler armoured cars. The Daimler is armed with a small two-pdr gun and a machine gun specially for anti aircraft defence. The armour is 11mm thick. The prisoners claim the entire 10th Armoured Division is up front. They know nothing about any other armoured divisions. Recently there are said to have been numerous changes in the bigger armoured units. When conversation turned to the next offensive they thought its commencement imminent. The 7th Armoured Division would act as spearhead in this event, that is, it would drive a wedge right through our southernmost positions, then turn north so as to cut of the supply lines of the Axis and throttle the units in the front line.

The main tank assembly and repair shops are near El Taga.

These men have known for some time that the 52nd Infantry Division has arrived in Egypt. But they believe that this division – one of the best

---

* Gott was commander-designate of the Eighth Army. He was on his way to take up the appointment when his plane was shot down. His place was taken by General Sir Bernard Montgomery.
† *Three Score Years and Ten*, privately printed, Chester 1976.

in the British Army – has not reached the front yet.

On 23 October 1942, at eleven A.M., i.e. on the very morning of the beginning of the battle of El Alamein, the POW cage reported:

> A prisoner captured in the northern sector was turned in by XX Corps. He belongs to the Cameron Highlanders, 51st Division. His battalion departed with the steamship *Richmond* on July 9. The ship later rendezvous'd with the rest of the convoy coming from Glasgow. The Black Watch is in the front line. According to the POW's statements the entire 51st Division came directly out to the Middle East. The prisoner confirms rumours of an offensive among the troops, who expect the British advance any day now.

On 26th October the same POW cage at El Daba phoned that 'a British POW who had lived in Paris for a long time firmly insisted that the main thrust would come next, not in the south, but in the north!' It added, 'He is "trustworthy" and has good reason for his statement.'

Mainly on the strength of this statement the G-2 answered Field Marshal Rommel's question on the evening of that day, as to whether 21st Panzer Division could be transferred from the south and sent north, that this could be done. The decision for this move could be taken on the basis of all the reconnaissance results, even though it meant the southern front was denuded of tanks.

Agents' Work

In the virtually uninhabited wastes of Libya and Egypt the kind of agents and spies who could be employed in Europe were naturally not available; they would in any case be useless, because of the vastness of the zone and the swiftly changing situation. Arab nomads have no concept of time, and cannot distinguish between types of vehicles – all cars are *wabur* (machine); nor can they remember or repeat exact figures.

The combat report from a Sinai Bedouin in 1935 on the battle of 1915 in the north of Sinai, where Germans and Turks had fought against English and Australians, ran for instance as follows: 'They came from there and came from here; then there was a clash and they went.' On the occasion of the advance into the Fezzan in March 1941 some Tibbu of the Tedjerri region were asked about the small Free French attack on the Fezzan. Apart from the fact that there were strangers that came from the south, they could say nothing either about the strength of the detachment or the number and types of vehicles. What came to light was quite meaningless although the Arab interpreter might of course have invented much of it.

Enlisting the native inhabitants of Cyrenaica as agents posed more difficulties for the Germans than for the British; although the Libyans probably had nothing against the Germans, they hated the Italians as an occupying power. Consequently they inclined more to the British. Naturally the German command in Africa would have found it valuable to get information from Egypt, and attempts were made to infiltrate agents, but they met with no success.

Enemy Behaviour

Everything, from the enemy's military methods and tactics in attack and defence – are they bold or inflexible? – to his national character is of legitimate interest to military intelligence.

Often it is a question of imponderables, but an understanding mind can grasp the essentials: observations drawn from previous military actions provide clues that are of importance for summing up the enemy and his intentions. The enemy's actions and reactions will reveal to the informed intelligence officer much about the character of the opposing commander and the morale of his troops. Many actions can be taken against a hesitant enemy that could not stand a chance against a commander capable of rapid resolve. One cannot ignore the possibility that the enemy may ape one's own behaviour and tactics if they prove the more successful like the use of surprise or the relentless exploitation of initial successes.

*

The primary task of intelligence was to observe the enemy's conduct and obtain information about him. But time and again the possibility and even desirability arose of influencing his conduct. For such actions the intelligence service was well qualified, as one example shows.

Bomb attacks on German and Italian field hospitals had increased sharply during September 1941 with heavy casualties and great damage. On 28th September Panzergruppe Afrika sent a wireless signal to the OKW Propaganda Department: Further British air attacks on German and Italian hospitals have been reported between 18th and 23rd September:

1. On 18th September at four-thirty P.M. an attack on main dressing station, 21st Panzer Division.
2. On 27th September at eight A.M. bomb attack on hospital, Italian Savona Division. Three dead, six wounded, total destruction of surgical department.
3. On September 27th at eleven thirty A.M. bomb attack on main dressing station 21st Panzer Division. Eleven dead, three seriously injured, five lightly wounded. Division regards attack as intentional as station was marked by giant Red Crosses on rocks and twenty Red Crosses very distinctly laid out. Fliegerführer Afrika has applied via X Air Corps to Supreme Commander Air Force for permission to execute retaliatory attacks.

On 27th September, we printed this warning leaflet: 'Englishmen,' it ran. 'Our patience is exhausted!'

In the last two weeks you have destroyed and battered installations and shamelessly murdered soldiers who had been wounded in fair combat: Your pilots have not hesitated to bomb and strafe hospitals, main dressing stations, and casualty tents clearly marked with the Red Cross.

There followed a list of attacks with their dates, then the leaflet continued:

We will not tolerate this improper military action one day longer. We are accustomed to a fair fight with legitimate weapons against proper adversaries. But if you intend to pursue these gangster methods then we will repay you in the same coin. If there is more cowardly attack of this kind our airforce will be ordered to bombard your field hospitals and clearing stations without pity!

Our Propaganda Company had written a draft in a considerably sharper language, which had in fact been 'softened' by us to the above wording.

The threatened reprisal attacks did not have to take place, the British attacks on hospitals now ceased.

The monotony of the daily intelligence work was sometimes indescribable. Visits to the front line from time to time with Field Marshal Rommel provided a welcome change. Close attention was always required in the laborious job of piecing together the stones to give a complete mosaic of the enemy. The general guidelines could not be lost sight of; yet at the same time we had to be prepared to shift our attention quickly. The job called for the precision of a skilled artisan as well as a sympathetic understanding of the circumstances and psyche of the enemy.

If an adversary is worked on over a period of time, the observer becomes accustomed to his habits and preferences and also to his weaknesses; in a given situation it was often possible to predict certain patterns of behaviour on the basis of this knowledge. Thus with the British the dominating factor was 'safety first'. The British generals were obsessed with this; Churchill reports from the Boer War that they even railed against those who wanted to pursue a defeated enemy. General Sir Redvers Buller is said to have referred to the damned pursuit, as he ordered back the British Cavalry who were all for pursuing the Boers sweeping back near Ladysmith! True, there were others among the British generals, like O'Connor, the victor of Sidi Barrani. In the winter of 1940/41 he had taken the fortresses of Bardia and Tobruk, and then Benghazi and the whole of Cyrenaica just by reckless pursuit of the Italian Tenth Army; but there were few British generals who acted as he did.

The British stereotype was represented by General Sir Bernard Montgomery: first he built up maximum superiority in guns, tanks and men; and then, only when nothing could go wrong, he attacked. Rommel dubbed him 'the Fox' because of this caution and determination not to fail as had 'the others', as Montgomery called his predecessors at Eighth Army headquarters.

The G-2 (Intelligence) officers engaged in North Africa had all undergone the same training. They were used to sizing up the facts clearly, to estimating enemy strength without illusions, and to depict it objectively and without undue pessimism. They were certainly not ominiscient, but they were unprejudiced and could acquire an insight into the enemy's intentions without drifting into the realms of fantasy. They kept a sense of proportion and a fine balance of judgment, and there was little if any exaggeration evident in their reports, the intelligence summaries. As their assistant, the author can testify to this. After Major von Plehwe left our staff in March 1941 and after the premature loss of Captain Count Wolf von Baudissin, who fell into enemy hands on 5th April near Tobruk after only a short period of service, from May 1941 onwards Captain Roestel became the DAK's intelligence officer. His period of office saw the great defensive battles on the Egyptian frontier and our victory in the battle of Sollum. On 15th August Major Friedrich Wilhelm von Mellenthin took over as intelligence officer of the newly formed Panzergruppe Afrika. He gave a fresh impetus to the intelligence work: he tightened up the channels of communication of intelligence and initiated an interchange of results with the Italian SIM. Mellenthin's peak responsibility would come during the winter campaign from 18th November 1941 to January 1942. While he assessed the enemy's intentions on the basis of a well-founded and realistic intuition, his successor – who would take up his post at the beginning of February 1942 – preferred to deduce from the 'logic' of the situation what the enemy might be up to.

The precision of his estimates of the enemy order of battle and intentions would become particularly apparent during our summer offensive of 1942; unfortunately ill-health forced Colonel Ernst Zolling to leave Africa at the beginning of October 1942.

After an interim in which the author was responsible for the intelligence work, on 25th November Captain (later Major) Leibl would take over as G-2 of the German-Italian Panzerarmee Afrika.

Leibl was imaginative but methodical. During the long retreat to Tunisia he would often correctly predict the enemy's intentions – usually an outflanking movement – although intelligence was very hard to come by. In this manner he provided his superiors with information that made it possible to evade capture by a superior enemy. Major Leibl would then be nominated G-2 of Fifth Panzer Army which fought together with the Italian First Army (successors of the German-Italian Panzerarmee) in Tunisia. From 8th March 1943 onwards Army Group Africa, commanded by Colonel-General Hans-Jürgen von Arnim, would direct the fighting. When the army group capitulated in May 1943 Leibl would be taken prisoner by the Americans.

On the Italian side, Major (later Colonel) Revetria was chief of SIM at Supercomando Libia: an energetic, intelligent and well-informed officer, Revetria contributed considerably to the ready collaboration, which Major von Mellenthin had begun. Of SIM's liaison officers to the G-2 staff of Panzergruppe and Panzerarmee Afrika, the most prominent was Lieutenant-Colonel De Carlo, who had been awarded the Gold Medal for his work; among the junior officers Lieutenants Ferri and Tozzi became close friends with the Germans. The cooperation between Italians and Germans was loyal at every level.

CHAPTER FOUR

Intelligence during the Campaign

First experiences when reconquering Cyrenaica
When the German Intelligence service began to function in February 1941, the only tool of reference it possessed was an Italian situation map dated 15th February. This showed the British two forces as consisting of corps – one armoured corps and one ANZAC-Corps, that is, an Australian-New Zealand army corps.

Little by little further light was shed upon the darkness that shrouded the enemy's battle order and dispositions: on 24th February the first prisoners (a lieutenant and two other ranks) were taken by our 3rd Reconnaissance Battalion near Agheila; they belonged to the King's Dragoon Guards (a reconnaissance unit that had relieved the 11th Hussars of 7th Armoured Division, which had been established until 17th February near Agheila) and to the 16th Australian Anti-Tank Company.*

This did not enable us to detect the subsequent departure of 7th Armoured Division from Cyrenaica to Greece. Major von Plehwe, G-2 at Rommel's Corps headquarters, tried every day to obtain access to the intelligence developed by SIM; but at that time the Italians guarded this very jealously and he could not dispel the fog that shrouded the enemy situation; there were too many contradictions.

When DAK's headquarters staff was transferred to Sirte on 13th March, von Plehwe had to return to Rome; until the end of March, when Captain von Baudissin arrived the post of G-2 remained vacant. At that time air reconnaissance was the most important source information; wireless intelligence was only just overcoming its teething troubles as was to be expected in a new theatre of war.

In March the Italians asked us to mount a reconnaissance operation into the Fezzan in the south of Libya as rumours of operations by the Free French against Italian forts in this region had come through. The rumours seemed to have some substance, insofar as the Italian garrison of Kufra capitulated to Free French troops

* B. Maughan, *Tobruk and El Alamein*, Canberra 1966.

from Chad. For this sortie Lieutenant-Colonel Count Gerd von Schwerin, OC of 200th Regiment, assembled a small motorised force and set out southwards on 15th March. This small force, of which the author was a member, advanced via Hon, Murzuk and Gatrun to Tedjerri, nearly up to the southern frontier of Libya; it found no trace of the purported enemies. There we received news that the Italians had fresh information on the spot, but it was all probably a belated echo of a British raid on Murzuk and other forts in the Fezzan in January and a simultaneous unsuccessful Free French attack on Tedjerri. Such news was liable to be exaggerated since it was usually passed on by isolated groups of simple people and even then only after some delay and with little regard for chronology either. Enquiries of the Tibbu nomads living there, questioned through Arabian interpreters, yielded nothing new.

The British raid against the Fezzan had been executed by the Long Range Desert Group in January 1941: two patrols under the command of Major P. Clayton had made a surprise attack on the Italian forts there at a distance of some twelve hundred miles from Cairo. They certainly caused confusion; but as they were only equipped with light weapons they could hardly operate effectively against the forts, and the Italians held out against nearly all of them. After destroying airfield installations and planes the two LRDG patrols carried on south to Lake Chad, to operate together with Free French troops from the south against the Italian-occupied oasis of Kufra, which was important for communications between Chad and Egypt.

Major Clayton, heading the lead patrol group on this sortie, was taken prisoner south of Kufra by the Italians, through some fine co-operation between the Italian airforce and the Sahara Company; both were under the command of Colonel Leo, commander of the Libyan Sahara. Clayton's column was severely mauled and had to retreat. The Free French then executed the operation against Kufra alone; it culminated with the seizure of the principal fortress in the Kufra oasis, at Al Jawf on 1st March.

Colonel Leo explained to the author in detail how he had deployed the airforce and Sahara Company from Kufra against the LRDG attack. He had moved out the Sahara Company, far to the south of Kufra, to intercept Clayton after Italian reconnaissance planes spotted the British column. Clayton himself was cornered on the last day of January. The first Italian planes to attack his column, immobilised his car; he assumed he had enough time to repair his puncture, and sent back the other vehicles. But this assumption turned out to be false: The Sahara Company arrived with superior fire power about half an hour later and Clayton had no alternative but to surrender. Through the good offices of SIM, the author was permitted to talk with Major Clayton on 3rd March, and he recounted the circumstances of his capture. The admiration shown by German officers for Clayton's achievement in crossing sand dunes a hundred miles and more in width – the 'Sand Sea' between Egypt and Libya – with a military column was some consolation to him in his captivity. It was incomprehensible to us that the Italian Sahara Company gave up mobile warfare a little later, when the Free French attacked, and after a short skirmish left the Al Jawf garrison to its fate. The attacking Free French column coming up from Chad, would have not been able to hold out for long if the fortress and Sahara Company had collaborated better. As it was, Kufra was lost and with it an important southern outpost for the Italians.

On the strength of von Schwerin's reports that Gatrun-Tedjerri and the region to the south was clear of the enemy, our corps HQ attached no further importance to the rumours about Free French troops and southern Libya. Von Schwerin was ordered to return. He reached Agedabia on 3rd April at six P.M. Rommel then gave him command of the corps' southern attacking column, which was to set out that same evening via Ben Gania and Tengeder to the north-east in the direction of Derna and Tmimi.

It will be of interest to record here the intelligence which we had received between mid-March and the start of this first advance and the immediately subsequent skirmishes that brought about the capture of Agedabia:

March 18th, 1941:
The report of a *Zerstörer* [long-range twin-engined fighter] pilot, i.e. air reconnaissance, confirms reports by certain Arab agents raising suspicions that the British have withdrawn key units from the area Agedabia—Solluch—Mersa-el-Brega. This creates the impression that they have no intention of holding Mersa-el-Brega;

March 19th: The impression hardens, that the enemy has left only strong rearguards at Mersa-el-Brega.

March 20th: It is not impossible that the British have completely gone over to the defence and have withdrawn the bulk of their forces into Cyrenaica.

March 21st: 'Y' reports the absence of between ten and fourteen enemy wireless transmitters; this can be taken as confirming the withdrawal of enemy forces. Overall reconnaissance report: At and to the south-west of Agedabia are assumed to be: one armoured scout car battalion, one tank battalion, one mechanized infantry battalion, one artillery regiment, and one French brigade.

March 24th: Agheila is overrun in the course of the Italian-German advance. Thereupon the British have withdrawn, apparently to the Mersa-el-Brega defile.

March 26th: The wireless picture suggests that after the fall of Agheila fresh forces of up to three formations were brought forward: one armoured car battalion and two artillery battalions. It is anticipated that the British will try to hold Agedabia at all costs.

After taking El Agheila, Rommel decided to attack the enemy's holding position at Mersa-el-Brega on the last day of March, to probe the enemy resistance. Only weak resistance was offered to this attack and on 1st April it was realized that only a small force was involved and that the British were conscious of this weakness. Air reconnaissance moreover reported that the British were pulling back. Learning of this Rommel decided to follow up and to test the enemy strength still further. The British retreated too rapidly to enable proper assessment, so Rommel pounded after them with 5th Light Division. He seized Agedabia on the afternoon of 2nd April, and on the next day the division was ready for defence between Agedabia and Zuetina. But it reported that it had enough fuel for another one hundred miles.

Characteristically, Rommel ordered all non-essential vehicles to be unloaded and to return to fetch fuel from the rear dump at Arco dei Fileni (between Sirte and El Agheila). It was to take one night and one day. 'This,' he said, 'will save blood and win us Cyrenaica!'

The pursuit that then began developed into the first German-Italian offensive. At first it met with anything but approval from the Supreme Commander, the Italian General Italo Gariboldi. On 2nd April he sent a wireless signal from Tripoli: 'From information received I learn that your advance is still going on. This is in contravention of my directives. I ask you to await my arrival before continuing your advance.'

But our appraisal of the situation on 3rd April suggested that the British withdrawal to the north and north-east was continuing; Rommel therefore decided to harass the enemy on his southern flank at Ben Gania and Tengeder, to find out whether they intended to hold Cyrenaica; and to push on still further round their flank and to the rear, if opportunity arose, that is, to the north-east in the direction of Tmimi.

Later, at nine P.M. that day, General Gariboldi arrived at Deutches Afrika Korps headquarters. He told Rommel to report on the situation first and not to advance until he gave the order. Rommel objected that he could not wait for such a protracted system of giving orders. As the German commander, he argued, he must give his orders in accordance with the prevailing situation. Towards the end of this conversation a signal arrived from the OKW which imparted to Rommel – so he maintained – 'complete freedom of action' in resuming his offensive advance; this General Gariboldi did not dispute. The next day he received in person a similar order from the Duce. A signal of 3rd April from the OKW's Wilhelm Keitel, strictly *limiting* Rommel's freedom of action, arrived only later by which time it had been overtaken by events.

Both Rommel and others have written narratives of the full scale offensive, into which this limited advance expanded. The sequence

of events is well known. It will suffice here to give a short survey. From Agedabia, his German-Italian troops pushed forward in three columns in an attempt at cutting the line of retreat of the British who had initially tried to hold Cyrenaica. One column, the Schwerin group and parts of 5th Light Division under General Johannes Streich, made a right hook from Agedabia via Maaten el Grar and Ben Gania to Mechili. Two columns under Colonel Olbrich with 5th Panzer Regiment rallied at Msus and advanced from the west against Mechili via Antelat and Solluch. A third group under Irnfried von Wechmar, consisting of the 3rd Reconnaissance Battalion, marched east via Benghazi, rolled back the Australian infantry at Er Regima and joined up with the other columns just before Mechili. Rommel led from the air. His troops made only slow progress as the going was bad, fuel was short and navigation errors delayed the far flung columns. The spearhead under Lieutenant-Colonel Gustav Ponath, which Rommel had launched against Derna, reached the hilly region south of the airfield there in good time; but it was too weak to block the Via Balbia leading out of Derna on the escarpment bordering the airfield, and was thus unfortunately unable to cut off the mass of British troops in Cyrenaica. The 9th Australian Division took the cross-desert route leading to Martuba and thence to Tobruk. The major part of the British troops flowing back via Derna and its two passes – which gave access to the escarpment – were able to escape, before Rommel could reinforce Ponath's advance force enough to seal off the Via Balbia highway south of Derna.

On 4th April Schwerin's group reached Bir Tengeder at nine P.M., making for Mechili. By early 5th April long columns of British troops were falling back along the Via Balbia from Cirene to Lamluda and Tmimi to Gazala. Planes sent by our Fliegerführer Afrika attacked columns of enemy tanks and motor vehicles near Msus, and we expected frantic attempts by these troops to break through to the east. At midnight Msus was reported clear of the enemy. Our appreciation of the enemy's situation on Sunday morning, 6th April was: 'The British have escaped total annihilation by us and are for the most part marching on Tobruk. It is possible that they will embark in the port of Tobruk.'

Our combat air reconnaissance (*2./[H] 14.Pz.*) reported at seven-thirty A.M. that day: 'Garrison has dug in at and around Mechili, partly behind wire barrier. In Mechili 230-300 vehicles, with fifty to seventy vehicles two miles to the east. Along tracks leading to east is a further big accumulation of vehicles.' Ponath's advanced detachment reached the hills two or three miles south of Derna airfield at about six-thirty P.M. and spent the night in one of the wadis east of the highway, which was however kept under surveillance. That night Generals Philip Neame, C-in-C in Cyrenaica Command, and Richard O'Connor, victor of the battle of Sidi Barrani, were captured: they had both chosen the southern track when heading east out of Maraua; after crossing the Mechili-Derna road they had turned north and run slap into Ponath. The commander of 9th Australian Division, Major-General Leslie Morshead, who had taken leave of these two gentlemen at about eight o'clock that evening, chose to use the main highway east, the Via Balbia via Derna, that night and arrived without hindrance at four A.M. at Tmimi. This was the night when, as mentioned, Ponath was still not in control of traffic flowing down the Via Balbia.

Rommel and O'Connor were commanders of comparable flexibility and energy. But in this way the duel between them never took place. O'Connor was not actually in command in Cyrenaica at the time, although Wavell had earmarked him for this on 2nd April. He had stayed as adviser to General Neame, considering it unfair to relieve him once the operations had begun. It was fortunate for the British that Morshead, who shortly excelled as the inflexible defender of Tobruk, had chosen not to accompany the other generals.

On the next day, 7th April, Ponath attempted an attack on the airfield, but the enemy artillery and anti-tank guns responded with superior fire and he had to retire southwards. Fortunately the British did not follow. After reinforcements arrived his detachment resumed the attempt about mid-day, attacking the eastern part of the airfield. The reinforcements consisted of one anti-tank and one anti-aircraft platoon, two machine-gun platoons and a field howitzer, with only three rounds. At first this attack made good progress westwards but about three P.M. eight British tanks cleared the way for a convoy, which escaped along the coast highway. Ponath resumed his push at about five P.M. and blocked the Via Balbia at Derna. 'Great booty,' Ponath reported, 'water and fuel'. The British owe it to the drive of their officers that their troops were not trapped at Derna; in the traffic jam on the serpentine road between the escarpment and the airfield, south-east of Derna they had ordered vehicles overturned and they had brought up artillery behind them. This halted Ponath's first assault and secured the escape route of the British columns through the town, though not without losses.*

Evaluation of 'Y' yielded the following enemy situation:

Forces near Tobruk, apparently not all that strong, have orders to defend themselves near Acroma and to send out only reconnaissance patrols to the south and west. Probable retreat by a major group early on 7th April at the latest from area south of Derna making for Gazala and points further east. Rearguards of a major group with logistics unit will be entering area from south of Derna to Mechili up to the morning of 7th April. We once more call attention to fact that the tank unit on which [Fliegerführer] Fröhlich of Luftwaffe inflicted serious defeat at Msus may arrive at Mechili early on 7th April.

In the meantime the Commander-in-Chief, Rommel, personally took charge of preparations to attack Mechili. No attack however took place on the seventh as Olbrich's group was still thirty miles away to the south-west, and the 3rd Reconnaissance Battalion was forty miles to the west and the bulk of Streich's force, the 5th Light Division, arrived at Mechili only after night had closed in.

Our airforce completed the picture of the enemy as follows: at three P.M. they sighted 'large tank and vehicle accumulations' at and to the east of Gazala; west of that, however, at Um er Rzem-Gazala, the routes were only lightly held and farther to the west there was no more enemy at all. All this made it plain that the British troops had evacuated Cyrenaica and were withdrawing into Marmarica with the bulk of their forces.

Ponath's group had fought continuously since late 7th April against the enemy's desperate efforts to break through. He was only partly successful, since the enemy could by-pass the airfield in the north. In the evening Rommel arrived at the airfield, and Ponath was able to report to him huge quantities of booty, including weapons, ammunition and fuel as well as eight hundred prisoners.

Unlike Rommel, neither Neame nor O'Connor had been actually with the fighting troops, so that given the bad signals communications the battle-inexperienced troops who had little enough combat experience anyway, lacked firm command. In consequence, Rommel pushed on relentlessly as soon as he detected that the British were not putting up a coherent resistance.

* Oral information to the author from one of those participating, Brigadier Hugh Mainwaring.

At eight o'clock on 8th April 5th Light Division and the 1st Battalion of 5th Panzer Regiment took Mechili. Here another general, Michael Gambier-Parry, commander of 2nd Armoured Division, was captured with sixty officers and about 1,700 other ranks. All kinds of booty was taken, and the documents that were captured were of no small importance. (They will be dealt with later.)

Captured British officers showed by their questions of the author that they had fatally overestimated our strength.

Rommel had contributed to this. At Tripoli he had commanded his engineer, Lieutenant Hundt, in February: 'Bring me a hundred and fifty tanks!'

Met with baffled silence he had continued: 'You have enough timber and canvas here, and Volkswagens too.'* The resulting dummy-tanks looked real enough, particularly to air reconnaissance: they left tracks, they cast giant shadows, they had long wooden gun barrels and regularly changed position just as real tanks would. Alas, the time would come when the boot was on the other foot, and the British learned to camouflage tanks as dummy lorries to deceive us.

Among the vast booty from Mechili and on the desert route from there to Derna, and at the airfield in particular, were vital enemy documents including orders and dispositions. These allowed us an excellent insight into the British army's order of battle in the Middle East. They enabled us to round off and update our 1940 picture of the British Field Army's structure. We now had a much clearer picture of their whole command structure in the Middle East. Unfortunately the intelligence officer of the German Afrika Korps – who would normally have evaluated these documents – had gone missing; Captain Wolf von Baudissin had been captured near Tobruk on 5th April. As soon as it was realised what a quantity of captured papers had fallen into our hands Foreign Armies West sent over Major Soltmann, the War Office expert on England, to DAK Staff headquarters to examine them. The DAK's chief of staff Lieutenant-Colonel von dem Borne ordered Lieutenant Behrendt (the author) to help Major Soltmann on account of his knowledge of languages.

From the captured documents we gathered that the following units had been on the British side against us: Under Cyrenaica Command (a territorial command coming under Middle East

* Author's recollections.

Command) were 2nd Armoured Division with 3rd Armoured Brigade and the 2nd Support Group; also 3rd Indian Motor Brigade (three battalions with light weapons), 9th Australian Division (without its artillery, but with 20th, 24th and 26th Australian Infantry Brigades, and three artillery units: the 1st Royal Horse Artillery, the 104th Royal Horse Artillery, the 51st Field Regiment, RA, and one battery of the 3rd Royal Horse Artillery (anti-tank unit). These formations represented the sum total of the two army corps that we had supposed to be in Cyrenaica in February. The reports showed British repeatedly complaining of the miserable state of their motor vehicles – the tanks and lorries were worn out and sometimes fit only for the scrapheap. A partial conversion to captured Italian M-13's had just begun, replacing the worn out British tanks. But the Italian tanks did not perform satisfactorily: their engine cooling systems boiled over after as little as ten to fifteen miles so their daily range was limited to only about fifty miles. Another factor was that 2nd Armoured Division was newly activated and lacked battle experience. The shortage of signals staff was a bad handicap; many of these had been sent over to Greece.

The German-Italian advance to the Egyptian western frontier was, so to speak, a series of clashes between 'stragglers' – small combat groups that formed on both sides from time to time. The British command was unsure; it suffered from inappropriate communications and constantly changing orders; the Germans and Italians came under Rommel's energetic command, constantly pushing and co-ordinating, so that every difficulty and minor reverse was overcome.

On the British side there was confusion: a dispatch rider whose motor cycle broke down on the desert road from Mechili to Derna asked a passing car for a lift back to 3rd Armoured Brigade. He got in, and remarked after a while: 'Strange car'. He only now learned that it was German! He took his fate philosophically. All the British vehicles suffered badly as they were all more or less on their last legs; but they could not be repaired for lack of time. Both sides suffered alike from shortage of fuel, navigation difficulties and the bad terrain which wore out all vehicles without regard for nationality. But there was a difference: the Germans, even in small groups, always knew where they were going or what to do, whereas the British did not. Their generals were prisoners of the unfolding situation; they left the initiative to us, the enemy, and they were nearly always too late with each decision they took. *Ducunt volentem fata, nolentem trahunt,* the appropriate Latin proverb: 'Fate guides the resolute, but drags the undecided.'

On the morning of 9th April air reconnaissance established that the whole region between Mechili and Gadd el Ahmar was clear of the enemy; some twenty-five miles east of Gadd el Ahmar, it detected a retreating British column, while the main British forces were located fifteen miles west of Tobruk and from there on to Tobruk itself. About ten ships were sighted in the harbour there.

On the next day Rommel's appreciation of the situation was as follows: 'I am convinced the enemy is avoiding contact. We must pursue him with everything we have. Our objective is to be made known to every man; it is the Suez Canal. To prevent an enemy breakout from Tobruk the offensive is to be pushed ahead by every means possible.'

Combat Air Reconnaissance was flown over Tobruk on the 11th, seven-thirty A.M.: 'German troops a little north of El Adem,' this found. 'The enemy at Tobruk has established a front to south-east close to B. el Azazi. He has manned positions on the mountain range thirteen miles south-east of Tobruk. Positions west of Tobruk abandoned.'

The 5th Panzer Regiment made an initial reconnaissance thrust, west of the El Adem-Tobruk road, pushing northwards. Afterwards it reported: 'South of Tobruk in the Sghifet el Chuer [is] an anti-tank trench with many anti-tank guns and mines.' This was all that could be stated at that time, in the absence of maps of the defences; it was too little, as shortly became apparent, for a successful attack against a tough opponent well dug in. Army Air Reconnaissance (2./H14) had reported 'an enemy group of 100 lorries, artillery and tanks hitherto located near El Adem, in hasty withdrawal eastwards on Trigh Enver,' but this did not unfortunately weaken the already considerable determination of the Tobruk garrison to resist. The German attackers could only counter with élan.

Not until 12th April would DAK be informed about the siting and layout of the permanent defence works at Tobruk. Our sole basis for giving orders was a 1:400.000 map; the Italian Supercomando unfortunately gave us no briefing. Count Schwerin's detachment had meanwhile sealed off the front around Tobruk on both sides of Sidi Daud on the 12th. According to our intelligence information at Afrika Korps the British did not have the troops available and ready for action necessary to hold off a serious thrust against Egypt. Our air reconnaissance reported that the British were weak on the frontier and that there were no more forces until far beyond Matruh. Therefore our intention was to continue the fast drive eastwards with advance detachments to overrun one by one all the reserves hastily brought up by the British before they could divert strong forces from Abyssinia or Greece. The bulk of the troops would follow after taking care of the logistics position. The precondition was the capture of Tobruk: it had to be achieved whatever the cost.

At six P.M. on 13th April 1941 the attack began. In support of 5th Light Division were 8th Machine-Gun Battalion and a handful of tanks, Colonel Grati's Artillery Regiment and the 1st Battalion of the 18th Flak Regiment. They attacked the crossroads south of Tobruk, which was of importance both as a jumping off point for the capture of the town and as an artillery observation post. On the right flank the Machine-Gun Battalion succeeded in taking the anti-tank trench and the barbed wire entanglement but the attack failed to attain its objective.

At four-thirty A.M. the next day the decisive attack by 5th Light Division began. The 8th Machine-Gun Battalion succeeded in breaking through the ring of fortifications on the west right by the road from El Adem to Tobruk, but it was unable to widen the breach. The attack by 5th Panzer Regiment was repulsed when still three miles south of Tobruk by concentrated artillery and anti-tank fire; nor could the 8th Machine-Gun Battalion follow up this attack. When the breach was sealed a large part of the battalion was cut off, captured or killed. Among the dead here was Lieutenant-Colonel Ponath himself, an outstanding commanding officer. In spite of Stuka and Flak artillery support, Korps headquarters had to admit that our attempt to take Tobruk by storm had failed; it ordered a change to siege tactics in front of Tobruk.

It must be reiterated that having reached Tobruk unexpectedly early the German troops were under the possibly fatal disadvantage that they knew nothing about the defences of Tobruk and repeatedly ran right into unexpected positions. Reconnaissance units kept stumbling across unsuspected tank-obstacles and positions that were so well camouflaged that they were barely visible even from only a few yards away; and all of them were fiercely defended, in contrast to the enemy's combat behaviour hitherto.

The lack of adequate maps resulted too in inaccurate reports, causing grave misunderstandings. The Brescia Division wrongly reported that it had occupied Point 187 north of Ras el Madawar, the south-western anchor post of the defences, without a fight. Only several days after we reached Tobruk, on 19th April did the Italian

Supercomando make available accurate map material; and this delay was instrumental in the serious failure of the first German-Italian assault on Tobruk.

If we had captured Tobruk the way on into Egypt would have been free. Given the enemy weakness after our thrust across Cyrenaica, it would have been a perfectly feasible objective to reach and block the Suez Canal if the attack had succeeded. So the Afrika Korps was correct in attacking Tobruk at the first opportunity. Even though these first attacks failed, it is proper to remember that at that time there were only 32,000 Germans in Africa, whereas General Morshead, the defender of Tobruk, disposed about 36,000 men – of which 24,000 were at the front (14,000 Australians and approximately 9,000 British); moreover he had an artillery strength of seventy-two guns.

Then the enemy counter attacks began. Intercepted wireless signals reported the first British attack at six-thirty A.M. on 22nd April. They came at the Fabris Battalion of the Brescia Division with about six or ten tanks (according to an Australian report they were only Bren gun Carriers):

> *7.50 A.M.:* Two hundred infantry surrender.
> *8.20 A.M.:* The fighting now seems to be over; about two hundred prisoners have been brought in. We destroyed three or four light guns and twenty or thirty motorcycles with side-cars.
> *9.00 A.M.:* Own losses: one light tank, one other rank.

In the course of another Australian counter-attack a battalion of the Trento Division was taken prisoner to a man, leaving behind its entire equipment, according to one Australian intelligence summary. Meanwhile we learned from British prisoners on 25th April that the British were planning to reverse their fortunes, if possible, in front of Tobruk, by launching an outflanking attack from Capuzzo.

We made preparations for a second attack on Tobruk from 26th to 30th April, executing diversionary raids during the latter days to persuade the enemy that we were about to attack the frontier at Sollum front and that an assault by 5th Light Division south of Tobruk was imminent. At six-thirty P.M. on 30th April Stukas delivered heavy attacks on Hill 209 and on the points chosen for 15th Panzer Division and General Kirchheim's group to breach the defences.

At seven-fifteen P.M. hours the assault parties moved in to attack the outer ring of the defences; and at nine-thirty the 2nd Machine-Gun Battalion took Hill 209, Ras el Madawar. In this opening phase of the attack, we had apparently succeeded in deceiving the defenders about our intended point of breakthrough. Meanwhile, our Radio Intercept Platoon reported anxiety over on the Sollum front on the enemy's part as a result of our deception manoeuvres.

After breaking through eleven positions in the outer ring of Tobruk's defences, and four of the inner defence ring, our attack was halted. The front around Tobruk consolidated for the time being. Late on 3rd May a counter-attack led by the Australian 2nd/18th Infantry Battalion collapsed under our fire and Morshead called it off altogether on the next morning. Prisoners later confirmed to us that this night attack was a large-scale attempt to recover the fortifications that had been lost to us.

Our Commander-in-Chief, Rommel, issued an Order of the Day which might be mentioned here:

On the evening of 30th April we attacked the enemy fortification ring on both sides of Ras el Madawar. In fighting of unprecedented violence lasting more than twenty-four hours, we succeeded in breaking out the dug outs of the strongly fortified bunker line one by one. In hazardous assault we captured numerous well-armed concrete strongpoints, one after the other, despite tough enemy resistance. Counter-attacks by tanks supported by fierce artillery fire, were repulsed. Heat and sandstorms hampered the fighting.

During the whole day our airforce was repeatedly in action with Stukas, and single- and twin-engined fighter planes. I express my profoundest admiration of the outstanding achievement of both officers and men. This battle will go down in history as one of the hardest of the war in Africa.

Our troops had thrown everything they had into the objective of taking Tobruk. But they had failed, and the way into Egypt could still not be opened. Tobruk remained a thorn in the flesh for the Afrika Korps until 1942.

Wireless Intelligence is reinforced: First Successes.
In the meantime 3rd Radio Intercept Company/56th Signals Battalion (at that time called *Horchkompanie*) had arrived in the forward area of the DAK. Part of this company, the Intercept Platoon (*Horchzug*) Africa had already been in action under

Lieutenant Gerisch having arrived at Tripoli on 25th February and reached its forward area in Sirtica on 6th March.

Contrary to some reports the whole company had not arrived in Africa in time for this first thrust through Cyrenaica. Only the one platoon under Gerisch was at DAK's disposal at the commencement of the advance. The rest of the company had reached Bolzano by Easter Sunday, 14th April and would embark at Naples; only on its fourth attempt did SS *Leverkusen*, the ship bringing it over with a section of 15th Panzer Division, enter Tripoli harbour on 24th April. The company then re-absorbed the *Horchzug* platoon, and its commander was transferred elsewhere.

The company issued its first report on 2nd May, Radio Monitoring Report No 1. It is apparent from those reports which survive that radio monitoring's picture of the enemy was not always perfect. At that time we did not bother much with wireless reconnaissance; it was of interest, but less important than either ground or air reconnaissance. The latter provided Rommel with particularly accurate data on the weakened enemy he was facing. It was his intuition, his instinct about his opponents' likely behaviour that was the decisive factor. 'I used to get this hunch that I knew where the enemy would give way', he would tell the author later on in the campaign. After the whole company's arrival in the forward area under their commanding officer Lieutenant Seebohm, radio monitoring became materially more productive than before.

From now on important new information was systematically acquired; it was of limited value on its own, but it could be supplemented, confirmed, or in some cases refuted by material from other sources, as occasionally happened when the enemy attempted diversionary manoeuvres. Wireless reconnaissance alone could not always supply the correct explanation; but when all the intelligence was in it could be pieced together to provide a reasonably accurate picture.

As the following messages show, it was only with the full company's arrival that radio monitoring became our best source of intelligence on the enemy. After dramatic battles on the Sollum front, vain British attempts to restore the situation by counter-attacks from Tobruk, and a further unsuccessful British attack on 9th/10th May we received wireless intercept messages indicating that reinforcements were coming from the south on the 10th.

Wireless intercepts after a German attack beginning early on 12th May around Sidi Omar, Sollum and Bardia had taken the enemy by

sreel picture of Rommel
his interpreter Wilfried
bruster on his right.

.5 centimetre gun crew in
n at the Battle of Sollum
leaxe) June 1941.

sh prisoners in April 1941.

Morale soars in the Afrika Korps as Rommel successfully fights off the first major British offensive against him—Battleaxe, June 1941.

After Battleaxe.

surprise, indicated a large sea relief attempt was likely on the 14th.
In Radio Monitoring Report No 12 of 13th May 1941 the events of
12th May are vividly described.

Sollum front: The German attack which began in the early morning
caught the enemy on the hop: he was still much occupied in restoring
order after his own unsuccessful attack on 9th/10th May. The
preparation of our own troops during the night had gone unnoticed by
the enemy. The first report from one of his reconnaissance patrols about
our western force came at 4.27 A.M. and it was followed at five A.M. by
further signals reporting our other assault groups. The British southern
force eluded the threatening encirclement by timely evasive action to the
east or south-east; the CO of this force ('Jock') made no appearance all
day having left the evening before for a conference. The 4th Royal Horse
Artillery suffered most of all from the rapid withdrawal; it evidently
sustained considerable losses, since twenty-two ambulance cars were
sent to it after the fighting finished. The infantry brigade brought up
from the north-east could not stop our tank advance and it withdrew
hastily as well. The 2nd Rifle Brigade retreated before our own relatively
weak forces as they advanced across the coastal plain. From the fact that
the signals intercepted all day long were mainly reports on enemy
movements and contained no orders for action whatsoever, it can be
concluded that organised command was out of the question.

By mid-day divisional headquarters had still not received any orders
at all by wireless. At this time only scouting patrols mounted by the
reconnaissance units were following our forces who were returning to
their original positions. The bulk of the enemy forces remained for the
time being in the positions they reached yesterday in order to re-supply
and regroup. It seems that under the new organisation, three combat
groups will be created.

Apart from the reinforcements presumed on 14th May to have
reached them there was no clue to further enemy intentions to attack
on the Sollum front.

However on 15th May at five-thirty A.M. the British unexpectedly
attacked our positions on the Halfaya Pass and on the Sollum front
with strong tank support. At nine A.M. Sollum 206 and Hill 191 were
lost, and later the important Fort Capuzzo. According to wireless
reports, our garrison on the Halfaya Pass was still holding out at one-
thirty P.M. Radio monitoring also reported that German tanks had
overrun a British company near Capuzzo, and that the situation
there was considered to be very critical. Thus our own headquarters
learned of the recapture of Capuzzo through surveillance of the

enemy radio nets before reports reached it from its own troops taking part. In the evening there were reports that the Halfaya position had fallen, and that a fierce fight was going on for Sidi Azziz.

Our headquarters feared that the British tank forces (7th Armoured Brigade) would concentrate near Sidi Azeiz and advance on Tobruk on 16th May. The situation was judged to be grave. But our reinforced 1st/8th Panzer Regiment, brought up for support, found early on that day that Sidi Azeiz was clear, the enemy having withdrawn to the south. Perhaps the British command, hearing of the loss of Fort Capuzzo, had been influenced by the unexpected strength of the German armoured forces and decided to call off the attack. Capuzzo would threaten their rear communication lines if their tanks were fighting near Azeiz. Only on the Halfaya Pass did the British leave a garrison.

The German attack was continued in the teeth of strenuous resistance. It had reached the line from Sidi Omar to Point 206, Sidi Suleiman and Upper Sollum by evening. But the assault group under Maximilian von Herff would no longer be capable of the major attack planned for the 18th. It was only when air reconnaissance on the morning of the 17th brought word that the British had retired with the bulk of their forces into the region south of Sidi Barrani, that it was realized that we had beaten off the attack led by General 'Strafer' Gott with 7th Armoured Brigade and 22nd Guards Brigade.

Our radio monitoring summary on the evening of 25th May stated: 'Garrison at Halfaya Pass one mixed anti-tank and anti-aircraft battalion with heavy artillery and few riflemen as hitherto, but weakened with the loss of one reconnaissance squadron. The group near Sidi Suleiman has made no further appearance. The group south of Sidi Suleiman has withdrawn to the area of Der el Hamra. North of Der el Hamra one tank battalion with two to three artillery battalions, one infantry battalion and one armoured car battalion. Two reinforced Rifle regiments in coastal plain between Alam El Barraq and Sidi Barrani, the whereabouts of one infantry and two tank battalions is unknown.' Our ground reconnaissance confirmed that the enemy forces near Der el Hamra were not yet numerous. On the other hand the front line of defence was still held by its original strength.

Wireless reconnaissance had so far produced some interesting details and had occasionally assisted our Command in its decision-making, but the latter had failed to recognize sufficiently clearly the auguries of an enemy attack on 15th May. In spite of the enemy wireless signalling the German name *Fritz* on the eve of the attack, they had issued no warnings. Yet experience accumulated and would bear fruit before long.

The German attack resulting in the capture of the Halfaya position on 27th May triggered an enemy operation 'Daffodil'; this provided for the likelihood of a withdrawal to the east, because from one signal it became evident that the necessary positions had already been prepared and that further orders were unnecessary.

One English wireless operator was heard to remark that 'other flowers would grow'. This caused the Germans to step up their surveillance over the next few weeks. From wireless intelligence on 6th June we deduced a complete enemy reorganisation on the Sollum front as is shown by the account rendered by Lieutenant Seebohm of *3./N56* on 24th June, of which the reader will learn more later. The pattern of enemy wireless traffic was similar to before their last attack on 15th May, and all leave was stopped for British units for the period 2nd to 10th June. Their air reconnaissance also became noticeably more active. The enemy regrouping south-east of Sollum was apparently concluded on 8th June. Because of repeated enemy restrictions on wireless signalling, further details could not be ascertained. Strategic air reconnaissance reported considerable rolling stock activity at the railroad stations east of Mersa Matruh and heavy railway traffic on this line.

Then our 'Y' and direction finding services revealed the possibility of a shift by British armoured forces to the west (from the area between Bir el Tlata and Habata). Moreover, scrutiny of aerial photographs showed a further increase in the number of British tactical aircraft between Matruh and Alexandria, as well as an expansion of the camp at El Hammam to nearly three thousand tents. Column traffic east of Bir el Tlata and Bir el Aneba was reported in both directions on recently used tracks.

The Battle for Sollum (British Codename 'Battleaxe')

On 14th June the enemy passed the codeword *Peter* down through all echelon HQ's down to the lower units; we concluded that just like the announcement of *Fritz* before the May attack this presaged an attack by the British forces assembled in the Western Desert on the next day, 15th June. The Afrika Korps consequently took preparatory measures from nine P.M. on the 14th onwards.

The Battle of Sollum that raged from 15th to 17th June was a classic in the history of wireless intelligence. Not only had we deduced the timing of the start of the British offensive, but during the fighting the radio monitors kept Rommel's headquarters rapidly supplied with the most important enemy signals: these gave him an insight into how the enemy saw the situation, and revealed their concern about ammunition supplies. This in turn inspired Rommel's confidence in the correctness of his own orders, despite the fierceness of the enemy resistance in the tank battles. Shortly, captured documents shed additional light on the British order of battle and intentions.

On 15th June the British advanced at four-thirty A.M. to the south and south-east of Sollum. Not until seven-thirty was a strong enemy column reported ten miles north of Sidi Omar, striking north. From this it seemed that the enemy meant to thrust into the west flank of our Capuzzo-Sollum position and having destroyed the German forces there to raise our siege of Tobruk. Radio signals identified 4th Indian Division as attacking at Halfaya. From air reconnaissance by the 2nd Army Reconnaissance Squadron at about eight o'clock it seemed certain that Capuzzo, and *not* a western envelopment by 4th Armoured Brigade, was the objective of the British attack. Later that morning we captured a list of British R/T code-names giving the exact distribution of attacking troops, the names of their commanders, and code names for tanks, guns and equipment.

By mid-day further signals analysis had revealed 7th Armoured Division attacking with 4th and 7th Armoured Brigades towards Capuzzo; the location of both enemy divisions and one brigade south of Sheferzen and Sidi Omar meant that the weight of the attack was on the western flank. From the Halfaya Pass the British reported taking numerous prisoners.

According to intercepted signals 7th Royal Tank Regiment of 4th Armoured Brigade were attacking north of Capuzzo. The 7th Armoured Brigade was fighting, on the left flank of the attacking troops opposite 5th Light Division, having advanced to Bir Mafid.

By evening the British had apparently broken off the attack against Bardia and were trying to capture our strongpoints in the Capuzzo area; the enemy were strong in tanks, with 150 or 200, nearly all Matildas, British wireless messages spoke of a great tank battle.

According to a captured operations order the main attacking force in the north was 4th Indian Division with 22nd Guards Brigade and part of 4th Armoured Brigade. To protect the left flank of this force 7th Armoured Brigade with 2nd and 6th Royal Tank Regiments and

11th Hussars, were engaged opposite 5th Light Division on the German right flank. (Our 5th Light Division had orders to advance north of Sidi Omar to Sidi Suleiman.) At ten A.M. we intercepted British messages ordering 21st Indian Brigade to advance along the coastal plain to Sollum regardless of what it left behind. But by 10.45 the brigade had already reported that it could not advance.

Our intercept showed how heavy the fighting and losses were on both sides. They often mentioned 7th Royal Tank Regiment, a unit armed with the Infantry Tank Mark II ('Matildas') and on 16th June still attacking north of Capuzzo. On the same day the commander of 7th Armoured Division was heard ordering a workshop unit to get to work on infantry tanks for his 7th Armoured Brigade urgently. At three-thirty P.M. 7th Armoured Division retreated ten or fifteen miles to the south-east. At 3.45 P.M. we picked up a report that Sidi Suleiman was occupied by sixty German tanks.

At three A.M. the next day, 17th June, the HQ of 7th Armoured Division was observed to move its command post and return to its starting point. Shortly, just before seven A.M. our radio monitors picked up an enemy message that a German force of seventy-five heavy tanks was advancing on Sidi Suleiman; that German infantry had reached a point four miles east of Sidi Omar; and that this column had to be stopped at all costs. At 7.45 A.M. the enemy's 7th Armoured Brigade reported that it had run out of ammunition; the situation was very serious and, the brigade asked for immediate ammunition supplies. A further message at eight A.M. confirmed that 7th Armoured Division was supplied on a 'division-axis,' probably the desert road between Der el Hamra, Habata and Sidi Suleiman. By 10.45 A.M. the British garrison at Upper Sollum and Musaid had received orders to pull out. At two-twenty P.M. 7th Armoured Division reported to Corps Command: '7th RTR and B-Squadron 4th RTR have attacked near Hill 207 and report considerable damage to enemy armoured cars. 4th Armoured Brigade reports its strength at 24 I-Tanks, Division hopes for more.'

In the early afternoon we intercepted the following cryptic message from *Silver*, the GOC, to *Jugo* the Corps commander: 'Send umbrella for *Proctor* 16.00 hours send *Attaché Case* to landing ground, arrange onward home passage.' This information was conveyed to Rommel quickly and with relief. It was a clear sign of the enemy's retreat. We had won a defensive victory after the fight had swayed back and forth for three days. Compared with this further intercepts were of only minor importance. A typical signal read: 'Tank

Command 7th Armoured Division is alarmed about slow repair of its tanks'. (This formation, in the opinion of the Afrika Korps, had probably had the task of protecting or helping the division as it disengaged from us.)

The following Radio Monitoring Report issued on the day after the battle, will give an idea of the daily work of Seebohm's company *3./N56*.

Intercept Company *3./N56*   18th June 1941
(56th Signals Bn)

SECRET
Radio Monitoring Report No 17
(17. 6. 1941)

EGYPT

a) *Tobruk:* No new observations

b) *Western Desert:* Corps Command was said to be at Sidi Barrani. It was probably mo ʲed forward to there from Matruh at the beginning of the offensive.

In the course of the day the former *Brighton* HQ, (probably 11th Indian Brigade, with a newly activated formation consisting of one Infantry Bn, 31st Field Art Regt, one anti-tank company and two unknown units (engineers?) came under the command of 7th Armoured Division.

It is presumed that after the enemy withdrawal 7th Armoured Division has taken over the whole front again and that this new formation job is to secure the coastal plain sector.

The losses in enemy tanks are heavy. About mid-day 4th Armoured Brigade disposes merely 24 heavy tanks. Newly brought up from Egypt and put under 7th Armoured Division command are 9th Rifle Corps (Rangers), with officers' names:

Captain Sharpe   'hu'-net on 3100 kHz
Captain Hatherley   'lo'-net on 5345 kHz
                                                   Signed: SEEBOHM

Although the enemy retrieved most of their damaged tanks during the retreat, their losses were heavy: out of about one hundred Infantry-tanks sixty-four were knocked out or abandoned; of about ninety Cruiser-tanks they lost twenty-three. These diminished British tank forces were still able to withdraw before or escape behind the no less exhausted German Panzer regiments; this could not be prevented, given the vastness of the desert. Wavell accepted responsibility for this defeat. He was relieved of command by Churchill and replaced by General Claude Auchinleck as General Officer Commanding-in-Chief, Middle East.

Thus *Battleaxe* had not attained its objective of relieving Tobruk after turning the German front line; the British had incurred heavy losses in men and matériel. 'Desforce' under the command of GOC Western Desert, Lt-General Sir Noel Beresford-Peirse, with 4th Indian Division (Major-General Sir Frank Messervy) on the right and 7th Armoured Division (Major-General Sir Michael O'Moore Creagh) on the left, had to retreat to their starting point in Egypt. What mattered more was that the British tank losses were total, whereas the Germans were able to salvage and repair some of their lost tanks, because the Afrika Korps had held the field.

Our jubilation after Sollum was suddenly doused by a cold water douche – the news one week later of the German invasion of Russia. Everybody now realized that any hope of reinforcements for Africa was doomed. The 5th Panzer Division, which had been rumoured destined for Africa, went off to the Ukraine still wearing its yellow desert camouflage. This clearly indicated that Berlin had never seriously examined the opportunities of deciding the war with Britain in the Middle East – of capturing the oilfields of Iraq, and of then holding the Soviet-Union at bay by the potential air menace of Baku.

Organising and consolidating wireless intelligence
After Battleaxe which had exhausted the forces on both sides, there was a period of comparative tranquillity which was characterised by mutual spying through ground, air and wireless reconnaissance, and patrol and artillery activity.

Thus German reconnaissance detected at the end of June the probable relief of 22nd Guards Brigade in the coastal plain and the locations of 7th Support Group of 7th Armoured Division in the front line on the escarpment, of 4th Armoured Brigade between Bir Sofafi and Alam Rabia, and of 7th Armoured Division to the east of Sidi Barrani. In July and August some good monitoring results were also obtained in spite of skilful screening methods and the widespread imposition of wireless silence which hampered our insight into the enemy's activities.

On the Tobruk front patrol activity was renewed at the beginning of August; bunker S7 fell to the enemy and was recaptured by our troops. After the failure of his counter-attacks the enemy apparently called off further attempts to recapture.

On 14th August 1941 the command structure in Africa was changed. A new General Staff unit that had put in an appearance as 'German Staff at Italian Supercomando in North Africa' was placed under General Rommel to direct operations of the growing number of Army Corps. It eventually became the General Staff of the Panzergruppe Afrika, in overall command of the Afrika Korps with its 15th and 21st Panzer Divisions and 90th Light Division; of the XX Mechanized Corps, with the Ariete armoured and Trieste mechanised Divisions; and of the XXI Corps, with the Pavia, Bologna, and Brescia infantry divisions and of the Savona Division, which garrisoned Bardia.

The G-2 of this new staff, Major von Mellenthin, organised the intelligence section in such a way as to give the intelligence service new impetus; he vigorously worked all its branches up to a high degree of efficiency. Several officers joined this new section of Panzergruppe Afrika: Cavalry Captain Hoesch came in as an intelligence officer seconded from the OKW counter-espionage Abwehr branch; his job would be to create an organisation of agents in Egypt; Lieutenant Behrendt, author of this work, joined from the Afrika Korps as G-3; Lieutenant Ferri came as liaison officer to the SIM section of the Italian Supercomando North Africa; there was Lieutenant Habel of *3./N56*, and Lieutenant Freudenberger as the Panzergruppe's liaison officer to the Luftwaffe, the Army reconnaissance squadron *2./(H)14* and the Italian airforce. To promote closer co-operation between the German and Italian intelligence services, Major von Mellenthin satisfactorily arranged with SIM's Major Revetria to exchange reconnaissance information particularly from the 'Y' service. Our own Radio Intercept Company was reunited after recovering a platoon that had been stationed outside Tobruk.

At the same time, in agreement with the Italian Supercomando, air reconnaissance zones were fixed; this arrangement came into effect on 17th August. As for 'Y', in a conference with Lieutenant Seebohm, it was determined that he was only allowed to furnish

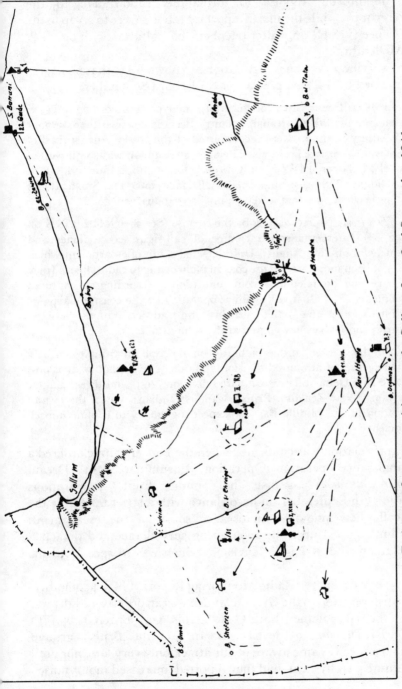

Estimate of enemy positions on the Sollum front 2nd September 1941.

See page 236 for key to symbols on this and subsequent diagrams.

radio monitoring reports to formations subordinate to the Panzergruppe, while the more important reports were to go up to the War Office (OKH) only after telephone consultation with our G-2, von Mellenthin.

An overview of the enemy situation as known up to that point was summarised in G-2's Appreciation No.1 of 3rd September:

Tobruk front: Enemy situation generally unchanged, according to POW statements of 20th Australian Infantry Brigade engaged there. About 115 battery positions were reconnoitred at the end of August; half of them were alternate positions. The main strongpoint was south-west of Ras el Madawar. POW from Tobruk belonging to 2/15th and 2/17th Battalions of 20th Australian Infantry Brigade stated that Stuka attacks had little effect, and that water supply and rations were good.

Sollum front: No regrouping by the enemy. (See sketch of 2.9.1941 on page 89) Intercepts reveal change of call-signs, code names and frequencies on 28th August. Unit detected south of escarpment which had not been monitored in the coastal plain owing to radio silence (they were relying on telephone communication.) According to captured documents 22nd Guards Brigade is operating on the coastal plain. Air reconnaissance: the active airfields and railway stations between Matruh and Daba show no preparations for attack.

General Appreciation: order of battle on the Sollum front essentially unchanged: one armoured division and one or two infantry divisions. In the Nile Delta still one armoured division (2nd) and three infantry divisions (New Zealand, British 12th, 1st Indian). Given the overall situation in the Middle East we expect the enemy to confine himself to defence.

This appreciation was confirmed when the Panzergruppe ordered a reconnaissance operation, Operation Midsummer Night's Dream (*Sommernachtstraum*) against the Sollum front. Preparations began on 7th September; in accordance with a strict timetable the Luftwaffe flew photo-reconnaissance south of the escarpment. Seebohm stepped up radio monitoring surveillance and detached one platoon to 21st Panzer Division, which was to spearhead the thrust.

As is shown from the Radio Monitoring Report of 14th September, the British reaction to the German attack was an orderly withdrawal under the code-name 'Bath-Chair': this was ordered by 7th Armoured Division at seven A.M. In fact the British ground reconnaissance became aware of our attack only very late; not until one minute past five A.M. had they reported 'increased motor noise'.

The enemy thereupon pulled back as ordered to the east, north-east and south-east.

On this occasion the capture of the command car of 4th South African Armoured Car Regiment complete with many enemy documents led to discoveries that were mentioned in Intelligence Summary No 2. It was here that we obtained a copy of the guidelines for motorised troops operating in the desert which have been mentioned earlier.

It could be stated that as a result of the thrust on the Sollum front it was no longer 7th Armoured Division in command but a 'Forward Group' with 22nd Guards Brigade on the coastal plain and two combat groups on the escarpment 'Big Brother' and 'Big Sister' with advanced security forces 'Little Brother' and 'Little Sister'. Reconnaissance was no longer carried out by 11th Hussars but by 4th South African Armoured Car Regiment, which for camouflage purposes had taken over all the wireless records of the 11th Hussars as well as their operating personnel. This was concluded from captured documents. Owing to very skilful wireless camouflage the withdrawal of the British 7th Armoured Division had escaped detection. On the other hand, the organisation of the combat groups 'Brother' and 'Sister' was now clear: each consisted of one or two artillery regiments, one or two armoured car squadrons, an anti-aircraft battery and anti-tank guns as well as the essential artillery.

British thoroughness in training their men was apparent from an order issued by their High Command in the Middle East sphere in which there was mention of schools of headquarters, war, wireless operators, transport, sports, medicine, infantry, armour, engineering, artillery, signals, chemical warfare and cooking.

As to British actions prior to and during the German advance, radio reconnaissance reported on 13th September: Enemy *ground* reconnaissance had not detected our movements on the night of 12th/13th September (a forward movement by the small forces closing up to the frontier). Enemy air reconnaissance reported a hundred vehicles at Sidi Suleiman on the morning of the 13th. The first British report on the beginning of our march into the assembly area, at 9:46 P.M., spoke of 'excessive motor noise'. The German attack was first reported by B-squadron of 4th South African Armoured Car Regiment, which was engaged in the north at 5:20 A.M. on 14th September, on the northern sector, and at seven A.M. the codeword 'Bath Chair' was thereupon given for the planned retreat. In spite of their rapid withdrawal they kept a running

Enclosure 10 of Intelligence
Summary Nr 2 as at 20.9.1941

Supposed British Organisation in the Middle East

General Sir Claude Auchinleck
Commander in Chief, Middle East

Gen. Sir James H. Marshall-Cornwall
C. in C. Military District Middle East

Gen. Sir Henry Maitland-Wilson
C. in C. British Troops in Palestine, Transjordan and

Lt. Gen. W. Platt
Commander British Troops Sudan

Maj. Gen. N.M. de la P. Beresford-Peirse
Commander Western Desert Force

Command British Troops Cyprus

Command British Army Troops Aden

Gen. Morshead
Commander Tobruk Fort

Contingents

BTE
British Troops Egypt

AIF
Australian Imperial Forces

NZEF
New Zealand Expeditionary Forces

UDF
South African Union Defence Forces

commentary on the latest position of 21st Panzer Division. The headquarters staff of the South African Regiment began to withdraw very late, ran into tank fire and lost its office truck, although it had received a warning from the 'Front Group' 'not to take things too easy'. Its report was: 'We regret to have to report that the enemy has grabbed important documents from my truck.'

At 12:30 p.m. there followed an advance announcement of an Operation 'Victoria', which was not however put into force at first. It probably meant a stage-by-stage retreat. This may have been a consequence of 'Daffodil' in May, when a withdrawal was initiated by the issue of a codeword and it then continued regardless of what the enemy might be doing and without an objective. At 5:18 p.m. Operation Victoria was begun. Before the German afternoon attack, the withdrawal to the east continued in accordance with Operation Victoria. Because of the possibility that the Germans might push to the north and the coast near Buqbuq, 22nd Guards Brigade was alerted. British wireless messages reported: One armoured car burnt out, one armoured car abandoned, one truck of the South African Reconnaissance Regiment fallen into enemy hands together with its documents, two British aircraft shot down, a German aircraft captured.

The Germans withdrew after their thrust, and the British followed though with some hesitation; only in the course of 16th September did they regain their old positions. Once again the British ground reconnaissance was seen to report back rapidly and thoroughly: the belated report of the beginning of Midsummer Night's Dream could be ascribed to the fact that the South Africans had as yet little experience of the desert. The co-operation of reconnaissance units with the artillery was particularly good, and the mobility of the latter was demonstrated time and again.

Enemy wireless activity from 22nd to 28th September suggested some reinforcement of the British forces covering the escarpment, probably because they had been shown by the German thrust to be too weak. The deployment of a further reconnaissance regiment on the Egyptian frontier, detected by radio intercept, was confirmed by air reconnaissance.

Counter-espionage (Abwehr) Activity and Organisation
During the initial weeks of the command of the Panzergruppe Afrika, the setting up, or rather the extension, of all its G-2 services provides a good example of the various means of obtaining intelligence;

excerpts from the first operational reports submitted by the Intelligence Department ('*Ic* reports') are worth quoting at length since they concern subjects that are rarely discussed later.

The following report highlights the activities of the Intelligence Procurement Officer (*Nachrichten-Beschaffungsoffizier*) to whom greater success was denied owing to the special difficulties of this area.

Major von Mellenthin is entitled to credit for having nurtured this branch and given it its duties; it was neither his fault nor that of the officers concerned that it could not fulfil all the hopes that were vested in it.

On 21st August 1941 Cavalry Captain Hoesch reported to G-2 of the Panzergruppe Afrika with orders to organise a network of agents in the Nile Delta. The report says:

Agents to be used in the Nile Delta should be equipped as far as possible with wireless sets so that the conveyance of information can be handled rapidly and they can receive Intelligence directives continuously. [Hoesch] is despatched to Berlin on 22nd August in order to report to the Foreign Intelligence and Counter-Espionage department (Amt Ausland/Abwehr) about this order. . . Upon arrival consultation with specialist from the 'Abwehr I H West' on the operation of agents in Africa.

On 1st September there followed a briefing of Director of 'I H West' on the directive issued by G-2, Panzergruppe Afrika.

Contact established with 2 agents. . .

On 2nd September, briefing of the Director of 'I H West' on the possibilities of employing and finding agents.

The following operational possibilities were discussed:

1. Dropping by parachute into Egypt.

2. Drop and pick-up by plane from Egypt.

3. Operation of a car patrol led by desert expert Count Almasy, north eastwards past Kufra to the Middle Nile, where the agents could be planted.

4. Operating through Turkey, Syria, Palestine, and from Crete by fishing boat to Egypt.

5. Official infiltration of Egyptians, Europeans, etc from Portugal or Unoccupied France via South Africa, Abyssinia or Port Sudan.

A further conference on these matters took place with the G-2 of Tenth Air Corps and the Intelligence Procurement officer of Tenth Air Corps. . . Subscription to Egyptian newspapers for Intelligence purposes . . . On 9th September instruction of agents. Attempt to recruit new agents. On the 10th, consultation in Vienna with Count Almasy on the planned drive by motor car to the Middle Nile in order to plant agents . . . On the 15th, report to the Director of 'I H West', Berlin, on actions so far. Captain Pretzl is appointed [Hoesch's] Liaison Officer to [Admiral Canaris]. Renewed meeting with two agents. Consultation with 'Abwehr II' [sabotage] regarding operation to disrupt the railroad from Alexandria to Mersa Matruh. The operation will have to be postponed as the aircraft flying the first mission crashed on take-off and some equipment was lost. On 16th September contact established with General Fauzi-Kauzi, the Iraqi rebel leader, who is now in Berlin, Fauzi-Kauzi will try to make available to us a diplomatic link between Egypt and Turkey. Took leave of the different department chiefs in Berlin. In Rome report to Abwehr Liaison Officer to SIM. Arrival at Panzergruppe Afrika on 23rd September delayed owing to fighter attack. On 24th report to G-2 on course of official journey. Discussion of the possibility of close-quarters reconnaissance operations. Major Revetria [*SIM*] is contacted for approval of this.

On 1st October an Intelligence Procurement detachment composed of the auxiliary officers Lieutenant Nordhaus, Second-Lieutenant Haeusgen, Second-Lieutenant Heymanns and three NCOs, and a wireless party of four men, arrived at headquarters, Panzergruppe Afrika. The interval between arrival at Tripoli and departure had been used to recruit agents. Out of three contacts that were opened only one was promising for close reconnaissance. Long-range reconnaissance from Libya seemed to be impossible. New contacts were to be found if possible in Tripoli and other Libyan towns, provided that the Italian counter-espionage department were agreeable to a German close-reconnaissance role.

On 4th October Second-Lieutenant Heymanns, with the agreement of the Italian counter-espionage department, got the order from G-2, Panzergruppe Afrika, to operate close-reconnaissance. In Derna contact was established with an Arab, who smuggled British whisky, cigarettes, etc out of Tobruk. In this way agents were to be infiltrated into Tobruk. The negotiations with the Arab were very difficult indeed and could only be carried on very cautiously.

On the night of 7th/8th October the Intelligence Procurement depot was attacked by one enemy bomber. Captain Hoesch was killed, Second-Lieutenant Heymanns died from his wounds and Accountant Corporal Busse was slightly wounded. The planned delegation of tasks could not therefore be carried out, the more so since Lieutenant Nordhaus, two NCOs and two other ranks fell ill with malaria between 9th and 14th October and had to be taken to hospital.

In view of this situation, which was reported to Abwehr I H by wireless, the senior officer was ordered to a major conference in Berlin from 29th to 30th October. At the same time the High Command announced the early arrival of two agents to be parachuted into Egypt. Consequently Lieutenant Nordhaus went by air to Athens with the G-2 of the Panzergruppe, Major von Mellenthin, and was ordered to report to Berlin.

After the G-2's return from Athens, the wireless operator Corporal Busch was sent there in order to establish contact between our own station and the Abwehr station in Athens. He was to ensure that wireless messages from agents in Egypt to Abwehr headquarters in Athens were also intercepted by our own wireless station.

Appreciation of Preparations for a British Offensive from the end of October to 22nd November 1941

According to statements made by prisoners of war on 9th October, relief forces for Tobruk were on their way; in detail, it was thereby confirmed that 24th Australian Brigade was relieved by the British 16th Brigade. As it could be assumed that the Australian division would stay together as one entity, the supposition was justified that the whole 9th Australian Division was being withdrawn. Moreover, wireless intelligence ascertained that the British 16th Brigade consisted of the following three formations: 2nd Queen's, 2nd King's Own Rifles, 2nd Leicestershires, all part of the British 6th Division whose wireless traffic in Syria had been noticeable by its absence these four weeks. On 12th October the New Zealand Division was picked up for the first time with its 1st Brigade in the region around Fuka, in the rear front line area. It was however assumed that the whole division which was still in the Delta would soon arrive. On 24th October the chief of *3./N 56*, the Radio Intercept Company, reported: 'British 7th Armoured Division have not had wireless communications for one week.'

The General Staff's Intelligence branch Foreign Armies West expected a British offensive at the beginning of October. The opinion of the Panzergruppe Afrika on the other hand was that no attack would take place in the near future. The British offensive was initially scheduled for 15th November, but postponed by three days, just as the German October attack on Tobruk was repeatedly postponed because of lack of reinforcements, especially in heavy artillery, finally to 22nd November.

German gun tractor towing 88 mm gun. From a roll of captured German film.

German gun in action. From a roll of captured German film.

Panzer III tanks prepare for action, May 1941. Note the spare lengths of tank-track strapped across the front to add to the armour thickness.

A Panzer III tank advances across the desert. From a roll of captured German film.

Under Colonel Ulrich Liss, Chief of Foreign Armies West, an intelligence conference was held at the end of the month in Athens. The participants were – the G-2's of Panzergruppe Afrika, of Twelfth Army and of Tenth Air Corps, and the commander of Wireless Intercept Troops South-East, the Abwehr station chief in Athens, the assistant Military Attaché in Ankara, and a staff officer from 'Special Staff Felmy,' operating in Syria.

According to what Major von Mellenthin reported, Colonel Liss's remarks did not make any basic changes to the enemy situation as seen by Panzergruppe Afrika. Liss re-iterated on this occasion that they had to reckon with the probability of a British attack in the near future. Reconnaissance operations were set up and the request was made for an agent to operate in the Mersa Matruh-Daba area, which was important for Panzergruppe, and to keep Panzergruppe informed of all enemy preparations in the Nile Delta and Western Desert. There then followed a discussion of the orders to be given to Hungarian Cavalry Captain Count Almasy.

As for Luftwaffe operations two tasks took precedence: preparation for the attack on Tobruk; and in particular, surveillance of the enemy in the Western Desert, and provision of up to date aerial coverage of Fort Tobruk. This would enable us to bring the former maps of the defences on the Tobruk front up to date.

Stepping up air reconnaissance of the enemy in the Western Desert gave a more accurate picture of the enemy dispositions centered on Bir Mella and Mersa Matruh. The rapid progress of railway construction from Mersa Matruh to the west – about one mile daily – was particularly noteworthy. The construction of this railway line and a considerable increase in the occupancy of stations and airfields (with fighters and bombers) supported the view that the enemy was planning an offensive, although air reconnaissance did not indicate that one was imminent.

Briefing-notes of 28th October recorded that the Luftwaffe was to produce aerial sketches and an aerial mosaic of Tobruk:

The PRU flights over Tobruk were to have begun on 10th October. One part, the south-east sector, had already been surveyed from 4th October onwards. Bad weather and cloud delayed these flights, so they could not begin as planned on the 10th but only on the 21st, 22nd, 23rd and 24th. The pictures are now with the survey teams of the observation batteries and astronomic survey units to collate the co-ordinates of the photographic datum points. This work will be finished in four to six days. Priority is being given to the eastern part of Tobruk. After survey of the photographic datum points, the pictures will be sent to X Air Corps, Athens, where they will be roughly collated. This work lasts about three days. The 1 : 15.000 picture sketch produced in Athens will thus probably not be available here before 10th November. A photographer's map complete with grid overlay can only be produced in Berlin. For that a further two to three weeks are needed. A 1 : 25.000 scale map produced in Berlin from the good photographic air cover of June 1941 is available, and the Artillery can fire, on the basis of this; it could arrive in a few days.

On 3rd November a sabotage troop that had been set ashore near Derna was captured; it consisted of four men. The group had been set ashore at Ras Hilal, thirty miles west of Derna, on the night of 22nd/23rd October; they had orders to find a suitable landing place and to discover whether there were artillery positions and beach duty patrols. They were unable to re-contact the submarine that had put them ashore.

The four prisoners belonged to a reconnaissance submarine. They stated under interrogation that Commandos were equipped with three 12,000 ton ships, which could take 15,000 men each and make twenty knots. These ships possessed 'Special Boats' capable of landing 1,500 men in 30 minutes, draught two feet, silent running electric engines, the bow equipped with landing ramps which could hold them fast on land. Other landings had been planned: one at the same time as an offensive at Sollum with more than 1,000 men and several of sabotage groups of 50 men each, independently of an offensive.

Meanwhile our wireless reconnaissance discovered a reorganisation in the Western Desert: while the British groupings had not changed, XIII Corps had been inserted* between Eighth Army (up till now Corps Command, Western Desert Forces) and 4th Indian Division, engaged on the Sollum front.

To protect our own southern flank, the Army planned, as per order No 4 of 26th October, to shift the bulk of 3rd and 33rd Reconnaissance Battalions into the area between Bir el Gubi and

---

* In November Eighth Army was divided into two corps: XIII Corps (New Zealand and 4th Indian Division with 1st Army Tank Brigade in support) and XXX Corps (7th Armoured Division, 4th Armoured Brigade, 1st South African Division and 22nd Guards Brigade).

Sidi Omar and to reconnoitre up to a line south of Bir el Chamsa and Bir Habata. Before this our G-2 had to examine the problems arising from this plan both with Rommel and at the front. He learned that both Rommel and his Chief of Staff agreed to the relief, but the Commander of the Savona Division requested that part of the holding forces should remain. The distribution of enemy forces, as issued on 10th November was broadly accurate as comparison with the British formations later detected shows.

In preparation for the attack on Tobruk, Intelligence Summary No 4 was issued on 11th November with a sketch of the defence works. It stated that the garrison's strength continued to be one division.

Radio reconnaissance revealed on 10th November South African division W/T traffic between Matruh and an area south of Sidi Barrani; the next day air and wireless reconnaissance were used to obtain a more accurate position. On the day after that the structure of 1st South African Division was clarified with Lieutenant Seebohm; it was stated that the onset of the ground-reconnaissance operation mentioned above, at about 3 P.M. on 1st November, all British patrols had been withdrawn behind the 'wire', that is the Egyptian-Libyan frontier. The British vehicles reported by air reconnaissance in the area north of Bir Kenayis had disappeared. No conclusions were drawn from that.

On 17th November there was total wireless silence by all British units. The evening report issued by our radio intelligence commented on the 'remarkably quiet wireless situation'. Air reconnaissance had not been flown in the last two days because of bad weather. It could not be flown on the 18th either. If therefore Panzergruppe Afrika intelligence was prepared for a British advance in the next days, nobody thought it would be a decisive offensive.

The Panzergruppe issued a detailed survey of Eighth Army's preparation, order of battle and intentions in its combat report:

In an Intelligence Summary issued mid-October, Panzergruppe pointed out that the possibility of an enemy offensive grew with each month, since the previous months had seen quantities of troops and materials transported to Egypt by convoy. The transfer of both the South African and the New Zealand divisions from the Nile Delta to the Mersa Matruh area – starting about the beginning of September – was detected by wireless intelligence and confirmed by interrogation of prisoners. The 21st Panzer Division's reconnaissance sortie in mid-September, into the region south of Sidi Barrani, did not yield any indications of an imminent British attack. In particular no supply dumps were found in the Egyptian frontier area. Furthermore, reconnaissance shortly before the beginning of the enemy offensive resulted only in an awareness of increasing enemy reconnaissance activity; serious preparations for an offensive were not noted. The reason that the build-up for the British offensive commencing on 18th November was not observed, is the following:

In sharp contrast to the Battle of Sollum in June 1941, the concealment of preparations for this attack were excellent. As wireless silence was ordered until the beginning of the attack, wireless intelligence had no way of detecting the advance from Mersa Matruh to the assembly zones. Wireless discipline by all British formations was also excellent. Nor did air reconnaissance detect the British build-up, in the first place probably because they only proceeded by night to the assembly areas, and then because the British covered themselves during the day by standing fighter patrols and excellent camouflage. On top of this came the fact that air reconnaissance could not be flown on 16th to 18th November as our airfields were unserviceable owing to cloud-bursts.

Furthermore, the Panzergruppe was insufficiently equipped with reconnaissance aircraft – it disposed only one reconnaissance flight – and this handicapped discovery of the British preparations for attack.

From captured enemy documents the order of battle and intentions of Eighth Army on 18th November 1941 can be seen in the following summary. The intention was to 'destroy the German-Italian forces in Cyrenaica.' The order of battle was given as XXX Corps, whose objective was to establish contact with Tobruk, with

1. 7th Armoured Division as a striking force (7th Armoured Brigade on the right, 22nd Armoured Brigade on the left, and 4th Armoured Brigade in the middle and behind them) in the area north and south of Trigh el Abd between Gabr Meliha and Bir Taieb el Esem. Thrust to Sidi Rezegh. Reconnaissance screen thrown out to north-east, north and north-west by 4th South

African Armoured Car Regiment, 1st King's Dragoon Guards and 11th Hussars.

2. 1st South African Division to protect the open flank to the west and south-west in the area south of El Cuasc. Reconnaissance to the north-west in the direction of Bir Hacheim and to the west against Maala er Rih. Thrust El Gubi.

3. 22nd Guards Brigade to protect the rear corps area, and to guard airfields and dumps, particularly in the area east and west of Bir esc Scegga.

The objective of XIII Corps would be to isolate the Tobruk front from the motorised German forces and their supplies, with

1. New Zealand Division, as a wedge between the mobile German troops and the Fort Tobruk front. Its route with 8th Royal Tank Regiment assigned to them is north into the area Sidi Azeiz where it divides: 5th New Zealand Brigade with one squadron 8th RTR attacks Capuzzo, 4th New Zealand Brigade with one squadron 8th RTR pushes northwards and cuts off the Bardia-Tobruk road, 6th New Zealand Brigade with one squadron 8th RTR marches on the Trigh Capuzzo in the direction of Gasr el Arid,

and 2. 4th Indian Division, with 1st Army Tank Brigade assigned to it, in order to surround the Fort Tobruk front line and to roll it up from the south-west. For that purpose 7th Indian Brigade and 42nd as well as 44th RTR are to attack Sidi Omar. 11th and 5th Indian Brigades to remain in their initial area, 11th Indian Brigade in the coastal plain, 5th Indian Brigade south-west of the escarpment (formerly Brother and Sister Combat Groups).

In addition there was the Oasis Group (later Gialo Group)

whose objective is to prevent all supplies to the German-Italian forces, in order to harass the enemy. It will advance with one infantry battalion, (3rd Punjabis), two reconnaissance units (6th and 7th South African Reconnaissance Battalions), one artillery regiment (2nd South African Field Regiments) and one anti-tank unit (1st Battery 73rd Anti-Tank Regiment) via Gialo to the north-west up to the coastal road.

Finally, there was the Fortress of Tobruk itself, whose objective was to 'endeavour to facilitate the task of 7th Armoured Division in engaging German-Italian forces by harassing raids.'

Comparison of forces on November 18th, 1941.
(excluding Italo-German siege units and
British garrison at Tobruk)

	German	Italian	British	Enemy Superiority
Battalions	15	20	46	+ 11
Tanks	260	154	648	+ 234
Armoured Cars	33	24	464	+ 407
Guns, light	36	104	400	+ 260
Guns, heavy	30	20	64	+ 14
Anti-tank	94	195	312	+ 23
Anti-aircraft	128	112	300	+ 60
Fighters	33	40	200	+ 127
Bombers (Stuka)	59	28	125	+ 38
Recce planes	10	3	30	+ 17

Playfair, Vol. III, page 30 gives the following figures for tanks:

German	244	British	477 Cruiser
Italian	146		132 I-tanks
Total	390		609

In addition, the British garrison in Tobruk had 57 Cruiser tanks and 69 I-tanks and tank reserves; the Germans there had nothing.

* * *

The Battle for Tobruk and the Defence of the Agedabia Line.

The course of combat during this British offensive (Crusader) is well known. It will therefore be touched on here only so far as necessary to give a picture of British actions and reactions.

Given his inferiority in men and matériel, Rommel planned to defeat the British formations in detail by concentrating his mobile forces, and taking the enemy on one after the other until the entire British striking force was annihilated. The British duly obliged by throwing their armoured brigades into the battle one by one. By the night of 19th/20th November, 7th Armoured Division was widely scattered: 22nd Armoured Brigade was still at Bir el Gubi, recovered from a sharp clash with the Italian armoured Ariete Division, which had stood its ground well; 7th Armoured Brigade and the 7th Support Group were distributed along the road to Sidi Rezegh, twenty-five miles to the north of Bir el Gubi; and 4th Armoured

Brigade was just near Gabr Saleh, forty miles south-east of Sidi Razegh!

The reasons for the wide dispersal of the forces are not evident. As the New Zealand historian John Connell wrote* it was not an auspicious start for a battle to annihilation.

It might have been supposed that in this battle British numerical superiority would carry the day; on the contrary, the 'battle fleet' was divided into small squadrons and flotillas, and these were attacked in turn and heavily defeated.

Nobody on the British side saw the battle as a whole, in contrast to Rommel and Crüwell, the Commander-in-Chief of the Afrika Korps.

The 4th Armoured Brigade had only ninety-seven tanks ready for action out of the 165 with which it had set out. The 22nd Armoured Brigade only came to its assistance after sunset and could no longer go into action.

The fighting prior to 22nd November was mostly for Sidi Rezegh and Sidi Muftah; from there 22nd and 7th Armoured Brigades and the 7th Support Group were repulsed. Thus weakened, all three armoured brigades had to withstand the mass attack by both German Panzer divisions and the Ariete armoured division on 23rd November, *Totensonntag*.† Although they laid down an effective and violent artillery barrage the British could not hold their positions; they escaped annihilation only by breaking out of the encirclement (which of course can never be total in the desert). As soon as 24th November Rommel started out across the desert to Sidi Omar, planning to repulse the enemy on the Sollum front, to induce the striking columns to withdraw by an attack in their rear, and to destroy the enemy dumps at Maddalena and Habata.

The plan did not succeed, for General Auchinleck was not to be so misled.

On the evening of 23rd November General Cunningham, C-in-C Eighth Army, learned, that 7th Armoured Brigade had no more tanks serviceable, and that the 22nd was down to only thirty; moreover he got reports that the situation on the XXX Corps front was very confused. He thereupon asked General Auchinleck to come and see the situation at once for himself as Commander-in-Chief Middle East. Cunningham believed the battle lost and underlined that a withdrawal was necessary if Egypt was to be saved.

---

* *Auchinleck: A Biography of Field-Marshal Sir Claude Auchinleck*, page 340.

† Sunday of the Dead in the Lutheran calendar, the Sunday before Advent.

Officers of Africa Panzer Group Command
on 18th November 1941

I. Commander-in-Chief and Chief of General Staff:

Commander-in-Chief	General of Panzer-troops	Rommel
Chief of General Staff	Major-General	Gause

II. Operations Staff:

Ia (operations)*	Lieutenant-Colonel (GS)	Westphal
01	Lieutenant	Voss
04	Second Lieutenant	Schmitz
Id (personnel)	Lieutenant	Bergerhoff
Ic (intelligence)	Major (GS)	v. Mellenthin
03 (3. Ordonnanzoffizier †)	Lieutenant (res.)	Behrendt
06	Second Lieutenant (res.)	v. Braumüller
Ic/AO (counter espionage)	Major	Eichler
Pz. Group Engineer Leader	Lieutenant Colonel	Hecker
Pz. Group Signal Leader	Colonel	Büchting
Repr. Foreign Ministry	Special Major	Frh. v. Neurath

III. Higher Quartermaster Group:

Higher Quartermaster	Major (GS)	Schleusener
	from 6.12.41 Major (GS)	Otto
Qu 1	Captain (GS)	Weiz
Qu 2	Major (res.)	Dr Pöschel
Group Doctor	Doctor General	Dr Asal
Group Engineer	Major (Ing)	Barthel
Group Commissariat	Higher 'Intendantur Rat'	Wilke

IV. Adjutantur:

1. Adj. (IIa)	Major	Scupin
2. Adj. (IIb)	Major	Oschlies
Commander of Headquarters	Major	Hiller

* GSO 1, Command Echelon
† GSO 3.

Despite the bad news, Auchinleck did not flinch in his resolve. He ordered the offensive to continue. To give weight to his order on 26th November he replaced Cunningham as Commander-in-Chief of Eighth Army by his own Deputy Chief of Staff, General Neil Ritchie.

So far only 7th Armoured Division and 1st South African Division had suffered heavy losses; 2nd New Zealand Division, 4th Indian Division and the Guards Brigade as well as the 70th Division at Tobruk were still intact. Thus the British still had reserves, and these they could deploy against the German thrust to the east from 25th to 27th November. As renewed fighting broke out at Tobruk, both German divisions returned to the west on 27th/28th November; this fighting to the east of Tobruk, after initial success for the Germans, ended with the lifting of the siege at the beginning of December. The Panzerarmee made a fighting retreat to Agedabia. Here, in a further tank battle near Agedabia, the British suffered heavy losses from 27th to 30th December, the reinforced 22nd Armoured Brigade losing 136 tanks and armoured cars. Rommel continued to fall back to the Mersa el Brega line and this was reached by the last formations, the mobile forces, on 12th January 1942. It was from this position that he and his German-Italian army began the counter-attack which ended in the recapture of Cyrenaica.

In the following description of events, the reader probably expects to find reports or opinions from the British point of view reflecting the heaviness of the losses in the battles of Sidi Rezegh, Bir el Gubi or Agedabia; but the British messages were masterpieces of understatement. From the British signals that were intercepted one seldom realised the real state of affairs in all its seriousness.

Virtually total wireless silence and the impracticability of air reconnaissance had enabled the British formations to advance unobserved up to 18th November and fan out from the Egyptian border at Maddalena to the north-west into the Bir el Gubi area, both south of Gambut against Tobruk, and also to the north against the Sollum front.

To this author's recollection, 21st Panzer Division was the first to report: 'Strong enemy reconnaissance forces striking first to the west, then to the north.' Similar reports came in during the day from the reconnaissance battalions, which avoided contact with the superior enemy forces.

By intensified air reconnaissance, our G-2 tried to ascertain the enemy's intentions. On 19th November these reports ran:

About 9:30 A.M. in the area Gabr Saleh-Maddalena-Gasr el Abid six hundred British vehicles clearly recognised as motor transport, heading north-west, the major part crossing considerably enlarged gaps in the frontier wire between Maddalena and Gasr el Abid.

Between 12 noon and one P.M. nine formations were reported, totalling one thousand including tanks, west of Maddalena and south-east of Bir Gubi heading north.

3:40 P.M.:
three large columns about forty miles south of el Gubi from direction of Giarabub heading in direction Tobruk; each column about seven abreast, length indeterminate.
4.35 P.M.: enemy tanks, twenty miles south of Bir el Gubi heading north; further large columns observed with lorries and artillery.

Given the sharply reduced enemy wireless communications only occasionally were signals transmitted; these broadly confirmed and rounded out the details of the enemy picture of the day before.

The British prisoners brought in on 20th November belonged to the 7th Hussars, 8th Hussars, Royal Gloucester Hussars, 22nd Armoured Brigade, the Northumberland Hussars, the 38th Royal Tank Regiment, 4th South African Armoured Car Regiment. Elements of 7th Armoured Division were recognised by emblems on the vehicles. At ten P.M. Lieutenant Seebohm reported:

1. 1st and 5th South African Brigades confirmed under 1st South African Division, located to the south behind centre of 7th Armoured Division,
2. British signal: POPY takes the lead . . . if you come across Popy, break through together.

From the enemy documents captured on 21st November the organisation of 7th Armoured Division was established. In addition to the brigades detected on the 18th, 7th Rifle Brigade was now observed.

Tactical reconnaissance reports radioed by British airmen were also intercepted and then yielded further information on the day.

At eleven A.M. a code-name list captured from 4th Indian Division was passed on to *3./N56* and this shed light on the intercepted messages. The G-2 assessment that evening ended with the words: 'Enemy seems to be preparing to break through to Tobruk.'

On the following day, 22nd November, the location of British forward airfields was discovered from captured documents and – of no lesser importance – the significance of the British tank identity pennants:

17th to 26th November: 2 pennants at top of antenna ('two up')
27th to 30th November: 1 pennant at top, 1 pennant midway up antenna (1 up, 1 down)

Only now was the meaning of signals like 'two up' grasped; such signals had been intercepted since the beginning of the fighting. The G-2 report for this day stated:

7th and 22nd Armoured Brigade tried to break through via Sidi Rezegh to Tobruk. Enemy Tanks engaged:

1st Army Tank Regiment at Sollum front under 4th Indian Division	150 I-Tank Mark II
4th Armoured Brigade and 38th RTR (Sollum front rear)	170 med. tanks
7th and 22nd Armoured Brigades south-eastwards Tobruk	260 med. tanks
In Tobruk units of 1st and 4th RTR	80 I-Tank Mark II
	230 heavy
	430 med. tanks
Total	660 tanks

How far the British ground reconnaissance aimed to get can be deduced from an intercepted signals reporting that 6th South African Armoured Car Regiment had made a scouting thrust into the region about Wadi Faregh, to the east of Agedabia.

On 23rd November, the day of the tank battle at Sidi Rezegh, a message intercepted 9:30 A.M. hrs was submitted at 10.45 A.M:

Large formation east of grid 450 (south of Gambut) reports that forward troops are fiercely attacked in the flank and from the south. Neighbouring formation west of the same grid asks eastern formation to thrust westwards as it would help *a great deal* by so doing. Same formation reports fifty German tanks six miles north-east of Bir Gubi.

Confused British messages confirmed the cauldron* near Sidi Rezegh, which was also mentioned in the G-2 report – the 'Encirclement of enemy forces located south-east of Tobruk' had been 'brought to a conclusion.'

On the following day, 24th November, Lieutenant Seebohm reported:

1. So far the following units have been detected under 7th Armoured Division: 4th Armoured Brigade with 3rd and 5th RTR, 11th Hussars and 4th South African Armoured Car Regiment, 1st Army Tank Brigade.
Not yet detected: 7th Armoured Brigade, 7th Rifle Brigade.
New formations detected: 22nd Armoured Brigade.

2. *11.00* A.M: front to the east engaging on hundred tanks at grid reference 430 400 (three miles south-east of Sidi Rezegh). One infantry baltalion marching north from there to the escarpment.

3. British ground troops making no report on any fighting in the cauldron.

4. *11.25* A.M: new commander of 4th Armoured Brigade reports to Division that his right wing has made contact and he would reinforce his left.

5. *10.42* A.M.: Reports of losses of a 22nd Armoured Brigade unit suggest heavy tank losses and officer casualties.

A report from the *3./N56* said: a 'Brigade of 1st South African Division which by its own messages believes itself in no man's land, is burning a motor vehicle, its cypher unit and its code documents.' Division orders it to assemble as many men as possible after completing the destruction.

In the evening, according to a report by Command Intelligence, the cauldron south-east of Tobruk was 'mopped up.' In it were found the 4th Armoured Brigade, whose deputy commander was captured; 22nd Armoured Brigade; 7th Rifle Brigade (Support Group); and 1st South African Brigade, some parts of which were of course able to escape in spite of the heavy losses, given the vastness of the open

---

* The name given by the British to the battle area of the Battle of Gazala in June 1942. The DAK gave the name (German *Kessel*) to Sidi Rezegh. In its military sense *Kessel* is an encirclement of troops.

spaces, insofar as their vehicles were still intact.

British radio operators were heard repeatedly asking after 'George's' and 'Uncle George's' 'eldest son', but in vain. That evening they continued to inquire after 'Uncle George's eldest son', i.e., 5th South African Brigade. It had been overwhelmed by a German tank attack, and thrown into disarray, losing many prisoners and suffering severe losses in killed and wounded. It was during this night that German ambulance men searched for wounded South Africans, and brought them blankets, rations and water.

From 9.22 to 9.57 A.M. on the 25th intercepted messages suggested some 'confusion' with the enemy, as a conversation between XXX and XIII Corps reveals:

Between Alec [4th Armoured Brigade] and Frank [1st South African Division] everything is settled and ready as far as their responsibilities lie. Frank [1st South African Division] has a fair number with him, but would welcome very much if you could assist him with armoured cars.

The enemy is now making the utmost efforts with two or three large columns, and we cannot wait any longer. Everyone is ready to go, including the RAF, so we can go ahead. It is difficult, but we've got to strike!

XIII Corps: I received a message that 22nd Armoured Brigade was being put under our command. But I haven't yet been able to establish contact with them.

XXX Corps: I don't know where Scotty [22nd Armoured Brigade] (is) – nobody knows!

At 12.45 4th Armoured Brigade reported to 7th Armoured Division 'that one of its lower units was all messed up and the situation was very obscure.'

The 4th Indian Division had stopped a German attack twenty miles east-south-east of Sidi Omar. The divisional commander was wounded. Repeated calls by British troops for air assistance were declined as no aircraft were available. According to prisoners' statements 1st and 5th South African Brigades were at Sidi Rezegh; this suggested that 2nd South African Brigade was probably with 7th Armoured Division. A G-2 memo that evening said that the majority of 1st Brigade of 1st South African Division had been captured, while the 2nd (with 7th Armoured Division) and the 5th had got away; the

2nd South African Division was supposed to be moving up, together with 3rd, 4th and 6th Brigades.

A report dated 26th November stated: 7th Armoured Division signalled 22nd Armoured Brigade; time of origin nine A.M.: '8:30 A.M., fifty tanks near Sidi Azeiz rolling west and north-west'. This message was repeated urgently four times.

Two examples will suffice to illustrate how important air reconnaissance was in addition to wireless intelligence, namely the air reconnaissance of 26th November: and the report by Air Command Libya of the 30th.

First Air Report
Mission: What is the enemy attack group in the area Gambut-Bel Hamed-Rezegh-Bir Bu Meliha doing? Are there any movements from the outside into this area?
Result: time 8:15 A.M.:
1) Enemy artillery group observed about three miles south-west of Rezegh. Artillery hits seen there and enemy tanks on fire.
2) Between Belhamed and Gambut a total of 400-500 vehicles observed in several clusters.
3) In area Sidi Muftah about 120 vehicles.
4) Six miles north east of NE Gabr Saleh 600 vehicles tightly closed up, heading north east, at standstill. North of this concentration a further 200-300 vehicles also at standstill.

Second Air Report:
Mission: What is the enemy doing east of Bel Hamed-Rezegh? Where are our own troops on the Trigh-Capuzzo in the Sidi Azeiz area and to the west of it?
Result: eleven A.M.:
To the south-east of Rezegh various concentrations, totalling 500 vehicles. Around Sidi Azeiz within ten mile radius about 500 vehicles observed in various concentrations.

Third Air Report:
Mission: Enemy east of Rezegh apparently defeated. Observe whether he is retreating and if so where to. Are our own forces from the Sidi Azeiz area advancing to west? Are any forces identifiable in the Bu Meliha area?
Result: 3:40-3:50 P.M.:
1) No eastward movements perceptible in the enemy group east of Bel Hamed and Rezegh.
2) About 150 vehicles near Gasr el Arid.

3) 200 vehicles around Sidi Azeiz. No westward movement observed.

4) About ten miles north east of Gabr Saleh 500-600 vehicles, of which some are making their own way.

5) Close to and south of Gabr Saleh 200 vehicles and tanks, of which some fanning out to north-west, north east and south east.

Comment: Report was submitted to Panzer Group at four P.M.

Fourth Air Report:

Mission: In the area south-east of Sidi Rezegh, are perceptible enemy forces making for Sidi Rezegh?

Result: time 5:05-5:45 P.M.

1) In the area Rezegh-Bir el Chelta-Bir el Gubi and farther east no enemy forces observed to be moving.

2) On the Trigh el Abd about four miles east of Bir el Gubi some vehicles were seen heading south-east.

Comment: Visibility was badly hindered by rain-showers and twilight.

Note: This report was submitted to Panzergruppe at 5:50 P.M.

*

Air Command Libya   *Command Post, 30.11.41*

Fifth Air Report

Mission:	Reconnaissance of area Bir el Gubi-Gabr Sciahebi (fifteen miles south south-east of Gubi)-Gabr Saleh-Hagfet el Nadura.
	Italian Air Reconnaissance reports in this area 800 to 1000 vehicles, mainly tanks, moving north west. Identification of strength and headings of enemy.
Result:	Time 12.30-12.45 P.M. Observer Lt. Kuhlmann.
	1. Fifty vehicles near Gabr Saleh.
	2. 100 vehicles near Bir Taieb el Esem.
	3. About ten miles south east of Bir el Gubi 250 stationary vehicles, among them tanks.
	4. From the above area (para. 3) 100 vehicles heading south-east, 20 vehicles west-north-west.
Addendum in writing:	Two sorties flown.

HASELOFF
Lieutenant

These examples show clearly how the airforce, by its daily reconnaissance missions in addition to those of *2./H14* (the Army Air Recce Squadron), enabled the Army command to detect enemy

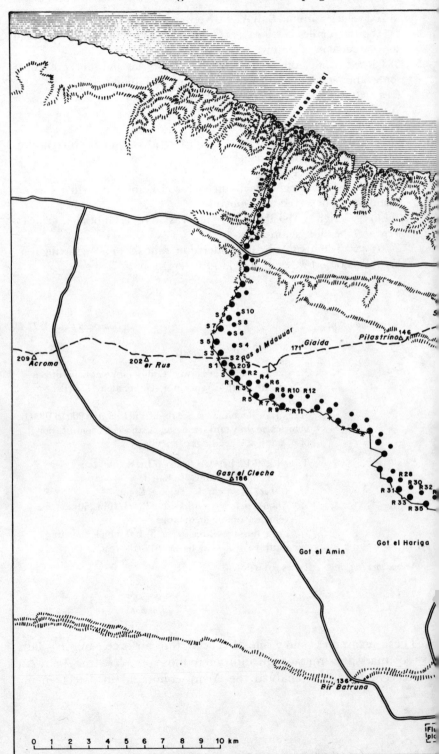

German plan of the defences at Tobruk

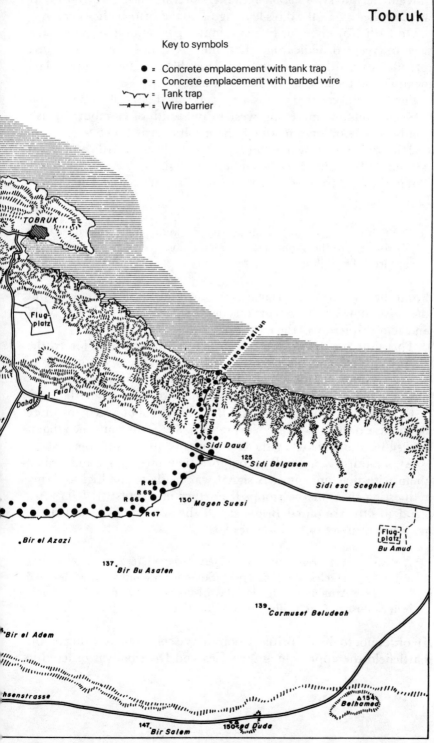

Tobruk

Key to symbols

● = Concrete emplacement with tank trap
● = Concrete emplacement with barbed wire
⌄⌄ = Tank trap
✳✳ = Wire barrier

movements quickly – *provided* that their aircraft could get airborne, as was not the case in the days leading up to the British offensive.

On 27th November at fifteen minutes past midnight, a message was intercepted indicating that the GOC-in-C, Eighth Army, intended to visit 7th Armoured Division that day, for he inquired its location and the nearest landing-ground.

Further intercepted messages confirmed British attacks on German columns marching west to the south of Gambut. British bombers were ordered to attack these columns at 1:55 P.M. and our G-2 informed our own fighter group. '3:40 P.M.: 4th and 22nd Armoured Brigade . . . engaged in heavy fighting.'

Later we interpreted a signal from 7th Armoured Division to Eighth Army:

> The fighting is over, the enemy scattered, twenty-eight tanks have been destroyed, the others routed to north-east. Some vehicles and some tanks captured. The fighting lasted three hours.

From these messages it is clear how much the battle see-sawed. But they also show how by seizing on enemy signals it is possible to build an accurate picture of the battle.

This time the thrust to the Egyptian frontier had not forced the enemy to abandon his offensive. On 27th November the Afrika Korps withdrew to the west to the area around Tobruk. During this movement, wireless reconnaissance still yielded important data.

For example, 5th New Zealand Brigade had not figured any more in wireless traffic since 28th November, 2 A.M. This confirmed that it had suffered badly during the German tank attack from the east.

At one-thirty A.M. the RAF bombed their own troops and strafed them with machine-guns. A signal was made to the Eighth Army requesting that this be stopped. Further intercepts: At 8.05 A.M.: 22nd to 4th Armoured Brigade: 'Of the sixty tanks reported the majority turn out to be dummies.'

7.53 A.M.: 7th Armoured Division to Eighth Army: Yesterday fourteen tanks and many vehicles were destroyed. Some lorries and vehicles deserted [sic] to 4th Armoured Brigade. The prisoners were hungry. The enemy is in confusion. Our artillery is very effective.

In order not to fire on British troops in the confusion reigning on the battlefield the approaching New Zealand Division was ordered to make itself known as follows: 'Wave helmets up and down rapidly on point of bayonet; aircraft lower landing gear and fire white flares.'

On 29th November the following signals were intercepted:

6:23 A.M. In combat area at 2.30 and 4.00 four A.M. engine noises and lights were noted. Some vehicles disappeared to north-east. It is assumed that the enemy was receiving supplies.

10:10 A.M.: *Report of 22nd Armoured Brigade:* German main body at grid ref. 448 396 (fifteen miles south-west of Gambut) marching west.

8:46 A.M.: *4th Armoured Brigade to 7th Armoured Division:* I am without ammunition and in urgent need of it.

In view of the British habit of understatement, this message was very revealing and was weighted accordingly.

12:40 P.M.: From a conversation of XIII Corps with the New Zealand division it transpired that the '7th Armoured Division will try by every means possible to prevent the approach of enemy columns from the east.'

1.16 P.M.: An intercepted German order from Rommel is transmitted:

The enemy is to be encircled in the area Belhamed-Safran-Capuzzo to which end Neumann goes via Via Duda to the north ridge Belhamed. Ravenstein (21st Panzer Division) is to prevent breakout with one unit on the north ridge Safran-Urano-Gebel-ridge (east of Sidi Rezegh). I myself am with Neumann [15th Panzer Division].

1:45 P.M. *An artillery formation in Tobruk signals:* 'Enemy tanks cut us off from the south. My ammunition situation is critical. Please help.'

3 P.M. *1st South African Brigade is attacked by the RAF and complains bitterly.*

4:25 P.M. *22nd Armoured Brigade to 4th Armoured Brigade:* Just captured German Panzer Division commander and staff. [General von Ravenstein, 21st Panzer Division, by the New Zealanders].

Italian wireless reconnaissance also made frequent reports, for instance at 5:18 P.M.: 4th Indian Division to formations under its command: 'All army and division code keys have been captured by the enemy and are compromised. New keys will be distributed.'

It was possible that this referred to the wireless documents of 4th Indian Division captured on 21st November.

And finally, at 7:30 P.M. a situation report from Eighth Army to XXX Corps provided an insight into the 'enemy situation' as seen by the British command:

We have indications that 21st Panzer Division and Ariete Division are in trouble. They report their location and heavy artillery fire in their rear. They say they will try to come directly behind the ridge to the north of the southern slopes . . . probably south-east of the NZ Division at grid line 447 (ten miles west of Gambut) . . . I consider situation of both to be serious. Do everything tonight to obstruct their supply, for which purpose 15th Panzer Division plans to use armoured cars which came from 1st SA Brigade.

The answer was: 'Have understood, shall act accordingly.'
Eighth Army: 'Splendid, good hunting!'
On 30th November at 8.35 A.M. XIII Corps was heard reporting to New Zealand Division: 'Ariete at point 175 (three miles south of Zaafran), offers a splendid target.'
Naturally, as soon as we picked this up everything was done by G-2 to warn the Italian division and insist that it spread out.

3:02 P.M. XIII Corps to Eighth Army: We have recaptured Duda, but are now staggering.
6:40 P.M. XIII Corps to XXX Corps: New Zealand Division has reported that Sidi Rezegh has now fallen into enemy's hands.

According to signals intelligence the British 70th Division was engaged at Tobruk; presumably it was composed of the brigades withdrawn from Syria and came under the command of XIII Corps. Late that evening a commander evidently experienced communication problems because the code-word 'Toast' was openly mentioned as 'Duda', since 'something important is about to happen there'.
The complexity of the military situation on Monday, 1st December was shown clearly in the evening report by our own G-2 and the BBC's afternoon bulletin from London.

BBC London four P.M.: 'In Libya General Rommel is throwing his last forces into the battle in order to penetrate the British corridor opened to the west. On Saturday evening 21st Panzer Division attacked from the direction of Belhamed, 15th Panzer Division attacked from the south-west, and Ariete northwards to assist 21st Panzer. The one and only success was the occupation of El Duda which was lost again the same night. Yesterday fighting continued without any enemy successes. The British troops are newly supplied and reinforced, whereas the German and Italian troops are labouring under serious supply difficulties.
Yesterday a thousand German prisoners arrived in Cairo.

G-2 reported on the evening of the same day:

> 7th Armoured Division with 7th Rifle Brigade, 1st South African Brigade and 4th Armoured Brigade continued its attacks between Bir el Chleta and Sidi Rezegh in order to relieve 2nd New Zealand Division. These attacks were repulsed and the bulk of the New Zealand Division destroyed. Only scattered remnants were able to escape to the south-east. Here they were taken in by 1st South African Brigade . . . 7th and 22nd Armoured Brigades did not participate in the battle.

From 18th November to 1st December 814 British tanks and armoured cars were destroyed, 127 aircraft shot down, and more than 9,000 prisoners captured.

Our intercept of British signals on 1st December yielded the following intelligence:

1.35 A.M. from XIII Corps to XXX Corps, 7th Armoured Division, New Zealand Division and Eighth Army:

> Enemy has taken Sidi Rezegh and is now attacking the New Zealanders' flank from the south and west with tanks. Consider it absolutely essential that 7th Armoured Division concentrate all efforts thereon to stop the tanks south and west of the New Zealander flank.
>
> *7.40 A.M. from 7th Armoured Division to Eighth Army:* New Zealand Division at present unwilling.
>
> *8.20 A.M. 7th Armoured Division to 4th Armoured Brigade:* South Africans still made no further progress.
>
> *9.02 A.M. Army Command to XXX and XIII Corps:* One enemy unit ordered at 8.45 hrs to attack our right flank in direction of the ascent of the axis highway (road bypassing Tobruk).
>
> *9.15 A.M.:* The enemy knows that we plan to attack Belhamed from the south-east.
>
> *12.21 P.M.:* Situation in New Zealand Division sector very confused.

At this time the Germans had precise knowledge of the enemy order of battle from signals intelligence, making full use of captured wireless documents:

A. *7th Armoured Division*
    4th Armoured Brigade   8th Hussars (Tank Battalion)*
                                  3rd RTR (Tank Battalion)
                                  5th RTR (Tank Battalion)
    7th Armoured Brigade   7 Hussars (Tank Battalion)
                                  2nd RTR (Tank Battalion)

* Units are here referred to by literal translation of the German intelligence description.

	6th RTR (Tank battalion)
22nd Armoured Brigade	2nd Royal Gloucester Hussars (Tank battalion)
	3rd County of London Yeomanry (Tank battalion)
	4th County of London Yeomanry (Tank battalion)
7th Rifle Brigade	1st Kings Royal Rifle Corps (KRRC)
	2nd Rifle Brigade (RB)
Divisional-Troops	2nd Royal Horse Artillery with 4th Armoured Brigade
	3rd Royal Horse Artillery with 7th Rifle Brigade
Divisional-Troops are largely divided into brigades; the command structure is constantly changing.	4th Royal Horse Artillery with 7th Armoured and Rifle Brigade
	102nd Royal Horse Artillery (Anti-Tank)
	60th Field Artillery Regiment (7th Armoured Brigade)
	1st Light AA Battalion with 4th and 122nd Batteries
	11th Hussars (Reconnaissance Battalion)
	Kings Dragoon Guards (Reconnaissance)
	4th South African Armoured Car Battalion Reconnaissance, etc, Transport, Engineer, San. troops.

B. *1st South African Division*

1st South African Brigade	1st Royal Natal Rifles
	1st Transvaal Scottish
	2nd Duke of Edinburgh's Own Regiment
	10th Brigade Signals Company (at present New Zealand Division)
2nd South African Brigade	1st Natal Mounted Rifles, Capetown Highlanders
	1st/2nd Frontier Battalion
5th South African Brigade	1st South African Irish Rifles
	2nd Botha Regiment
	3rd Transvaal Scottish
Divisional-Troops	President Steyn Regiment (MG Battalion)
	3rd South African Reconnaissance Battalion
	7th South African Field Artillery Regiment with 19, 20, 21 Battalions
	3rd South African Field Artillery Regiment with 7, 8, 9 Battalions
	7th Medium Artillery Regiment
	1st South African Anti-Tank Battalion
	one Light AA Battalion, etc

C. *2nd South African Division*   up till then only appeared with 6th South African Infantry Brigade; also 3rd and 4th Infantry Brigades belong to this division which is probably engaged in the rear operational area.

D. *4th Indian Division*

5th Indian Infantry Brigade	1st Buffs
	3/16th Punjabis
	4/6th Rajputana Rifles
7th Indian Infantry Brigade	1st Royal Sussex
	4/16 Punjabis
	4th Sikhs
11th Indian Infantry Brigade	2nd Camerons
	2nd Mahrattas
	1st Rajputana Rifles
Divisional-Troops	CIH (Central India Horse)
	Reconnaissance Regiment, Artillery, Anti-Tank, AA, etc.
1st Army Tank Brigade	8th RTR
	42nd RTR) Parts also with
	44th RTR) New Zealand Division

E. *New Zealand Division*
4th New Zealand Brigade
6th New Zealand Brigade
(5th New Zealand Brigade   directly under XIII Corps, no longer exists)

F. *Oasis Group*   3/2nd Punjabis
2nd South African Field Artillery Regiment
3rd South African Anti-Tank Battalion
6th South African Armoured Car Battalion
7th South African Reconnaissance Battalion
21st Indian Engineering Company
29th Indian Transport Company

G. *Army Troops*
12th Anti-Aircraft Brigade   with 68 Heavy AA Battalion
88 Heavy AA Battalion
94 Heavy AA Battalion
25 Light AA Battalion

According to a wireless report from *3./N 56* on 2nd December, originated at 12:42 P.M., 22nd Guards Brigade received orders from its commander, who was then at XXX Corps, to prepare to move. (The chief operations officer Colonel Westphal ordered G-2 in a memo to follow this up.) The headquarters of 2nd New Zealand Division had been located since nine A.M. on 1st December in the western sector of Fort Tobruk.

Mention was made of a 1st Division at Mersa Matruh; this must have been a reference to 1st South African Division, which had not been detected since 1st December on the Command Wireless Net of XXX Corps. This division, which came to North Africa with high expectations after its triumph in Abyssinia, was mauled so badly by the Afrika Korps in the first phase of the offensive that it had to be pulled out of the front after only two weeks.

As a result of this day's fighting and the mopping-up operations in the cauldron north of Sidi Rezegh, the number of prisoners and the booty further increased. From G-2 came information based on radio reconnaissance that showed the possibility of a transfer of some enemy headquarters in easterly and south-easterly directions. 7th Rifle Brigade, engaged on a wide front, might well have orders to screen an enemy *retreat*. Because of bad weather air reconnaissance could not be flown to confirm this speculation.

On the following day the enemy did not continue the disengagement towards the east and south-east that had been noticed on 2nd December. G-2 assumed that the battered enemy formations would be regrouped for a continuation of the offensive under the protection of a reinforced security screen (by 1st South African and 5th Indian Brigades).

It has already been mentioned with what dedication the Luftwaffe flew its reconnaissance missions, particularly at this time; up to seven missions were flown daily, and this prevented our command from being taken by surprise.

G-2's estimate of the forces at the disposal of the enemy yielded the following picture:

Marmarica:	The rest of 7th Armoured Division (one tank brigade)
	1 motorised division
In Tobruk:	1 to 1½ divisions and 1 tank battalion
Western Desert:	2–3 divisions (semi-mobile)
	plus 2 tank battalions
Egypt:	2 infantry divisions

On account of the strong pressure from Tobruk through El Duda to the south-east, the German south-eastern front against Tobruk had to be abandoned on 5th December; in fact we had the clear impression that the British had brought up further formations.

According to G-2 on 6th December, in pushing forward to El Gubi the enemy adopted a very cautious attitude towards the Afrika Korps. This was highlighted by one partially intercepted conversation.

Eighth Army to XXX Corps: 'I am sorry that I must trouble you once more, but it seems that the enemy *may be changing.**'

Eighth Army: 'You were in contact with him south of El Gubi.'

Eighth Army: 'I understand that Alec (4th Armoured Brigade) will deal *with party* tomorrow morning (. . . .) He has failed badly today; it is extraordinarily significant to act in this manner, and let me know how 'Chicken' will be with regard to 'Alec' (4th Armoured Brigade). Everything should be ready as far as possible so that it can go ahead suddenly.'

Eighth Army: 'I must leave that to you as you are the only one who can judge whether it is right for you.' . . .

Eighth Army: 'And please repeat this to Godwin† (XIII Corps?) and don't forget the great *want*, "Fetter" (at grid ref. 495 356 Alam el Abiad, five miles south-east of Gabr Saleh). Thank you, and as for meeting the needs for this purpose – I understand the situation which keeps changing so completely.

Deployed were: 22nd Guards Brigade, 11th Indian Brigade and 4th Armoured Brigade. Signals Intelligence revealed that 1st South African Brigade was being brought up and the headquarters of 4th Indian Division was detected.

Radio intercept: 7th Rifle Brigade to 7th Armoured Division: 500 enemy vehicles, twenty-five tanks moving west on the Trigh Capuzzo to El Adem (. . . .) In Wadi 429 401 (Sidi Rezegh) a German position was attacked at 15.30 hrs. The Commander [General Neumann-Silkow, commander 15th Panzer Division] was killed, the rest was scattered . . . At Sidi Rezegh 120 prisoners captured, 800 Schwimmer [New Zealanders] rescued.

The 7th Armoured Division reported: 'Both German divisions assumed in El Gubi area.'

In the opinion of G-2 the enemy had not yet realized that we had discontinued the siege of Tobruk on the south-east front.

On 7th December at 12.08 P.M. signals intelligence reported: 'There are indications that 21st and 15th Panzer Divisions have joined forces.'

According to G-2 the enemy was reinforcing in the area around Gubi. Wireless reconnaissance recognised the partly reorganised 22nd Armoured Brigade there.

---

* Italicised words in the conversation indicate those taken down in English by the interception operator.

† Lt General W. Godwin-Austen, commander of XIII Corps.

Wireless message Eighth Army to XIII and XXX Corps (handed in on 8th December, 6.30 A.M.: Advance ordered for 03.00 hrs.

7th Armoured Division to all subordinate units, 7.18 P.M.: 'All codes compromised.'

Air reconnaissance was especially important on 9th December for following the movements in the rear of the enemy lines. Sorties were flown as ordered but only with partial success as some planes did not return, including two Ju 52s shot down by Italian fighters.

The G-2 report said that the enemy pursued the Panzergruppe as it retreated north-west and reached the Bir Hacheim-Acroma line on 10th December. By wireless reconnaissance it was now clear that 4th Indian Division had been transferred from XXX Corps to XIII Corps. The 2nd South African Division, with 1st Army Tank Brigade under its command, was assembling for an assault on Sollum.

On the wireless net of the air liaison officer of XIII Corps a message was intercepted on 11th December that 400 paratroopers had been put ashore at Mrassas (west of Tobruk) at 10:50 A.M. An Italian combat group which had been cut off was in combat with the 23rd New Zealand Battalion. The New Zealanders were fighting Italian paratroops west of Mrassas. The Italians, mostly without tank support, were putting up fierce resistance.

At 9:56 A.M. on the following day, 12th December, 7th Armoured Division reported to XIII Corps: 'Carol dispersed a column of 100 German vehicles, destroying several and causing great confusion.' By 7.30 A.M. '15 vehicles and 40 prisoners had been captured', whereupon XIII Corps instructed 7th Armoured Division: 'Personally from "Godwin" to "Strafer"* (OC, 7th Armoured Division): I have just delivered your good news personally to the Army C-in-C, who is delighted!'

Wireless reconnaissance unit *3./N56* (pieced together at this juncture the following enemy order of battle: XIII Corps at Tobruk with under command:

70th Infantry Division

4th Indian Division with 5th and 7th Indian Brigades in the area south-south-west of Acroma

32nd Army Tank Brigade

* Lt-General Gott.

XXX Corps: with headquarters in the area around El Gubi, commanding:

> 7th Armoured Division with 4th Armoured Brigade and 7th Rifle Brigade in an area from south-south-west of Acroma to north-east of Hacheim;
> 1st South African Brigade west of El Adem;
> 22nd Guards Brigade south-east of Bir Hacheim;
> 2nd Royal Gloucestershire Hussars (formerly 22nd Armoured Brigade);
> 2nd South African Division with
> > 3rd South African Infantry Brigade;
> > 5th New Zealand Brigade;
> > 11th Indian Brigade, probably still on the coastal plain east of Sollum, and
> > 42nd Army Tank Brigade

From the reports concerning the South African troops it could be concluded that 1st South African Division no longer existed as an entity, and a temporary fusion of 7th and 22nd Armoured Brigades could equally be assumed.

From messages intercepted on 13th December the following are of interest:

> *The Eighth Army's operations staff radioed its second echelon between 5:20 and 5:39 P.M.:* 'Can you give me your requirements as a result of the conversation with "Bernard" (New Zealand Division) and "Uncle George" (1st South African Division)?'
> *Answer:* Equipment for a reserve company for each of these.
> *Operations staff:* In future 'Bernard' is no more under our command.
> *Answer:* Be careful if you explain why Bernard is already in this part of the world.

From G-2's calculations the enemy still disposed 40 heavy I-Tanks at the Sollum front, the 1st Army Tank Brigade; 40 I-Tanks Mk II at Tobruk, the 32nd Army Tank Brigade; and of 60 Cruiser tanks (med.) of 4th Armoured Brigade and 7th Armoured Brigade of 7th Armoured Division, and 50 Cruiser tanks (med.) 22nd Armoured Brigade (not yet engaged).

On 14th December air reconnaissance reported the railhead south of Sidi Barrani occupied by 4,000 vehicles, including tanks. This could be a formation being brought in from the Middle East.

At 7:45 A.M. from Commander, 4th Indian Division: 'Do everything you can to help.' Previously 7th Armoured Division had transmitted to XIII Corps: 'Further delay of the . . . (part not understood) may well rule out ultimate success.' According to the intelligence report only local enemy attacks took place and then were repulsed.

But on the wireless network of XIII Corps' air liaison officer a signal was intercepted at 4:07 P.M. which said:

> Position at Point 204 (six miles south-east of Bir Temrad) strongly attacked by tanks and from the air. Request immediate assistance.

Late in the evening Major Revetria of Italian Military Intelligence reported that an officer of 4th Indian Division captured at km 110 on the Via Balbia had stated that the British believed they had annihilated two German armoured divisions, and that only 40 of their tanks remained.

According to prisoners interrogated on 15th December the British 2nd Armoured Brigade was on the way from Cairo to the operational region (it was part of the British 1st Armoured Division).

Radio monitoring at 10:27 A.M. shed some light on the mood of the British higher command:

> *Chief of Staff XIII Corps to Chief of Staff, Eighth Army:* That's how things are here at present. I don't have any further news from 'Donald' (4th Armoured Brigade) on what will happen by midday . . . 'Michael' is farther from the objective than one might have expected. I hope he does something soon. I fear that there's not much else to be done. . .
>
> *'Sandy' of Eighth Army:* I'll check up and let you know. But *meet* 'Coffee' (C-in-C) *yourself*(?). I'm going where 'Arthur' is.
>
> *XIII Corps:* I'm gravely concerned and wish you good luck. Godwin (Corps commander) feels the same way, and I hope to see you again.
>
> *Eighth Army:* Thanks. All the best to Godwin. Don't forget 'Coffee' [C-in-C] is on your side. That's all.

At 1:32 P.M. 4th Armoured Brigade signalled to 7th Armoured Division,

> Visibility very bad; things are going bad for the boys. 'Ditch' [5th RTR] is at a standstill. We are doing our best. Get cracking with 'Storm'.

At 3:45 P.M. 7th Armoured Division replied verbatim to 4th Armoured Brigade: *'Carry on, Frank's boys* [4th Indian Division] *pressed. Your activity should help.'*

Our own G-2 report summed up: 'South-east of Bir Temrad the Afrika Korps was able to smash the greater part of 22nd Guards Brigade in a counter-attack, during which about 500 prisoners including a brigadier were brought in. Twenty-five guns, numerous tanks and anti-tank guns were captured.'

At four P.M. radio reconnaissance had picked up a message from 4th Indian Division to XIII Corps: '"King" (Indian Brigade) overrun at . . . [figures]. I believe the rest can hold on.'

At 3:13 P.M. Eighth Army asked XIII Corps to report; the reply was that the whole thing had moved off rather late.

Eighth Army: 'Then everything is satisfactory, don't you think?'
XIII Corps: 'There is no reason why everything shouldn't come off okay. It's all a bit late, but knitting together well.'
Eighth Army: 'That's excellent! The next thing I wanted to ask you is whether a signal from Uncle George's eldest son [5th South African Brigade] has reached you yet?'
XIII Corps: 'Not so far.'

On this day radio monitoring yielded one important fact: the New Zealand Division (without 5th Brigade) and 1st South African Division (without 1st Brigade) had been pulled out of Eighth Army Command area and now came under Commander-in-Chief, Middle East. Thus it was no longer necessary to reckon with them for future operations.

The enemy column reported at Bir Tengeder on 17th December (probably 7th Armoured Brigade) rolled westward and south-westward in an attempt to cut off the German main force. The following intercepts beginning at 8:10 A.M. show that they did not succeed:

C-in-C, Eighth Army to XIII Corps: It seems to me that the bulk of the Teapot-Yellow-Group has escaped between . . . and Mechili. Do you agree? What have you arranged, or what are you going to do?
XIII Corps: I have no information to confirm what you say. The only news I have is that the situation before the front of 4th Indian Division remains unchanged. I have reported that to you and ordered 'Natty' . . . to do everything humanly possible. More cannot be done.
Eighth Army: I have information from two other sources, according to which there are reports that Teapot-Yellow-Group have escaped! Their midnight situation report says that, closely watched by *food-light*

[footlights? Probably armoured cars] they are making for Kremlin [Mechili]; so there is no doubt that they have managed to get away!*

. . . The quickest way is, I believe, through 'Fetter'; get the hell out of it!

XIII Corps: I believe it's true. I thought you had pulled aside those people at Kremlin. . . .

Eighth Army: We must follow hard, and for my part I'm counting on you. They (the enemy) are occupying some very weak positions and they've probably left behind some *Foodlights* before Frank's front. Do everything you can to destroy the Teapot-position!

XIII Corps: I propose to attack on each front.

Eighth Army: 'That's good and fits in with my future plans. Has 'Ricky' [7th Armoured Division] sent somebody into the Juan area?

XIII Corps: No, not yet. I just received a message from him which says that he can hardly send anybody there tomorrow before 1800 hrs. I thought he had had someone already there.

Eighth Army: I agree, it's very *sticky indeed*. He should put on a bigger show. He has to put on a maximum effort. Otherwise we're going to lose a great opportunity.

Our air reconnaissance confirmed on 18th December that 7th Armoured Brigade was moving west from Bir Tengeder. On the 19th our G-2 reported that the enemy was only advancing cautiously, and that 7th Armoured Division had moved forward only a little way from Mechili to the west, without coming in contact with the Afrika Korps.

Radio reconnaissance on 20th December detected the headquarters of 1st Armoured Division apparently at Maddelena. The enemy's northern group advanced only slowly; in contrast the 7th Armoured Division headed west with fresh tank forces via Mechili. This may well have been a result of the admonitions of their superiors as reported in the radio conversation reproduced above.

Lieutenant Seebohm phoned with the news that 7th Armoured Division was moving west, but was reporting no contact with the enemy so far; there were no enemy or combat signals, and the British were having difficulty establishing communications between formations.

At 12.55 P.M. a new wireless net came on the air: it was 1st Armoured Division reporting to Eighth Army (new net); until now it

---

* Careless indications like these that Eighth Army was reading almost simultaneously Rommel's daily situation reports to Berlin should surely have caused the Germans to re-assess the security of their Enigma machine ciphers. – *Editor's Note.*

had signalled only in cypher, but this intercept was in clear, repeating a cypher-message that could not be solved.

Radio reconnaissance reported on 21st December that the enemy in the north (4th Indian Division) was apparently having difficulties with supply. 7th Armoured Division was following toward Benghazi only slowly.

On 22nd December it was realised that the British plan was to cut off the German forces' retreat south at Benghazi; on for example 23rd December a report in 4th Armoured Brigade area said that everything pointed to an evacuation of Benghazi and that numerous explosions had been observed.

From the combat area south of Benghazi a signal from 7th Armoured Division to XIII Corps was intercepted at 9:50 A.M.:

Repeat for the third time that Code Name [is] in at 'Bagpipe' [probably north of Antelat] and has orders to establish contact with 'Dawney' [22nd Guards Brigade]. But Dawney can't be raised by wireless.

At 7:20 P.M. 7th Armoured Division issued these instructions to the KDG reconnaissance unit (King's Dragoon Guards): 'Upon reaching Benghazi, your main task is to secure the petrol dumps.'

On 24th December at 3:04 P.M. the KDG reported to 7th Armoured Division: No petrol whatever to be found in the whole of Benghazi. According to mayor it was destroyed yesterday.'

'Frank,' 4th Indian Division, transmitted to XIII Corps: 'A Happy Christmas to you all! I hope you will not leave us behind in the good hunting!'

On 25th December Eighth Army signalled to everyone:

There is no possibility of celebrating Christmas as we would like to do. But our efforts during this Christmastide of 1941 may well mean that Christmas 1942 will look different. I send you my best wishes – may success be granted to you all!

G-2 was working on the basis of the following XIII Corps command structure at this time: 4th Indian Division; and 7th Armoured Division, with 22nd Armoured and 22nd Guards Brigade, and the Polish and 1st South African Brigades, the latter both echelonned behind 4th Indian Division. The evening G-2 report said:

Bulk of 7th Armoured Division with 22nd Armoured Brigade and 22nd Guards Brigade in area Saunnu-Msus-Antelat. 4th Indian Division in area east and north-east of Benghazi made only slow progress owing to bad road conditions and road blasting.

One signal had spoken of an 'enormous German ammunition- and bomb-dump' found at Benghazi and the airfield as being 'serviceable.'

From all the intercepted signals of 26th December G-2 summarised that the energy was disengaging, regrouping and replenishing units, and that there was little likelihood of a decision attack on the next day.

But on the evening of 27th December an attack by 22nd Armoured Brigade was expected against the east and north-east front of the Agedabia position, and this did take place on the 28th. It was thrown back onto Haseiat by a group of General Crüwell's Afrika Korps. The 22nd Armoured Brigade lost 58 tanks. From a British air liaison net the following message was intercepted about this at 1:10 P.M.:

Request maximum air support as soon as possible at Chor El Sufan. Furious tank battle raging there.

By the time that G-2 made his evening report on the 29th, the number of enemy tanks destroyed the day before had increased to 65. The 22nd Armoured Brigade withdrew with heavy losses to Giof el Matar; it pulled back to the north-east on the 30th – still harried by Crüwell, losing a further 48 tanks. Total losses in the last three days were 136 tanks and armoured cars. During this period there were further signs that 7th Armoured Division had been disengaged and transferred east, though without its 7th Motor Brigade which remained deployed in the battle area.

According to G-2, on 29th December 1941 the enemy Eighth Army Order of Battle was probably this:

XIII Corps (Combat Corps):
22nd Armoured Brigade
22nd Guards Brigade
Polish Brigade
7th Motor Brigade
4th Indian Division
disengaged for reforming: 7th Armoured Division with 4th and 7th
    Armoured Brigades

The author, March 1942.

Air reconnaissance sketch, 23rd November 1941.

XXX Corps (Garrisoning Corps):
1st South African Brigade, Derna
70th Infantry Division, Tobruk
2nd South African Division, Sollum front
5th New Zealand brigade
1st Army Tank Brigade
HQ, 1st South African Division) both without
HQ, 1st Armoured Division) troops

According to P/W interrogations and captured documents the structure of 22nd Armoured Brigade at the end of December was as follows:

3rd CLY (County of London Yeomanry) (tank regiment)
4th CLY (tank regiment)
2nd RGH (Royal Gloucestershire Hussars) (tank regiment)
2nd RHA (Royal Horse Artillery) (artillery)
102nd (Northumberland) RHA (anti-tank regiment)
9th Rifle Brigade (infantry battalion mot.)
12th Lancers (reconnaissance regiment)

Surprisingly 4th Indian Division did find petrol and other valuable booty at Benghazi after all. They reported on 30th December to XIII Corps and 7th Armoured Division inter alia:

> The following dumps were found: on the Benina airfield 3,000 gallons of petrol, perhaps more. On the airfield and in the hangar two complete aircraft, fittings and spare parts. New Ju 88 engines in crates; the following airworthy planes: one Ju 52, four Ju 88s, two Ju 87s, two Me 109s, one Me 109F, one Me training airplane.

No reason was found for the non-destruction or removal of these planes even after the reconquest of Benghazi at the end of January 1942.

In the wireless picture there were signs of the arrival of a new formation from the east; it might refer to the headquarters and elements of 1st Armoured Division, which had not been seen in the command wireless nets of XIII Corps since 29th December.

The operations report of *3./N56* at the end of December noted: 'Enemy attacks and regroupings were detected from signals, and the corresponding sectors and axes of attack.'

By manufacturing continuous contact with the operations staff of

Panzergruppe Afrika, this unit had rendered valuable assistance. In spite of the withdrawal this was achieved by the company being almost constantly on duty, and leapfrogging backwards. Only from 10 A.M. on 18th December to 3 A.M. on the 19th did it have to forego its scrutiny of the enemy signals and that was because it was changing position from east of Benghazi to west of Agedabia.

Withdrawal and Defence of the Mersa-el-Brega Position
This was the situation at the beginning of January 1942: The British had available for the continuation of their offensive one armoured division and four infantry divisions, either motorised or semi-motorised. The 1st Armoured Division, with 2nd and 7th Armoured Brigades, had 250 tanks. The infantry consisted of 4th Indian Division, Polish Brigade, 2nd South African Division, 22nd Guards Brigade, 5th New Zealand Brigade and Free French Brigade.

Bardia was still holding out, but on 2nd January the following message was sent from the 1st Army Tank Regiment sector at 8.56 A.M.: 'Bardia offers to discuss terms of capitulation.' By 11:05 A.M. Eighth Army was heard signalling to XIII Corps: 'Capture of Bardia completely effected. General Schmidt in our hands. Unconditional surrender.' They had liberated 1,100 British prisoners.

A subsequent message reported that fighting for Halfaya was continuing.

A wireless conversation between 7th Motor Brigade and 3rd Royal Horse Artillery Regiment on 4th January showed how military principles applicable to every army were enforced:

> *7th Motor Brigade:* I want you to get moving this very night, not just tomorrow!
> *Answer from 3rd RHA:* Is it not enough if I move only by daylight?
> *7th Motor Brigade:* You are to reach your destination as quickly as possible. I have nothing else to tell you.

On 6th January G-2 reported that owing to the sandstorm the enemy had evidently not noticed the break-out of the German-Italian forces from the area around Agedabia; bad weather had prevented any air reconnaissance.

According to radio monitoring it seemed likely that the forces hitherto engaged on the Bardia front would now be regrouped for an attack on the Sollum front.

At 8.06 A.M. the New Zealanders were heard saying farewell in a signal from 2nd New Zealand Division to 2nd South African: 'The New Zealanders are saying goodbye. May your battles in 1942 be as successful as ever.'

This wish was not to be fulfilled, as will be seen later.

Only on the morning of 7th January did the enemy begin their advance on the now evacuated Agedabia position. According to our G-2, Major von Mellenthin, the British were too weak for a major offensive, as yet, but this might well be resumed once further forces had been brought up. This hint, in conjunction with the arrival of a convoy at Tripoli on 5th January bringing him 54 tanks and 20 armoured cars, may well have induced Rommel to exploit the enemy's temporary weakness to make a counter-attack.

As Agedabia had been heavily mined and mine-clearing was making slow progress, G-2 was able to report on 8th January that 22nd Guards Brigade and 7th Motor Brigade had not advanced very far. In the following days there were persistent British warnings about mines laid by German sappers 'trained' in Russia, and messages like 'Avoid all old tracks, especially at bottlenecks.' or 'Only the roads are safe, the airfields not yet'.

Particularly significant was the signal from 1st Armoured Division to 2nd Armoured and 7th Motor Brigades, both under its command, reporting that the Corps ordered the strictest economy in petrol consumption.

A typical message intercepted on 9th January from Eighth Army to XIII Corps shows how well British surveillance of the enemy was functioning at that time.

From MXQ = Eighth Army, tactical time 9.1., 12.47 hrs
to ORQ = XIII Corps, transmitted 9.1., 12.58 hrs

Earl	*– Italian*
Yell	*– German (?)*
Cheat	*– Headquarter*
Probably biology	*– moving to*
sourpuss and	*– five*
drill	*– half*
baseball	*– miles*
geeble	*– west*
mormon	*– El Agheila*

This cryptic message, reporting the change of position of a German-

Italian headquarters, reached G-2 only two days later, on 11th January at 2:40 P.M.: which was not typical. It is not clear why there was this delay. That it was accurate is shown by a handwritten comment by Major von Mellenthin. '*We* will transfer to 5 miles west of El Agheila', confirming that the headquarters of Panzergruppe Afrika was referred to as 'Earl-Yell' staff by the British at that time.

On 10th January G-2 appreciated that as 5th Indian Brigade had begun a weekly training programme of formation exercises and reconnaissance activities, 4th Indian Division was unlikely therefore to become engaged in fighting in the near future.

On the Halfaya front a strong British attack on Lower Sollum began early on 11th January. While 22nd Guards Brigade reported, 'Mines cleared on all roads except from Agedabia to south, south-east and east', 4th Indian Division still warned its brigades the next day that the area all around must be regarded as dangerous.

A conversation between two radio operators on 12th January shows how valuable such self-important dialogues could be for us as the 'enemy':

> *Operator, 11th Indian Brigade:* Do you know when we're going to set off? . . . And as for where we're going, some even suspect (?) that it might be Gubi again.

This reference to Gubi, far south of Tobruk, triggered off – in the author's recollection – all sorts of speculation about British relief operations and the thinning-out of the enemy's battle front.

> *Operator, 4th Indian Division:* I don't think that you'll be coming here . . . then you'll go straight through!
> *11th Brigade:* Ten days ago we were told that we would go to Derna, but I have my doubts. . . .
> *4th Indian Division:* But at 2400 hrs . . . PUKA is just going back now . . .'
> *11th Brigade:* . . . and away. Might . . . in Cairo, I suppose the next place will be Malaya.

Probably because it was frequently mistaken for 22nd Armoured Brigade, as from 13th January 22nd Guards Brigade was renamed 200th Guards Brigade.

During the next few days the enemy groupings were unchanged. According to G-2, the enemy appeared to be winding up for an attack, but on 14th January a signal from 1st Armoured Division to 7th Motor Brigade, which Rommel himself initialled, spoke of 'change-over time' and of 'the day following our relief' which did not suggest an attack.

The 7th Motor Brigade signalled to 1st Armoured Division on 14th January at 6:40 P.M.: '12th Lancers have occupied Burruei; road conditions here are the worst yet. Heavy wear on vehicles.'

Experience so far gathered was summarised in a basic order on wireless intelligence issued on 14th January. It must be considered in conjunction with the planned counter-offensive that duly began on 21st January. Its purpose was to ensure that wireless intelligence was carried out only by the experts of the Italian and German intercept companies while the signals troops were limited to the transmitting of communications between their respective commands.

Despite sandstorms alternating with rain, British ground reconnaissance reported on 16th January on the German-Italian troop concentrations, on large numbers of infantry with vehicles and tanks, and on trenches covered by tanks and artillery. Signals about tank replacement crews and their relief or employment led us to think a tank brigade was to be reinforced, but then came a signal which widely discussed throughout the entire headquarters of the Panzergruppe. It was from the commander of 1st Armoured Division to XIII Corps, 3:12 P.M.:

'It is just possible that commander 7th Motor Brigade will reach "Humbug" on the 18th at 1600 hrs, but more likely not before the 19th at the same time. Confirm the date. I take the view that this *joy ride* does not, I repeat not, help to win the war.'

This seemed to indicate the withdrawal of 7th Motor Brigade of the 7th Armoured Division. The commander of 1st Armoured Division was certainly right in what he said, especially when one considers that comparable 'joy rides' to Egypt or Greece in the spring of 1941 had proved disastrous in their consequences.

On 17th January the British broadcast the news that our troops in the Halfaya sector had capitulated, having held out there since the beginning of the British offensive on 18th November.

The 7th Motor Brigade, which was still engaged at the front, reported to 1st Armoured Division, among other things at 4 P.M.:

Taking advantage of yesterday's sandstorm the Germans brought six armoured cars and six guns to the plateau west of Burreui. These prevent our reconnaissance west of Burreui where a considerable accumulation of vehicles is positioned.

On account of bad weather air reconnaissance was barely possible for either side.

On 20th January, eve of the German-Italian counter-attack from the Mersa-el-Brega position, the British reported that enemy activity was 'normal'.

The Second Re-Conquest of Cyrenaica

According to prisoners' statements, the German offensive which began on 21st January at 8:30 A.M., took the enemy completely by surprise. Radio reconnaissance reported the situation at 2nd Armoured Brigade as completely confused; it was not ready for action, apparently for supply reasons. The rear service echelons of 1st Armoured Division were given the order to get ready to move off. Such reports were naturally grist to Rommel's mill, confirming as they did the rightness of his offensive approach, of which at first the Italian Command disapproved.

In the afternoon, 200th Guards Brigade was heard to report: 'Enemy continues to advance very rapidly eastwards. We are changing position.'

The G-2 reports of 21st and 22nd January also spoke of a hurried retreat by the British. On the following day they still avoided contact and withdrew quickly northwards in the Msus-Solluch direction. The 1st Armoured Division reported to XIII Corps at 7 P.M. on the 22nd: '1st Rifle Brigade considerable drama (2 words garbled) stuck fast in the sand. No details yet available'.

The RAF emphasized over its wireless nets that it had made maximum efforts throughout the whole day.

The 1st Armoured Division sent this order at 9:05 P.M. to 200th Guards Brigade, and for the information also of 2nd Armoured Brigade:

Positions of your combat groups are not suitably convenient. Your main task is to delay the advance of the enemy on the Agedabia-Antelat road. Nothing must distract you from that task.

The answer at 10:55 P.M.:

I'm carrying it out, but I had no petrol to advance till nightfall. 'Arthur' [reconnaissance unit] and Group are moving into 'Measly' [between Agedabia and Bu Fettah] tomorrow morning at daybreak.

In view of what G-2 had called the 'hurried retreat' by the British in its reports after the beginning of our counter-attack, the following signal from 1st Armoured Division to XIII Corps on 23rd January can only have been meant 'psychologically': 7.50 hrs: 'Harrow' [2nd Armoured Brigade or part of it] is now moving towards Antelat in order to destroy the enemy reported in that area.

And at 8 A.M.:

2nd Armoured Brigade is heading north to destroy the enemy in the Antelat-Saunnu area. Ergh Group will advance on the Grara-Saunnu track and occupy Saunnu. 1st Rifle Brigade will advance on the right flank of Ergh Group. 200th Guards Brigade will proceed to Antelat by the shortest route.

200th Guards Brigade informed 1st Armoured Division at 8.52 A.M.:

We are firing at everything on the main road; we are attacking the enemy, about 60 vehicles with guns. We are short of petrol. Supplies will take some time.

1st Armoured Division: Last night you said you had enough petrol. Go back on the direct road and fetch it.

In the evening wireless reconnaissance learned that XIII Corps had placed two units newly under the command of 1st Armoured Division, one of them 11th Hussars and/or Royals. XIII Corps reported to Eighth Army at 7.41 A.M. on the next day, 24th January:

You cannot break through with your forces. Is that understood?

Eighth Army: Many thanks. I will give you further details in code.

1st Armoured Division to Ergh Group (special combat group on the left flank) at 7 A.M.: Saunnu occupied by the enemy. Go on, go on, go east to (coded). (I.e. otherwise you will fall into the enemy's hands.)

The urgency of this signal is probably explained by the previous day's signal to XIII Corps that Ergh Group was to occupy Saunnu.

1st Armoured Division to Ergh Group, 200th Guards Brigade and 1st Rifle Brigade, 8:30 A.M.: First group of 'Harrow' [2nd Armoured Brigade] is retreating northwards, followed by enemy guns and vehicles.

Eighth Army (C-in-C), 12.54 P.M.: '*Scotty's Boys*' [22nd Armoured Brigade] are expected here in this programme. Can you tell me how I can channel them into your 'crafty'?

XIII Corps: The answer is that you can't! All you have to bear in mind is 'Raymond'.

Eighth Army: All right. If you don't say anything to the contrary, '*Scotty's Boys*' remain here . . . .

XIII Corps: I have two or three reports about the latest situation on the way up to you. I don't want to say more; we are quite happy, more than we were.

G-2 confirmed that evening, 24th January, that the 1st Armoured Division, encircled in the area east of Agedabia, had suffered heavy losses as we tightened the pocket and they redoubled their efforts to break out, especially south of Saunnu. Since 21st January we had destroyed or captured 143 tanks and armoured cars, and eighty guns. Ground troops had shot down 14 planes and taken 1,000 prisoners.

At 5.20 A.M. the next morning, 25th January, the battle group of 1st Rifle Brigade and 2nd Armoured Brigade was heard making a situation report on the previous day:

> In contact with the enemy at pinpoint 7060 [eight miles east of Antelat] throughout the whole day. Repeated artillery ducks . . . . Up to dusk our advanced units were fired on by artillery . . . . The area was twice attacked by Stukas . . . one plane shot down . . . we are short of ammunition, petrol, water, rations.

At 9.40 A.M. XIII Corps signalled: 'Very heavy fighting at pinpoint X 5070 (2,000 yards east of Antelat). Details follow.' There were many reports of enemy tanks east of Antelat, some even heading to the north-west. At 10:07 A.M. we heard a signal, 'We are retreating.'

According to G-2, 1st Armoured Division sustained very heavy losses at the hands of German motorised forces advancing north to Msus: 96 tanks and armoured cars, 38 guns and a large number of vehicles were captured or destroyed.

Air reconnaissance reported remnants of this division fleeing back north and north-east, apparently towards Mechili.

On the same day radio reconnaissance reported disagreements arising over the continuation of operations; the loss of Benghazi was said to be within the realm of possibility! This was testified to by the following wireless conversation intercepted at 1:15 A.M. on 26th January:

> *XIII Corps to Eighth Army:* I was in contact with 'Windsor Lad' [a unit of 4th Indian Division] yesterday evening and the situation is clear as far as the Tonic line. South of Tonic no enemy movements.
>
> *Eighth Army:* I'd like to believe that you are right, but that does not alter the plan that I have set out for you. . .
>
> *XIII Corps, 1.45 hrs:* To secure 'Rattle' I understand your point of view, but . . . I think that an attack by Windsor Lad is the right thing.
>
> *Eighth Army:* If the details have already been issued and those people have been officially put in charge, then it *is out of my hands.*
>
> *XIII Corps:* I take full responsibility.
>
> *Eighth Army:* I have understood your signal, but *I don't believe* the attack is a practical possibility. It might not be possible to carry it out.
>
> *XIII Corps:* It depends on whether the enemy attack continues. I notice you would rather 'Windsor Lad'. . . .

On the basis of the enemy intelligence over the last few days the G-2 of what had now been upgraded to Panzerarmee Afrika transmitted to the German and Italian units substantially the following information: The 1st Armoured Division which had been defeated at Msus had sidestepped to the north. Air reconnaissance had sighted reinforcements being rushed to Cyrenaica. Wireless reconnaissance had detected for the first time the 1st Free French Division. One intercepted signal spoke of a planned enemy advance from Benghazi to the south-east in the event of a further German advance on Mechili. On the other hand, considerable disagreement about how to continue the operation was discernible among the various British headquarters because of this renewed defeat. Therefore, some said, the evacuation of Benghazi could not be ruled out.

After a somewhat calmer day on 27th January the enemy, now mainly the 4th Indian Division, changed their dispositions in Western Cyrenaica. Their order of battle was now as follows:

5th Indian Brigade	–	mainly near Barce
7th Indian Brigade	–	defensive position south of Benghazi
11th Indian Brigade	–	at Maraua
Central India Horse	–	(CIH) Reconnaissance unit, parts with 5th Indian Brigade

The 8th Royal Tank Regiment moved early on 28th January via

Tocra to Benghazi, in order to be at the disposal of 5th Indian Brigade in securing the defensive position.

> *Eighth Army signalled to XIII Corps at 2:30 P.M.:* Can you give me the latest news on the movements of enemy columns in the Mechili region and the track from it to the north?
> *XIII Corps:* Apart from air reconnaissance we have no further news.
> *Eighth Army to XIII Corps, 6:25 P.M.:* I am proceeding to 'Gilbey', further orders follow.
> Comment by *3./N56:* the bulk of 1st Armoured Division had retreated to 'Gilbey'.

Panzerarmee Afrika reported that major units of 4th Indian Division (5th and 7th Indian Brigades) had been routed by the attack of Combat Group Marcks on Benghazi – which had been taken in the morning – and by the Italian Motorised Corps attack on Ghemines. Scattered enemy units had managed to escape to the north-east and east.

According to air and radio reconnaissance, G-2 continued, the impression persisted that the remainder of 1st Armoured Division had retreated to Mechili. The 11th Hussars, detected north-east of Bir Melezz, had ordered their patrols to withdraw.

On the next day, the 30th, G-2 issued this appreciation at 9:45 A.M.: Attempts to break out of Benghazi eastwards had been repulsed during the night of 28th/29th January; more than 1,000 prisoners had been made, and the booty was immense. G-2 reported during the day:

> Continued retreat of the enemy observed by air reconnaissance to-day. Around Maraua and south of it, according to signals intelligence, only 11th Indian Brigade and possibly elements of 5th and 7th Indian Brigades are still located, whereas 1st Armoured Division is heading through Mechili further to the east. Overall impression: enemy appears to be evacuating Middle Cyrenaica.

According to POW statements, 7th Indian Brigade was holding the security belt south of Benghazi on 31st January. Whilst 1st Welch of 5th Indian Brigade moved up to Sceleidima on 23rd January, the other battalions of 5th Indian Brigade remained near Barce, as they were not motorised. Only part of the 8th Royal Tank Regiment, destined for the protection of Benghazi, had actually arrived there as it had transport difficulties and the I-tanks were very slow.

At 12.05 P.M. 1st Armoured Division was heard to signal to XIII Corps and Eighth Army: Reports suggest that the enemy is at Charruba [sixty miles east of Benghazi, south of the Gebel] and heading north or north-east.

Our first air reconnaissance report that day found the area south and north-east of Benghazi clear of the enemy. The second, flown between 10 A.M. and mid-day, reported, 'At El Abiar . . . about 400 vehicles; . . . twelve miles south of Gazala 200 vehicles stationary; 500 on the route east; at Tmimi 100 vehicles; the Trigh el Abd is clear.' The evening report by the Panzerarmee G-2 noted that the British retreat had continued under strong rearguard protection, and that 1st Armoured Division were proposing to retreat to twenty-five miles south-east of Mechili.

The overall impression was stated by G-2 late on 1st February thus: 'Enemy continued on 1st February with the evacuation of Cyrenaica.'

In spite of the precipitous nature of their retreat, the British did not omit to keep an eye on their own enemy situation reports. This is shown by a signal made at 6:51 P.M. on 1st February by XIII Corps to 4th Indian Division, L-Force, Polish Brigade and 150th Brigade:

For information of Eighth Army and 1st Armoured Division: Two prisoners captured today twenty miles south-east of Msus, belonging to 8th Panzer Regiment. They state that the regiment is at Msus. A captured map of 21st January shows Afrika Korps headquarters at the multiple crossroads at Bir Malezz (twelve miles east of Msus).

I assume that Afrika Korps is now in at Charruba, but that 15th Panzer Division is still back at Msus. 21st Panzer Division is probably at Charruba.

On 2nd February our G-2 assessed: 'After evacuating Cyrenaica the enemy is bringing up reinforcements west of Tobruk, apparently to form a defensive front there.' Signals Intelligence reported that one brigade of 1st South African Division, hitherto supposed to be at Bardia, had appeared at Gazala and that 1st Armoured Division was at Mechili.

On the 3rd the British retreat continued. A defensive front was in the making in the Tobruk-Gazala-Bir Hacheim triangle. The Panzerarmee's G-2 estimated that available for this purpose were: 1st Armoured Division, badly mauled; one brigade of the 1st South African Division; 4th Indian Division; 150th Brigade; Polish

Brigade; 22nd Armoured Brigade reconstituted; 1st Free French
Brigade; 32nd Royal Tank Regiment, to garrison Tobruk; remnants
of 70th Division, and with 2nd South African Division, being
retained as a garrison on the Bardia-Sollum front. For a mobile
defence of the front west of Tobruk there were consequently now
operational: '150 tanks, 18 battalions, nine light and three medium
artillery regiments.'

Under cover of a security screen beginning at Ain-el-Gazala, the
enemy established their defensive front from 4th to 6th February
between Bir Hacheim and Acroma and points further north, and
improved it as time went on. As the enemy resistance stiffened, the
German-Italian offensive slowed to a halt west of Ain-el-Gazala.

The British autumn offensive that had begun on 18th November
1941 thus ended on 6th February 1942 with the loss of Cyrenaica to
the German-Italian counter-offensive. In its overall report on the
events of this campaign, the Panzerarmee Afrika offered the
following comment:

> Basic to the British autumn offensive was their intention of annihilating
> the German-Italian forces in North Africa, gaining possession of Libya,
> and thereby establishing contact with Gaullists in French North Africa
> in order to gain eventual control of the whole North African coast line as
> a base for attacks on the southern part of Europe. The British autumn
> offensive of 1941 was thus determined by one long-range military and
> political aim.

In preparations lasting for several months, the British high
command had assembled every available unit under Commander-
in-Chief, Middle East, in order to ensure the success of its offensive.
Not only were those formations already engaged and with experience
in the Libyan battle zone brought fully up to strength, but
particularly in artillery they were reinforced beyond that point. In
addition, three infantry divisions and one armoured division – also
supported by very strong artillery – had been freshly brought in. At
the start of the offensive the Eighth Army was superior to the
German-Italian forces in tanks by about 75 percent, in armoured
cars by about 750 percent, in light guns by about 180 percent. Only
in infantry and heavy artillery were the British inferior – they had
only about thirty percent. 'The British airforce', the report
continued, 'had been brought up to a hitherto unequalled high level.'

It had three times as many fighters and fifty percent more bombers and reconnaissance planes. The Mediterranean fleet lay with a number of its heaviest units in Alexandria harbour ready to support the operations of the army. It later covered the transport of troops and supplies along the coast and its guns joined action during the fighting for Tobruk-Bardia and Halfaya, without having to fear any kind of resistance.

The assembly of all the forces earmarked for the autumn offensive of 1941 had been carried out with skilful screening and also wireless deception and was aided by bad weather. They were therefore largely successful in maintaining the element of surprise.

'Though the British high command demonstrated skill and circumspection in its preparations for the offensive,' the Panzerarmee subsequently assessed, 'in the execution of the offensive they were less successful.' Wilfully flouting the principle that all available forces must be brought into action at the decisive point, on 18th and 19th November only part of the Eighth Army was committed to the attack. The consequence was that individual formations were so heavily battered in the course of the fighting that they had to be withdrawn piecemeal as they became no longer battleworthy. 'At no place and at no time during this battle in Libya was the British High Command able to take control of the fighting by concentrating all available forces when it mattered.' The Panzerarmee regarded this 'fundamental error' as one reason why the British offensive ultimately failed.

In detail, the Germans allowed themselves the following comments: The British had certainly endeavoured to exploit to the full the battle experience they had already gained. They were conscious of their inferiority to the German command, and in theory had tried to learn from them. In practice they proved, however, barely able to abandon their former methodical and heavy handed command tactics.

Their orders were schematic and went into the smallest detail. The middle and lower command were consequently allowed little freedom of movement. The higher command usually adapted only slowly to the changing situation resulting from the flux of battle. The British soldier generally gave a good account of himself, even if he never attained the German punch in attack. His officers fought with gallantry and devotion; a certain shyness of independent action existed. His NCO's were uniformly good. The reconnaissance units were numerically strong and since they were equipped with self-propelled guns especially strong in battle; they carried out their tasks with extraordinary flexibility and efficiency.

The German analysis offered serious criticisms of British tactics. The offensive was usually led by numerous spearheads, which considerably diminished its strength. It was heavily supported by artillery, sometimes five or six artillery regiments for each division; evidently the British hoped to compensate for the inferiority of British tanks vis à vis the Germans in this way. They preferred reverse slopes when establishing defensive positions and these were always protected by a strong screen of armoured cars, in which the British had vast numerical superiority.

A special element was introduced by the Long Range Desert Group, a troop equipped and trained for long-range reconnaissance and nuisance raids far behind our lines, and by the Commandos who carried out sabotage and other raids in our rear.

> Panzerarmee Afrika moulded its operations so as to deploy our own numerically inferior forces at the most decisive place, in maximum concentration and if possible only in an offensive manner. Certain limitations were imposed on this aim by the niceties of coalition warfare and of the often precarious supply situation. Yet we always adhered to the principle that precisely because of our numerical inferiority *only offensive action* would produce results. For this reason we opted for a mobile defence during such times as we were forced onto the defensive.

In following this principle, the Panzerarmee stressed, its sole aim was to defeat, and if possible destroy, the enemy. The capture or occupation of territory was of no importance. 'It was immaterial therefore throughout the entire operation whether the Marmarica or Cyrenaica was temporarily in our hands or the enemy's. What mattered was solely the need to preserve our own forces, in order to be able to deploy them for a counter-attack at the right moment.' The recapture of a previously lost region was the inevitable consequence of a successful counter-attack.

The German soldier had fought magnificently throughout the nearly three months of fighting. Officers, NCO's and other ranks all contributed substantially to the success of the operations through their enthusiasm and sense of responsibility, and not infrequently by their independence of action.

The gallantry of the German soldier in Africa, facing an enemy who was acclimatized and better equipped, will always merit a glorious page in our history concluded the Panzerarmee's self congratulatory report. Even during the retreat he never lost his sense of superiority over the enemy. How high the morale of our soldiers was, is shown by photos of German prisoners in Cairo, in which they proved by their bearing that the German soldier knows not only how to endure hard fighting, but also how to face the hard fate of captivity with dignity.

The co-operation between Panzerarmee and Air Commander, Africa, was good. It was deepened and enhanced still further by frequent visits by Field-Marshal Kesselring, who attached particular importance to constant personal contact with the Panzerarmee. The Luftwaffe always supported Panzerarmee operations excellently, in spite of enemy air superiority, except when their operations had to be curtailed by supply difficulties.

In addition to the outstanding work of the German fighter pilots this report praised the untiring service of the reconnaissance pilots, who had always helped despite the most unenviable operating conditions.

Towards the end of the counter-offensive, our G-2 developed the following order of battle of enemy forces in North Africa, as of 5th February 1942: under the command of Eighth Army, he concluded, came

a) XIII Corps (Combat Corps) in the Tobruk-Gazala-
   Bir Hacheim area with:

	estimated fighting strength		
	Inf.Bn.	*Art.Regt.*	*Tanks*
4th Indian Division:			
5th Brigade) heavy			
7th Brigade) losses		2 lt	
11th Brigade	6	1 med.	–
8 RTR (of 1st Army Tank			
Brigade)			40(I)
1st Armoured Division			
2nd Armoured Brigade	–	1	30(m)
1st Rifle Brigade	2	1	–
200th Guards Brigade	3	1	–

Ergh Group	–	1	–
150th Brigade	3	1	–
Polish Brigade	3	1	–
1st Light Free French Division, mechanised	5	2	40(m)
70th Division, Remains of 32nd Army Tank Brigade	9(garr)	Fort	25(I)
(Tobruk Garrison)	3	Art.	–
1st South African Division	6	2	–
(b) XXX Corps in Sollum-Bardia-Tobruk area and south with:			
2nd South African Division	9(garr)	2 lt	–
Remains 1st Royal Tank Regiment		2 med	–
22nd Armoured Brigade (under reorganisation)			30(m)
	31 and	10 lt	100 (m)
	18 (garr)	1 med	65 (I)
		2 lt and	
		2 med	
		=Bardia	
		and	
		Tobruk-	
		Art.	

c) In Delta region and Western Egypt:
   7th Armoured Division
      (1st Brigade ready mid-February)
   2/3 50th Division (Occupation Troops)
   7th Division (Occupation Troops)
   12th Division (Occupation Troops)
   Parts 5th Indian Division (Occupation Troops)
   2 Greek Brigades (Occupation Troops)

G-2's conclusion was that in the Marmarica Britain had at present about six or seven infantry divisions, of which two divisions were held as garrison troops for Tobruk, Bardia and Halfaya; and one armoured division with, at present, a total of about sixty Cruiser tanks, and army tank units with about ninety I-tanks. The enemy formations positioned in the Delta area and Western Egypt were based there only as occupation troops, except for 7th Armoured Division of which one armoured brigade would become ready for

(*Left*) The Afrika Korps advances. In middle distance a Panzer III tank. Note how visible are the tracks left in the sand, affording possibilities for spoofing the enemy. (*Right*) The German infantry digs in—the ground is hard and gravelly, allowing little depth for foxholes. Note the hand grenades on the lip of his shallow trench, steel helmet ready for action. (From a captured roll of German film.)

Typical of the low hills in the desert that were of such vital tactical importance in the battles. (From a captured roll of German film.)

Administration under desert conditions.

Wireless communications in the desert.

operations at beginning of February, according to information from the German War Office (OKH).

'It follows', concluded G-2, 'that the British troops actually *available* for action at present (four to five infantry semi-motorised divisions, 150-Cruiser tanks and 90 I-tanks) are only in a position to wage a defensive battle.' From what the OKH stated the predicted arrival from Great Britain of eight infantry and two armoured divisions had not yet taken effect in the Middle East. 'The armoured divisions are said to have not yet embarked.' We must accept that the infantry divisions will soon arrive followed by replacements for the reconstitution of the worse hit formations.

> Whether the British formations transported from the homeland will be engaged in the Middle East or in the Far East can not yet be ascertained; in any case we need not anticipate the start of a new British offensive before early April, if at all.

The 'Good Source'

It was not only the usual intelligence sources, such as air and wireless reconnaissance, that confirmed Rommel's opinion that at the beginning of 1942 the British were weak after their autumn offensive, and were encountering severe problems in replacing their huge personnel and matériel losses and in reconstituting their formations after the capture of Cyrenaica. He knew of their supply difficulties from intercepted signals.

But equally important was what he called the Good Source. This had begun to flow in the winter of 1941/2. By Good Source were indicated all items in Africa that had been cabled by the American Military Attaché in Cairo, Colonel Bonner Frank Fellers, to Washington. These cables were also being read in Berlin.* SIM, the Italian military intelligence service, had succeeded in August 1941 in persuading a clerk in the American Embassy in Rome to open the safe containing the 'Black Code', the secret American Military Attaché code, to purloin that code, make a photocopy of it and the relevant code-key tables, and to replace it without arousing suspicion. As a result from the autumn of 1941 all messages encyphered in this code could be read by both the SIM and the

---

* A long series of Fellers' telegrams from this period will be found in the 'office diary' of General George C. Marshall, in the National Archives, Washington DC. Examples can be found on page 233ff of this book. Editor's Note.

German Abwehr in Berlin. It was a magnificent coup by Italian Intelligence.

Of all the code telegrams, which included some from the US military attaché in Moscow, those sent by Colonel Fellers from Cairo were the most important; because they carried vital information on the Middle East battlefields. In view of the great frankness between the Americans and the English, this information was not only strategically but tactically of the utmost usefulness. In fact it was stupefying in its openness.

Colonel Fellers committed to these telegrams the most secret data on military affairs in the Middle East – things that he had witnessed for himself on visits to the front line or gleaned from the headquarters in the desert or in Cairo. He was most assiduous in his inquiries and was inevitably furnished with top secret information by the British who were desperately angling for the entry of the United States into the war. This vital information, enciphered in the Black Code, was deciphered in Germany, translated, re-coded, and was in the hands of the General Staff and Rommel only a few hours after its transmission from Cairo.

The author well remembers that the Good Source was already playing a role by January/February 1942, but as it was forbidden to make notes, German documents do not exist. To his knowledge however the information about British tank losses, the number of tanks operational, and general enemy strengths reproduced from January to May 1942 in the intelligence surveys and orders of Battle were largely due to the Good Source. David Kahn has published* some examples of the information contained in Colonel Fellers' reports, for example, the following:

January 23: 270 airplanes and a quantity of the antiaircraft artillery being withdrawn from North Africa to reinforce British forces in the Far East.

January 25-26: Allied evaluation of the defeats of Axis armour and aircraft.

January 29: Complete rundown of British armour, including number in working order, number damaged, number available, and their locations; location and efficiency ratings of armoured and motorized units at the front.

February 1: Forthcoming Commando operations; efficiency ratings of various British units; report that American M-3 tanks could not be used before mid-February.

* *The Codebreakers: The Story of Secret Writing* Weidenfeld & Nicholson, 1968, p 473. Reproduced by kind permission of the publishers.

February 6: Location and efficiency of the 4th Indian Division and the 1st Armoured Division; iteration of British plans to dig in along the Acroma–Bir Hacheim line; recognition of the possibility that Axis forces might reach the Egyptian frontier once the armoured divisions had been re-grouped.

February 7: British units stabilized along the Ain el Gazala-Bir Hacheim line.

This and similar information transmitted over the following months gave our High Command vital clues as to the enemy's strategy, strength and plans; it confirmed intelligence from other sources, especially signals intelligence. We shall return to the Good Source again during the course of the German offensive that began on 26th May 1942.

Reconnaissance activity on both sides

During the period of consolidation on both sides that lasted until the end of February, it became clear that the enemy was planning to defend neither Acroma nor Tobruk but the so-called Gazala position, and here he completed preparations. Enemy patrol activity became intense.

At this time discussions took place with Captain Count Almasy about a special operation to infiltrate agents into Egypt using captured vehicles, which will be discussed later. On 18th February Almasy drove to Tripoli to overhaul the vehicles and train the agents and escort party.

Meanwhile *3./N56* reported details of the construction of field fortifications, gun positions, minefields and obstacles. According to wireless intelligence, British Field Command 88 at Tobruk was consuming 500 tons of petrol daily, whereas according to German records the consumption rate of a British armoured division for every 100 miles was only 250 tons.

The following reports show the excellent co-operation enjoyed by signals intelligence: on 23rd February, at 9:40 A.M. British air reconnaissance was heard to report, '1,000 vehicles near Um er Rzem. Excellent bomber target'. This intercept was received at 10:30 A.M., and bears the handwritten notes:

1033 hrs informed Afrika Korps (Captain Laubinger).
1036 Air Command (Major Knapp), asked for fighter protection.
Postscript by Major (GS) Zolling: Six British bombers with fighter escort appeared about 2 P.M. over Um er Rzem. Four British fighters shot down by our own fighters; bombers aborted attack.

At 3:05 P.M. our monitors at *3./N56* heard the British Air Liaison net report: 'Returning bombers report no bomb targets between Gazala and six miles west of Um er Rzem.' The document bears the marginal note in handwriting: 'To DAK.'

At the end of February 1942 we obtained the complete British minefield plan, and this was of great importance in spite of the time that had elapsed as it could possibly become of immediate interest again given the frequency with which the battlefields changed hands.

Reconnaissance activity on both sides continued throughout March, though accompanied now by heavier raids. In a typical British operation, battle groups of three brigades (1st South African, Polish and the British 150th Brigade) attacked the German strongpoint of Aleima, twenty-five miles west of El Gazala but was repulsed.

On 16th March enemy forces fell back before our own advance, losing prisoners, weapons and equipment until they reached the Segnali-Temrad line. The enemy was certainly vigilant as the following intercept showed:

1st Armoured Division to 12th Lancers, 0.00 hrs: Suspect vehicle concentration this evening near Mechili. This may be an indication that German forces are about to take over this point. Watch out for anything that confirms this assumption.

Prisoners and documents captured during this raid confirmed the prevailing enemy picture.

On 21st March the British carried out forward assaults from the Segnali-Temrad area, throwing several battle groups at strongpoints south of Tmimi and at Martuba, when they were repulsed. On the next day the enemy fled before a German counterthrust – especially from the area south of Martuba – with considerable losses – at least according to G-2's report later that day. But a British signal transmitted to 4th South African Armoured Car Regiment described the 21st March attack in different terms: 'First news about our successful attack by three mixed columns is as follows: Tmimi taken and occupied, airfield near Martuba shelled, 250 army prisoners and 16 Luftwaffe prisoners.' So it had been regarded as a success by the enemy, even though the withdrawal had been hasty – as it often was with the British: once a retreat was ordered, they were so quick about it that it easily looked like a headlong flight; but for all that, it was not often that they lost control of a situation!

The involvement of 1st Armoured Division, 50th Infantry Division and 1st Free French Division was confirmed on this occasion by radio monitoring; furthermore, the long 'absent' 7th Armoured Division appeared for the first time at the end of the month with an address c/o XXX Corps – important information!

Air reconnaissance and Luftwaffe operations were stepped up, particularly at the beginning of March. On 8th March a fighter-bomber attack was flown against Gambut airfield, with the consequence that the same day we intercepted a British order to the effect that 'all personnel going on leave can only start from the Capuzzo station and return there'; this was farther to the east than British men going on leave had been accustomed to.

The following example shows how relatively closely on occasions the descriptions by the Luftwaffe and RAF tallied with each other. The Luftwaffe reported on 15th March:

> Enemy air activity 14th March: 13.09 hrs, Attack by 12 bombers, 8 Curtiss, on airfield Martuba. At JG 27 (Fighter Group 27) five Me 109s, one Me 108 and one other slightly damaged, otherwise small material damage.

The RAF signalled in cypher on 14th March:

> Executed successful bombing attacks on Mechili. . . . Very successful daylight attacks on bomber and fighter base at Martuba. Enemy lost . . . three fighters and three probables.

The figures very closely correspond; while actual damage caused, is usually overestimated by the attacker in view of the speed of an air attack.

In southern Libya light Free French reconnaissance forces attacked the Italian strongpoints of Um-el-Araneb, Gatrun, and Tedjerri (to the east and south-east of Murzuk in the Fezzan) at the beginning of March; they were repulsed. The attack was undertaken from Zuar in Tibesti (in Chad). Elements of the enemy forces were still in the Fezzan when they were attacked by the Italian airforce on 16th March; some days later they were detected sixty miles south-east of Gatrun, probably on the retreat into the Tibesti mountain range.

These and similar Free French raids had no influence on the

fighting on the coast, as long as the campaign was being waged in Egypt or Libya. Only when the fighting reached Tunisia were General Leclerc's troops more closely involved.

In April 1942 the mutual close observation by the opposing armies was continued, with patrol activity and air reconnaissance. At the beginning of the month signals intelligence detected a degree of enemy regrouping, but the details were not ascertainable for the time being because of the enemy's enhanced wireless discipline and frequent code and cipher changes. The 7th Armoured Division had maintained wireless silence until 9th April and after that transmitted deception or wireless training traffic in conjunction with XXX Corps under whose command it now came; direction finding (DF) placed the division east of El Adem.

In addition, the remoter fields of inquiry, like railroad traffic which had to be timetabled differently because of the shorter nights (with earlier arrivals at and later departures from Capuzzo), as well as suspensions of leave – allegedly because of a shortage of railway carriages – were detected by wireless reconnaissance. Normally suspension of leave would set the alarm bells ringing: one was announced for the period 16th to 24th April but on this occasion when taken in conjunction with other reconnaissance information it was considered not to be a cause for alarm.

At the end of the month parts of 7th Armoured Division were DF'd north of Bir Hacheim, to which they had now advanced. At that time XXX Corps had under its command 7th Armoured Division, 1st Armoured Division, 22nd Armoured Brigade, and 5th Indian Infantry Division. XIII Corps disposed of 1st South African Division, 2nd South African Division, 50th Infantry Division, and 1st Army Tank Brigade.

In G-2's view not enough attention was being paid to the interrogation of prisoners. If handled skilfully this could be one of the most valuable sources of intelligence. He accordingly issued an order on 8th April as to how POW interrogations were to be carried out. In general they were to be conducted by the Division's G-2. The order reminded officers concerned about the principles laid down in Appendix 6 of Army Regulation g.89, setting out the duties of the G-2. As this order is of basic interest, the salient points are worth repeating.

The divisional G-2 was to write an interrogation report containing:

a) name   )
b) rank   )   The POW is obliged
c) number)   to disclose this information
d) place and time of capture;
e) any uniform badges and vehicles emblems on the vehicles used by P/W;
f) unit to which the prisoner belonged.

If possible the interrogation was to be extended to include questions on command structure, deployment, operations, plans, names of commanders, chiefs of staff, etc.

Officers were to be held separate from other ranks; all papers other than military identity cards were to be taken away from POW at once, marked with the POW's name, and given to the escort party for handing in at division headquarters. Airforce personnel were to be interrogated only by Air Commander, Africa (Fliegerführer Afrika).

Abwehr operations

The OKW's counter Intelligence, the Abwehr, tried to assist the German-Italian campaign in North Africa with operations against Egypt in the summer of 1941. They met with no better success than had their attempt to set up a network of agents in the Nile Delta.

A plan was made to abduct the former Chief of General Staff of the Egyptian Army, El Masri Pasha; the attempt failed because although the Pasha was fully informed and agreed to go along, he did not appear at the pre-arranged rendez-vous in the desert south-west of Cairo, where a He111 was to pick him up; he had been arrested in the meantime.

The second attempt, Operation Condor, fared no better. The plan had been to set down two German agents by plane in the desert between the Farafra oasis and Upper Egypt. The mission was flown on 16th July 1941. The He111 with the two agents on board arrived there at nightfall, found it already too dark to land, and was lost at sea on the return flight; the escort plane made it safely back to Benghazi.

A Hungarian air force officer from the First World War, László, Count Almasy, had been attached to the Abwehr in Berlin as an adviser, and given the rank of Luftwaffe captain. He had been released for that purpose by the Hungarian forces, and had assisted in this operation in an advisory capacity. After its failure he proposed – to the initial amazement of the Abwehr – that he drive overland from Cyrenaica, around the deep south of the Libyan desert to Assiut in Upper Egypt, some two hundred and fifty miles south of Cairo, and set down two agents there.

Coming from any other man this would have been dismissed as loudmouthed braggadoccio. From Almasy, however, it made sense. He knew what he was talking about; on innumerable expeditions to the desert of southern Libya he had come to know the terrain and the difficulties of these vast empty spaces. He was familiar with its hardships and dangers. He had made a name for himself before the war as an explorer and leader of expeditions, and was considered one of the finest experts on the Egyptian desert.

His plan was approved by the Abwehr. In detail, his idea was to drive via the Gialo oasis three hundred miles south-east of Benghazi, to the group of oases at Kufra far to the east, then by-pass in a wide sweep to the south the mountain massif of the Gulf Kebir, then strike eastwards and head for the Kharga oasis where he would head north again, to reach the town of Assiut 150 miles away, or rather the slopes of the Libyan desert some miles west of the town. From here both agents would infiltrate into the Nile Valley.

After lengthy preparations in Berlin and Africa and the special overhauling of the vehicles at Tripoli for the long journey across the desert, Operation Salaam set out. The vehicles selected were captured British stock – two Ford cars, English command cars and three one and a half ton lorries (known as *Flitzer* to the Germans in Africa). Passing through Agedabia, a hundred miles of Benghazi, the group reached Gialo first and finally arrived at the dropping point west of Assiut on 24th May, 1942. Here two agents, Eppler and Sandstede, were set down.

As the crow flies, the distance covered by Almasy was over 1,300 miles; taking into account reconnaissance and inevitable detours it must have been closer to two thousand. It was a unique achievement both by Almasy and his German companions, as only the initiated who know the physical and psychological burden associated with long desert travel can appreciate. Almasy himself later said that he had a sixth sense for the desert and that this had guided him. But credit was equally due to the preparations made by Hans von Steffens, whose planning took all the difficulties of the journey fully into account and obviated needless risks.

This great achievement deserved a comparable degree of success in acquiring intelligence from Egypt. Unfortunately these hopes did not materialise, as Steffens later revealed.* Circumstances were to blame for which the organisers of this operation could hardly be held responsible. Although both agents escaped arrest by the British in Cairo until the end of July, the two Panzerarmee wireless operators whose job had been to decipher any messages sent by 'Salaam' fell into British hands at the end of May together with all their secret documents. Thus for security reasons any messages coming from Cairo were neither confirmed nor answered after that. As for the two agents themselves, they are said to have aroused suspicions in Cairo by squandering money and throwing lavish parties. In such circumstances once one is under surveillance – and the British are very punctilious in such things – intelligence-gathering and transmitting are soon finished. Thus what had seemed an impossible journey had been crowned by success at first, but it resulted in no useful information whatever reaching Germany from these agents.

While the events of the ensuing months – the prosecution of the German offensive right up to El Alamein, the first British counter-attacks in July, the last German attempt to invade Egypt at the end of August, and the mounting signs of an impending British counter-offensive – still did not make intelligence gathering in Egypt pointless, there was just not enough time to make the necessary preparations for a fresh shot at infiltrating agents into Egypt, and the attempt was not repeated.

The Second German-Italian Offensive
In spite of violent sandstorms, which became more frequent than usual in May 1942, the enemy continued his normal reconnaissance patrols and disruptive artillery fire.

Our reconnaissance were now reporting the enemy's tank and motorised formations steadily closing up to the west. There were reinforcements to the enemy northern front at Ain-el-Gazala as reflected in the increased motor vehicle activity and multiplication of tents in the El Adem-Bir Hacheim-Gazala-Tobruk area.

Meanwhile, by intensifying the air raids since the beginning of the year against Malta our air force had succeeded in all but neutralising the island as an obstacle to the passage of German-Italian convoys through the Mediterranean; this had improved the sea transport

---

* H. von Steffens, *Salaam: Geheimkommando zum Nil - 1942* (Neckargemünd, 1960).

situation, so that the Panzerarmee could be reinforced and supplied. One rumour circulating at that time said that the number of fighters ready for action in Malta on 10th May had dwindled to only one.

Field-Marshal Kesselring had briefed us on 18th April as to the air force's intentions in the Mediterranean. The Italians were planning a surprise assault on Malta, for which they would be loaned German paratroops and equipment.

Kesselring proposed on this occasion that we dislodge the British from their Ain-el-Gazala position before the summer heat set in.

The Chief of Comando Supremo, General Ugo Cavallero, believed however that as the Italian paratroopers were not yet fully battle-trained they were not ready for the surprise attack on Malta proposed by Kesselring; accordingly the following sequence of events was agreed upon on 30th April, in order to exploit the air raids on the island. First the Panzerarmee should launch an offensive at the end of May; it should if possible take Tobruk, but halt on the Egyptian frontier so that by the July full moon at the latest Operation Hercules – the capture of Malta – could be carried out.

To underline this, the Comando Supremo directed Panzerarmee Afrika on 5th May to

defeat the enemy west of Tobruk and thereafter, assuming favourable conditions, take Tobruk at a rush, and only once this categorical precondition has been met continue the advance to the Sollum-Halfaya line. This frontier line is in no event to be passed.

The offensive was to begin at the end of May.

Summarising the preliminary history of this attack, the Panzerarmee would write as follows:

Although continuing his active reconnaissance and marching activity the enemy had gone on the defensive after the heavy losses of his counter-offensive. He had continued to strengthen the Bir Hacheim-Gazala position and in particular its two anchor posts at Bir Hacheim and Gazala, which were rebuilt as fullscale fortresses. Between these two fortresses the enemy had laid out extensive minefields interspersed with powerful strongpoints. The number of mines laid in the Hacheim-Gazala position alone exceeded 500,000. The total number of mines laid in the fortified positions of Marmarica exceeded a million.

To the rear of the Gazala position lay the Tobruk fortress with its efficient harbour. Tobruk gave both backbone and suppliers to the Gazala position. In order not to rely solely on the sea-route the enemy had extended the military railway – initially only as far as Matruh – and then by May as far as Tobruk. He could also use the coastal road for motor transport and supply.

The report of the Panzerarmee explained that the enemy was well provided with supplies and transport, our own supply position was at rock bottom. The petrol situation was always particularly critical. As late as March it would only have allowed a brief mobile defensive operation. The situation improved in April and May, as we established air superiority over the Central Mediterranean, enabling an increase in supplies to the ports of Tripoli, Benghazi and Derna. After Malta had been successfully held down for some time, the reorganisation and stockpiling of reserves for the German-Italian troops was vigorously pressed ahead. In spite of this there could be no doubt that the enemy would be able to reorganise his Eighth Army more quickly than we could ours. It was to be assumed that he would then resume the attack in an attempt to return the Benghazi-Malta link by conquering Cyrenaica, thereby winning control at least in the Eastern Mediterranean.

> We had to assume that the enemy would attack early in June. Taking all this into consideration the Panzerarmee decided to steal a march on the British and take the offensive themselves at the end of May. For this the previous capture of Malta would be highly desirable. But even if this proved impossible the Panzerarmee's offensive should still be undertaken.

Prior to the beginning of this German-Italian offensive, our Army G-2 issued an intelligence summary dated 20th May 1942 (signed by Major Zolling). This depicted the current enemy situation fairly accurately, and it is of particular interest because of the way that the Good Source, the American Colonel Fellers, shines through behind the statistics on the enemy Order of Battle, and the evaluation of the tactical efficiency of various enemy units and the appraisal of their commanders.

The Panzerarmee's offensive began at 2 P.M. on 26th May 1942 with a diversionary attack on the Gazala front. The Afrika Korps and the Italian XX (Motorised) Corps, meanwhile assembled at Segnali North in order to reach a point south of Bir Hacheim by a night movement starting at 8:30 P.M.. From there the attack would be carried into the enemy's deep flank on an axis from El Adem to

Acroma. The author still remembers an intercept of the first report made by a British armoured unit at about 5 A.M. on 27th May: 'Enemy Panzer columns are bearing down on us. It looks like it's the whole damned Afrika Korps.'

During the following days signals intelligence like this was immediately sent over to General Rommel, greatly facilitating his direction of the battle. Unfortunately no copies of the intercepts survive as all the files of 621 Radio Intercept Company* were later lost and the G-2 files of that period are also missing.

The excellent insight that the Good Source afforded into enemy command intentions will be dealt with later. But Ultra also influenced events, and these will be briefly summarised first. It was incomprehensible that in spite of the continuous stream of British reconnaissance messages our tanks flooding round to the east of Bir Hacheim were able to overwhelm 7th Motor Brigade as it moved into position, to destroy parts of 4th Armoured Brigade and to overrun the staff of 7th Armoured Division, with the result that it was not until the next morning that the Eighth Army learned what had happened. The Ariete Division encountered and defeated the newly arrived 3rd Indian Motor Brigade; by 10 A.M. the 90th Light Division had already reached El Adem, so that it appeared that the timetable foreseen by the German operations order was actually going to be observed. The American Grant tanks were a nasty surprise, even so, since their main armament outranged both the Panzer III and IV.

While the Afrika Korps was able to win ground northwards to as far as eight miles south and south-west of Acroma, it found its supply columns cut off by British tank attacks; and the supply track skirting around Bir Hacheim had become a hunting ground for the British and was therefore unusable. The fighting brought heavy losses; soon over a third of the German tanks were out of action. The 90th Light Division was cut off from the rest of the army at El Adem and in a precarious situation.

The British situation improved on 28th May, since the Panzerarmee was now widely scattered and running into severe supply difficulties. The next few days could have been decisive, but General Ritchie missed the bus – he fumbled this glittering opportunity presented by the German weakness. Rommel rushed supply convoys to the Afrika Korps and took command of it himself. In order to secure supplies he had to find and open a route through

---

* Formerly 3rd Radio Intercept Co. of 56th Signals Battalion. Renamed in April 1942.

the minefield to the west; but the minefield was guarded by 150th Infantry Brigade of British 50th Infantry Division, which was dug in at Got-el-Ualeb.

Rommel's plan to break this stalemate was as follows:

1. to open an aisle through the minefields and at the same time to destroy 150th Infantry Brigade;
2. to take Bir Hacheim, and
3. to cut off the two divisions at the northern end of the front (1st South African and the British 50th).

Given the inability of the British Eighth Army to seize the initiative that beckoned – on 29th, 30th, and 31st May – Rommel gained time to reinforce his troops. He went over to the defensive; the enemy counter-attacked but failed with heavy tank losses.

On 30th May Rommel personally opened up a route through the minefield so that his supply columns could reach the Panzerarmee. The 150th Infantry Brigade was encircled and overrun by storm on 1st June. During the same night the other 'thorn in the flesh', Bir Hacheim, was encircled by 90th Light Division and the Trieste Division.

A British counter-attack on 5th June failed, again with heavy losses; the number of serviceable Cruiser tanks available to Eighth Army dwindled from 300 on 4th June to 132 on the morning of the 7th. The 32nd Army Tank Brigade lost fifty of its seventy I-tanks.

By 10th or 11th June General Ritchie had lost control of events. Bir Hacheim was occupied on the 11th after its battered defenders, the French Brigade, had pulled out the night before.

The Panzerarmee now resumed its offensive. In the ensuing tank battles, and particularly those of 12th and 13th June, the British lost most of their remaining tanks; about 120 were strewn about the battlefield, and the number of those operational was put at only about seventy – no longer a serious menace to General Rommel's army.

On 14th June the enemy abandoned his Gazala position. Its defenders, the 1st South African and the 50th Infantry Divisions, only barely escaped because the remnants of the armoured brigades aided by an English and a South African battalion and some artillery managed to hold up the German Panzer divisions thrusting northwards towards the coastal highway, the Via Balbia, until the evening.

The 29th Indian Brigade gallantly defended the El Adem box

until 17th June, but then broke out and escaped during the night. This cruelly weakened the defences of Tobruk. We attained Tobruk on the 20th and it capitulated on the 21st.

Since the opening stages of the battle of the Marmarica had been trumpeted by the British as a victory – for the Panzerarmee had formed itself encircled in the so-called 'Cauldron', and London was confident of its annihilation, Norman E. Dixon has asked in his book *On the Psychology of Military Incompetence:** the question, 'Why did it happen?'

> A popular explanation was that Rommel had the advantage in equipment – better tanks and guns. This excuse lacks validity. The Eighth Army had a four-to-one advantage in tanks (including 400 in reserve) which were on average of superior quality to those of the Panzerarmee, a three-to-two advantage in artillery, and six hundred as opposed to five hundred and thirty aircraft.
>
> A truer answer is inadequate generalship. The Army Commander Major-General Neil Ritchie, a fine-looking man, has been described by his contemporaries in ways strikingly reminiscent of Elphinstone, Raglan and Buller.

General Elphinstone was responsible for the disastrous British retreat from Kabul in 1842; General Lord Raglan was the no less inadequate commander of the British Expeditionary Corps in the Crimean War, and General Buller was Commander-in-Chief during the Boer War.

Dixon cites, among others, the general who commanded XIII Corps up to February 1942, Godwin-Austen: 'General Ritchie had a great air of decisiveness, yet was really rather indecisive. He had a tendency to ask your advice and having received it act in the opposite way.' He also cites General Messervy, commander of 7th Armoured Division from February 1942; Messervy gives one example of Ritchie's irresoluteness and his muddled orders for the defence of El Adem: 'I got via Corps an order:

> on no account was El Adem to be evacuated – they were to fight it out to the last. It was already surrounded. I was told by Norrie† that these were the Army Commander's personal orders. Then I had a message: it might be evacuated if I thought it couldn't be held. I said I was quite sure it could not be held for long; then I was told to pass this message on to 29th Brigade. Then I got another order – the Army Commander says it must

---

* Jonathan Cape, 1976. Reproduced by kind permission of the publishers.
† Lt Gen Willoughby Norrie, GOC XXX Corps.

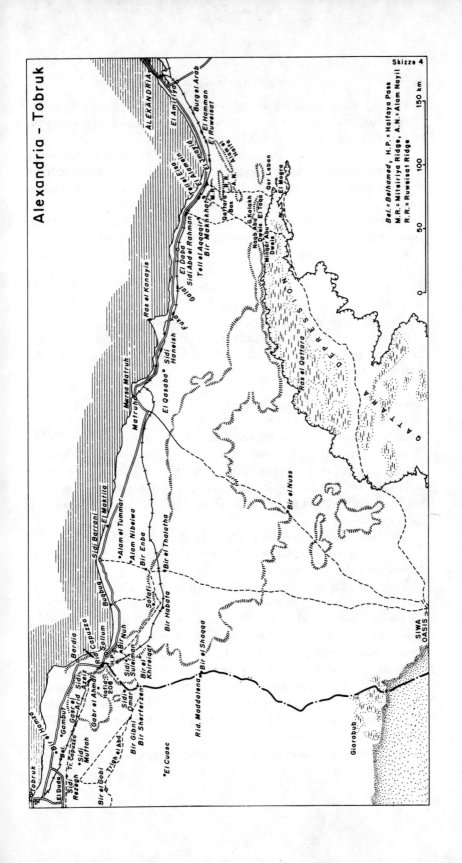

be held. Then yet another: that it was to be evacuated if the brigade could get out. I passed this on to Denis Reid [the Brigadier] and they got out. This was an example of what was happening all the time.'

The upshot was the flight of Eighth Army to Egypt; General Ritchie wanted to defend Mersa Matruh, but General Auchinleck did not consider the strongpoint tenable and relieved Ritchie from command. As Commander-in-Chief, Middle East, he was ultimately responsible and he himself took command of the Eighth Army.

Regardless of the directive laid down by the German High Command (OKW) and Italian Comando Supremo that Operation Hercules – the capture of Malta – should be undertaken, Rommel succeeded on 24th June in securing the permission of both Hitler and Mussolini to pursue Eighth Army right into Egypt.

On the last day of June his advanced units reached the region west of El Alamein, where a fortified front had been prepared by the British.

The Fighting for the Alamein Position
According to one of the last reports of Colonel Fellers to be deciphered by the Germans, the British planned to pull their Eighth Army into this Alamein position. This had been providently worked up during the previous year in the forty mile wide neck between the sea in the north and the salt marshes of the Qattara depression in the south. It afforded the last real chance to defend Egypt against German attack.

The entire British position in the Middle East depended upon the successful defence of this line. The German-Italian advance had to be stopped ahead here.

There was bitter skirmishing on this front throughout the whole of July.

Rommel got cracking. On 29th June his 90th Light Division had occupied Mersa Matruh; on the 30th he was already sixty miles further east, coming up to the Alamein position. This consisted at first only of three fortified rings, or 'boxes': the first at El Alamein in the north, the second near Bab el Qattara in the middle, and the third near Naqb Abu Dweiss in the south. They were each about fifteen miles apart, so for the time being there was no coherent defensive line whatever.

As a result of the Eighth Army's rapid retreat the Panzerarmee's

Information in the desert. *Above:* Name, rank and number . . . a German soldier interrogates a British POW, April 1941 and *below* listening to the news by radio in the desert.

Water presents a problem in the desert.

A desert wadi.

G-2 naturally had no precise information about the operational areas of the British units now fighting in the Alamein position. In the north XXX Corps had command; but our G-2 took it to be X Corps (which in reality had organisational duties for the defence of the Delta.) He took the British 50th Infantry Division to be at Alamein itself; nobody realised that 1st South African Division was in the front line; one brigade was engaged in the Alamein box and the two other brigades stationed between Alamein and Deir el Shein on the west of Ruweisat Ridge. An Indian brigade was thought to be at Deir el Abiad, but it was engaged further east. Instead of one brigade, the whole New Zealand Division was assumed to be in the Qattara box and 1st Armoured Division to the west of it, whereas it had gone directly from the retreat to a reserve position on the Ruweisat Ridge.

The Afrika Korps struck east on 1st July from its assembly area ten miles south-west of El Alamein; it took Deir el Shein that evening after its defenders, the inexperienced 18th Indian Brigade, were wiped out. Nevertheless, their stubborn fight had gained one day for Auchinleck. The 90th Light Division attempting to cut off Alamein encountered heavy artillery resistance from the South Africans south of that box and dug in. On top of that a violent sandstorm on this 'real horror of a day' badly hindered the Afrika Korps and 90th Light.

By the evening of 1st July the prospect of snatching a rapid victory had dwindled to zero; instead of out-manoeuvering the adversary Panzerarmee found itself bogged down in a battle of attrition, which was right up the street of the British Command and troops, because it was what they had been trained for. For mobile warfare, in which the Germans had hitherto excelled, the British Command was too orthodox and rigid. Through the respite won on 1st July, which may well have been decisive, the British 1st Armoured Division were able to regroup after its four-day retreat and beat off the exhausted Afrika Korps attack. Exhausted and below strength, the 90th Light Division attacking Alamein had no chance against the South Africans.

On 2nd July the entire Afrika Korps was forced onto the defensive in the evening when it had to check a thrust by XIII Corps from the south. On 3rd July, the Afrika Korps was still on the defensive; it had to save the Ariete from the New Zealanders. A renewed attack at the Ruweisat Ridge brought only limited territorial gains.

That day the order was given to dig in; the offensive, and with it the invasion of Egypt, were suspended for the time being.

On the same day, 3rd July, Churchill sent the following telegram to General Auchinleck. It contained perhaps the first time explicit published reference to Ultra, the use of intercepted German signals of the highest security classification:*

> On July 1 we told you our special information that enemy after feinting at your southern flank would attack centre of your position about where 18th Brigade lay and thereafter turn northwards to cut off El Alamein strong point. This is exactly what he appears to be trying to do. Are you getting these priceless messages (which have never erred) in good time? Every such telegram ought to be in your hands without a moment's delay.

General Corbett, Auchinleck's CGS, answered that same day:

> Am answering for Commander-in-Chief to avoid delay. Your message being passed to him with this reply. 'Every special-source message goes direct Eighth Army received there as early as at CHQ. These messages of great value. Some arrive in time to be operationally of use, others not so. Timings can be checked your end.'

However, Rommel just did not have the strength to carry out his plans as described in his signal (and intercepted by the British). On July 4th the Afrika Korps had only 36 tanks ready for action.

Auchinleck planned to pit XXX Corps against the German-Italian northern sector west of Alamein whilst XIII Corps enveloped our right wing in the south and then thrust north, to cut off the Panzerarmee. But the British corps commanders were not up to this task and on neither 4th nor 5th July was it carried out. One consequence was the relief of General Norrie, at his own request, as commander of XXX Corps on 6th July by Major-General W.H.C. Ramsden, at that time commander of 50th (Infantry) Division.

During the night of 7th to 8th July the New Zealand Division evacuated the Bab-el-Qattara box, whereupon Rommel gave the order to resume the advance eastwards.

But on the 10th an attack by the Australian 2nd/26th Battalion thwarted this plan: early that morning they overran the Italian

* John Connell, *Auchinleck: A Biography of Field-Marshal Sir Claude Auchinleck* (Cassell, 1959).

Sabratha Division in the coastal region, and captured Tell el Eisa only just short of the Army Command Post. This attack signalled the collapse of Rommel's plans to attack in the south, as he had to detach parts of the Afrika Korps from this to counter-attack in the breach made by the Australians. Despite this the Australians held on to the ground they had gained here, at Tell el Eisa. Nor could this Australian salient be pinched out on the 11th, as the Australians held onto their newly gained positions against all counter-attacks. Rommel had to content himself with consolidating the situation in the north; the ground lost at Tell el Eisa and Point 33 was ceded to the 'Aussies'.

After this there was no way to carry out the planned attack by the Afrika Korps in the central sector; nor did the German attacks launched on 16th July enjoy greater success. On the contrary, an Australian attack on 17th July broke through the positions of the Trieste Division and were only halted by throwing in our last reserves.

Further enemy attacks on the 21st and 22nd, executed by 5th and 6th New Zealand Brigades and 161st Indian Brigade, failed because they lacked tank support and were unable to break through the German front; the ground gained was lost to German counter-attacks.

During the night of 26th/27th July, 2nd/24th Australian Battalion attacked in the northern sector and the British 69th Infantry Brigade of 50th (Infantry) Division in the centre. Both attacks were thrown back as the British tanks pushed off too late or not at all or – in the case of the 50th RTR – had to retreat after losing twenty-two tanks.

In spite of great difficulties in warding off these strong attacks on the 26th and 27th the Panzerarmee front held out. However, and this was of greater significance for the course of the campaign, the German-Italian offensive had been finally stalled.

Later in July a bulletin issued by General Auchinleck in March fell into our hands. It has often been quoted since then though not always in full. Quite apart from the psychological importance attached to Rommel by the enemy command, it shows by its final paragraph that at the time of issue a very generous attitude existed in British minds towards the Rommel phenomenon. And to Auchinleck fell the honour of being the general who succeeded in checking Rommel's advance into Egypt, an honour that every German *Afrikasoldat* who knows what happened does not hesitate to award to him.

To: All Commanders and Chiefs of Staff.
From: Headquarters, BTE and MEF.
There exists a danger that our friend Rommel is becoming a kind of magician or bogey-man to our troops, who are talking far too much about him. He is by no means a superman, although he is undoubtedly very energetic and able. Even if he were a superman, it would still be highly undesirable that our men should credit him with supernatural powers. I wish you to dispel by all possible means the idea that Rommel represents something more than an ordinary German general. The important thing now is to see to it that we do not always talk of Rommel when we mean the enemy in Libya. We must refer to 'the Germans' or 'the Axis powers' or 'the enemy' and not always keep harping on Rommel.

Please ensure that this order is put to immediate effect and impress on all commanders that, from a psychological point of view, it is a matter of the highest importance.

(Signed) C.J. AUCHINLECK
General
Commander-in-Chief, MEF

P.S. I am *not* jealous of General Rommel.

It was Auchinleck who had organised the resistance to the German-Italian offensive at Alamein. It was his attacks at the beginning of July that brought that offensive to a halt; indeed, his attacks of 10th July and especially the 27th nearly brought defeat to the Panzerarmee. It had to dig in, and call off the offensive.

Signals Intelligence May–July 1942
During the fighting which had lasted from 26th May until the end of July 1942, worthwhile results had been obtained almost daily by Signals Intelligence but all relevant documents were lost when the 621 Radio Intercept Company was overrun and wiped out on 10th July. One interesting detail is known from Lieutenant Habel, who was at that time engaged near Bir Hacheim with one platoon of the company.

The fighting for this cornerstone of the British line west of Tobruk was all but over; under our artillery and Stuka bombardment and repeated assault by our shock troops the Free French defenders had been crowded closer and closer. In one book, Paul Carell has described how

* Paul Carell, *Die Wüstenfüchse* (Hamburg, 1960) p.208.

on the night of 10th June a patrol brought in a prisoner captured while clearing part of a British minefield. Interrogation elicited dramatic information: the surrounded troops had been ordered to break out through certain pre-selected minefield lanes that would have been cleared in advance.

According to Habel this was not so: 'On the contrary, my platoon had intercepted a coded signal, decoded it and sent it on to our G-2 and operations staff. The signal contained exact data on the break-out routes and on the reception points where the British lorries would approach the outer perimeter of the pocket. We took our own precautions in the light of this information.'

The result was that the ensuing breakout caused heavy breakout casualties among the Free French brigade. The abandonment of this fortified system around Bir Hacheim had very serious consequences for the British command; in Auchinleck's words, Rommel's reaction to it was 'immediate and determined'.

Signals intelligence had given us the British battlefield layout by the evening of 11th June:

1st Armoured Division:	Headquarters with 22nd Armoured Brigade and 2nd Scots Guards across the Trigh Hacheim road about four miles south of Knightsbridge;
2nd Armoured Brigade	was moving south-eastwards across the Trigh Capuzzo;
201st Guards Brigade	was in the Knightsbridge box;
4th Armoured Brigade	was stationed where it could cover the left flank of this box, to the south-east; and
29th Indian Brigade	holding the El Adem box, was fifteen miles farther east.

The headquarters of *7th Armoured Division* was to the east of the El Adem box.

Rommel had such a thorough knowledge of all these dispositions from his signals Intelligence that he often had a clearer picture of what the British C-in-C planned than some of the British subordinate formation commanders. Our radio reconnaissance reported for instance that 4th Armoured Brigade had declined to carry out an attack to the south-east. While this was not strictly accurate, Rommel thereupon ordered 15th Panzer Division to stand on the defensive, whilst the 21st advanced south of the Knightsbridge box to take the British armour in the rear.

The result was a tank battle that developed on 12th June, and ended with the annihilation of a great part of the British tank force; about 120 tanks were lost. On the 13th his victory became certain; the remaining British tanks had been all but ground to pieces between the German Panzer divisions – it was a 'Black Saturday' for Eighth Army.

The Good Source had yielded particularly useful information during the weeks following 26th May*. It came up with the number of British tanks ready for action and it reported on the atmosphere in Cairo, including details of a 'flap' that set in there and reached such proportions that the RAF offices in Cairo had thrown their files through the windows onto lorries waiting in the rear to transport them away. Arnold Cauer, one of our men who managed to escape captivity briefly and moved freely around Cairo at this time, later confirmed this to the author.

It was the British tank losses in mid-June before the attack on Tobruk in particular and this flap in Cairo that had caused Rommel to pursue the beaten and demoralised Eighth Army regardless of earlier plans to halt on the Egyptian frontier.

At the end of June moreover, the Good Source reported that the British had initially intended to restore their defensive line at the completed line of defences hinging on Mersa Matruh; but that when Auchinleck had realised this position was untenable he had decided that the Eighth Army must fall back on the Alamein position. The intercepted telegrams of Colonel Fellers from Cairo to Washington kept Rommel informed about the British change of mind.

On 29th June this source of intelligence suddenly ran dry. It does not matter much today why this stream of intelligence was suddenly cut off. Probably the British cryptanalysts had detected that the Fellers telegrams enciphered in the Black Code were always set out in the same format, enabling them to decode them in the end, and they had recommended the Americans to modify the code. Perhaps Fellers' outspoken pessimism was what brought about change.

According to one a fantastic story told about the cessation of these messages, the German radio broadcast presented a play on 27th June at 8:15 P.M., announced with the words: 'We bring you a radio play with scenes from the British and American secret services!' The American military attaché in Cairo was the central figure in this radio play. The story has it that through an indiscretion at the deciphering agency housed in the Matthäis church in Berlin, signals

* See page 233-5.

of Colonel Fellers which were in fact translations of authentic Fellers telegrams had been provided to the broadcasters, and these had written finis to his reporting from Cairo.

If true, then messages broadcast over the German radio can at most have confirmed the British in what they already suspected, and speeded up their decision to warn the Americans that the Black Code had been broken. In reply to his own inquiry the author learned from Mr Edward Thomas, a former member of the Bletchley staff now working at the Cabinet Office Historical Section in London and co-author of the official history *British Intelligence in the Second World War* as follows:

> As regards our knowledge of the leakage of information through Fellers I can assure you that it did not come through our reading of Fellers' telegrams. The story is long, not uncomplicated, and will one day come out. In brief, it is that our suspicions were aroused through our reading of Luftwaffe and Panzerarmee Afrika Enigma, and that we were finally – but somewhat late in the day – able to trace the source of the leak.

Whatever the reason, from 29th June onwards the Good Source fell silent. We now no longer had this incomparable source of authentic and reliable information, which had contributed so decisively during the first half of 1942 to our victories in North Africa. Whereas for the Germans the Good Source had been forthcoming little over six months, for the Allies Ultra was a much more enduring source of intelligence of the utmost importance and highest classification.

Ultra, Britain's own cryptanalysis, had played its part in defence against our sparring offensive from May to July 1942. According to *The Ultra Secret* Auchinleck and Ritchie were privy to Rommel's plans of attack and objectives for the end of May 1942: Rommel had reported them to Berlin; Bletchley Park had intercepted and deciphered them.

The well-timed British tank attack against the columns ferrying supplies to the Panzerarmee as it advanced, largely separating them from the tanks as they turned northwards on 27th May, supports this contention. On the other hand, Ultra was not the only help in appreciating German-Italian tactical plans that month, May 1942; the excellent British ground reconnaissance, particularly by the armoured car regiments, has already been mentioned; they certainly also gained information that suggested a German attack at the end of May. An entry in XXX Corps Signals war diary for 23rd May mentioned much enemy air activity which was considered a prelude to the expected enemy attack.* After a similar entry for 26th May it says on 27th May that the expected enemy attack was on. Anthony Cave Brown writes in *Bodyguard of Lies* that on 11th June Field-Marshal Rommel informed the OKW by cipher signal of the situation and of his intentions after the capture of Bir Hacheim – that he was not going to attack this time but wait for the enemy to come to him. Rommel's plan was revealed in an Ultra intercept and brought to the attention of General Auchinleck, to his chief of staff and to Brigadier Frederick de Guingand, his G-2 (who later became chief of staff to Montgomery.) Auchinleck sent de Guingand out to General Ritchie to brief him on Rommel's plan, without of course disclosing the source of the information. General Ritchie, however, vested more confidence in his own on the spot judgment of the tactical situation, and went ahead with his attack. By nightfall on the 13th he had, as already described, only seventy of his original three hundred tanks left.

Thus the battle in the Marmarica was lost; for Rommel the way ahead into Egypt seemed wide open.

The End of 621 Radio Intercept Company

No sooner had the Good Source dried up, than a catastrophe took place of even more serious consequences for Panzerarmee Afrika. On 10th July 1942 most of 621 Radio Intercept Company was overrun and annihilated at its possibly too far advanced operations point near Tell el Eisa, west of El Alamein; its entire documentation was captured by the enemy.

How did it happen? As been mentioned earlier, that morning the reinforced 26th Australian Brigade with 2/24th and 2/48th battalions of 9th Australian Division had attacked in the Tell el Eisa area. The operations report of Panzerarmee Afrika relates:

> Whereas in the south the attack was making good progress and promised well for the next day, on 10th July 1942 at 0600 hrs the enemy attacked the [Italian] Sabratha division north of the coastal road with a reinforced brigade after laying down a preparatory artillery barrage for one hour and with tank support. Italian troops here whose artillery seems to have consisted of one light artillery battery and one heavy artillery battalion, either surrendered without resistance or took to their heels. The Sabratha division was largely wiped out or captured and lost

---

* Public Records office, London: WO 169/4042.

its entire artillery except for the heavy battalion. Barely two miles south-east of the Panzerarmee Command Post itself was it possible for us to restore an improvised line of resistance using the machine gunners and Flak units attached to the Army headquarters and some elements of the 382nd Infantry Regiment which was just arriving along the coastal road and kept the enemy from advancing farther.

A regrettable consequence of this route was that the enemy advanced so quickly that they were able to destroy nearly the whole of 621 Radio Intercept Company.

The author's enquiries of the Australian War Memorial, Canberra, about the events of 10th July have elicited that there exists no special report about this day, with all its serious consequences for 621 Radio Intercept Company, and the exceptional good fortune of the British in capturing the company complete with equipment and all its documents.

These enquiries in Australia included an investigation of the war diaries of 9th Division and 2/26th Infantry Battalion. The only reference found was in 9th Division's Intelligence Summary No 245 of 13th July. This states under 'Enemy Identifications':

POW's captured night 9th/10th July included POW from 2nd Bn 86 Inf Regt Sabratha Div, 4 Bty 75/273 Mob Art Regt and 7 Bersaglieri Regt 21 Corps. Some 1,556 prisoners were then captured by 26 Inf Bde in coastal sector. 69 of the German POWs captured at the same place and time were identified as belonging to Nachrichten-Fernaufklärungs-Kompanie 621 (3 Coy 56 Sig Bn). Some very valuable documents including wireless intercept messages were captured from this Coy.

Based on the recollections of British and Australian soldiers who participated in the attack and on a contemporary British account, the following version can be offered of the loss of this vital unit and the irreparable damage it caused to Rommel's campaign.

Second-Lieutenant Wischmann, one of the unit's officers who had the good fortune to be attached to Rommel at that time, assesses Captain Seebohm's fateful decision to station his unit so close to the front line as follows, in a letter to the author in 1974:

Captain Seebohm was extremely ambitious and always wanted to win glory in Rommel's eyes by obtaining impressive results from our company. For that he needed above all, given the prevailing circumstances:

a) a site for our radio monitors offering good reception conditions and the possibility of picking up all the important enemy wireless nets loud and clear;

b) a site ensuring good connections with the DF-Stations; and

c) A site guaranteeing constant wireless contact with Rommel's forward headquarters (he was always on the move).

Since the beginning of June, I had been assigned to Rommel as liaison officer with two operators. Any important message intercepted by the company reached me a few minutes later and thereby Rommel. I kept the wireless situation map for him. Not infrequently, the intercepted enemy signals had been deciphered and were in Rommel's hand whilst the [less well positioned] enemy signallers were still querying them. Rommel thus often had signals in his hands before the enemy commanders to whom they had been addressed. It was to achieve such brilliant results that Seebohm had taken the risk of putting our company in such an exposed position by the sea, just a few hundred yards behind a sector defended by Italian troops. In the event, when the enemy attacked, the Italians fled.

When Rommel asked me at about 9 A.M. on 10th July, for the latest intercepts I had to tell him that we had still not established radio contact with the company yet.

'Where is the company positioned?' he asked.

I showed him on the map.

'Then it is *futsch* – lost!' he said, absolutely furious.

He was right. A few minutes later my operators monitored an enemy signal on a Division-Corps net: 'A very important officer named Seebohm has fallen in our hands.' He had gone, pistol in hand, against the British and had been captured severely wounded.

Seebohm told the author shortly before, rather apologetically, that he knew that his position was very far advanced, but he would get much better results from there. One of Captain Seebohm's platoon commanders, Lieutenant Heinrich Habel – who later took command of the reactivated 621 Company – was at the time with his platoon under the orders of 90th Light Division; thus he too escaped the catastrophe. He has told this author that he asked Seebohm earlier in July why he had sited his 'Circus' – as the soldiers dubbed their unit with all its antennae, tents and buses – so far forward. The answer was a cynical – 'A fine thing to tell me now!' Habel later learned that a 'colonel' had reprimanded Captain Seebohm because (perhaps at Matruh) he had left his position too early. The colonel concerned had evidently not realised that this company was not a rearguard combat unit but a precious and even irreplaceable intelligence gathering operation.

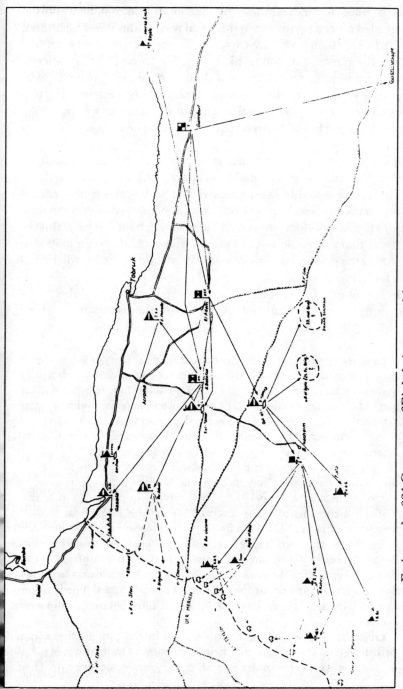

Estimate by 621 Company of Eighth Army positions as at 30th April 1942.

It is hard to understand why Seebohm could not swallow a misguided officer's criticism in the usual way, without feeling himself pushed to such an obstinate extreme. The more so as Seebohm was bright (he passed out top of his class). He came from an officer's family and was naturally ambitious to acquit himself well. Everybody who knew his work held him in high esteem. He was outwardly severe and seldom thawed, but when the ice was broken in personal conversation between equals he could be relaxed and open-minded.

It is a pity that he did not discuss with others the colonel's affront to him, but this too was probably in character.

The author is to this day depressed that Seebohm was not ordered to pull back to a less exposed position immediately when he paid a visit to the Army's forward command post on about 7th July. But the fact was that one could not tell from a divisional flag on a map that the Sabratha division was so inexperienced, had so little artillery and was far below strength.

In October 1974 Seebohm's successor, Lieutenant Habel, gave the author this account of the end of the company and its consequences for him.

101 soldiers of the company fell into Australian captivity or were killed in action. In addition to these high casualties the enemy captured extensive written material and documents which enabled him to work out the methods and organisation of 621 Company and to revise and reorganise his entire signals procedures accordingly. From what Lieutenant Herz (since deceased) told me after the war, I gathered that methodical destruction of the documents, etc, was no longer possible.

How great was the concern of the British to round up every member of the company even after the final surrender of the Afrika Korps can be judged from my own experiences in captivity. Immediately after that British officers turned up at several POW camps looking for soldiers from the company. My own name in particular was read out time and again. As the prisoners had not yet been registered it was easy for me to lie low. Of course this changed after we were shipped to America. At the end of November 1943 I was taken out of the Mexia camp in Texas, flown in solitary splendour from Dallas to Canada and shipped back to England by sea. There I ended up at an interrogation centre near London.

Over the next five or six months several interrogation officers from British signals Intelligence did their damnedest to squeeze out of me as the last company commander everything they might not yet know. Their interrogation methods are well known and there is no need to go over them again here. From the questions and remarks of the British officers I gained the impression that our working methods and wireless intelligence successes in North Africa had literally dumbfounded them, and that afterwards there had been a substantial reshuffle at the higher levels inside the Corps of Signals.

How great the shock was to the British, and how much they mistrusted the people of the intercept service, I realised after my release from captivity. From that moment in March 1946 until the end of 1948, I was under police surveillance at home. I had to report to the police from time to time, could not leave my home town without police permission and on British orders was subjected to random checks by the police in my private dwelling.

After the company was reactivated we succeeded in breaking a British supply code and we again delivered some valuable results but there was no way of regaining the consistently excellent results that had been obtained before 10th July, 1942. But the flow of good results resumed upon our arrival on Tunisian soil [in December 1942] when we came within range of the American wireless traffic. They were still happy-go-lucky and careless of their signals procedures; they had not had the bad experiences of the British.

In the author's conversations with Habel more details about Alfred Seebohm came to light. He was born on 4th June 1916. After matriculation, he initially studied electrical engineering, but soon joined the army (having served voluntarily before.) He passed out top of his class and advanced rapidly. His youngest brother, the only survivor of the three Seebohm brothers, has told the author that Alfred took his profession seriously and with dignity. He was company commander of *3./N56* in France from 1940 on. Early in 1941 this company was transferred from the observation of England to Africa, where it arrived in April. At the beginning of May it began operations.

He was generally considered to be dutiful but over ambitious. He was over-sensitive and lacked the proper degree of self-confidence. After the fateful dressing down by the anonymous colonel, he flipped to the other extreme.

In Rommel's Africa diary, discovered by David Irving, there is for 27th June an entry about nightly attempts of the New Zealanders to break out to the south from Matruh:

Artillery duels arise in which the participants are in particular AA

[Recce Rgt] 580, Battle Squadron Kiehl, the Littorio division, army artillery and finally Seebohm's Company. . . .

Perhaps this was when Seebohm earned his 'reproach'. A little while later he took his company right into the front line, far too close to the enemy – only six or seven thousand yards west of El Alamein.

Because the company had been activated originally in the Chemnitz area, now behind the Iron Curtain, it took some time to locate a survivor of the 10th July attack. But after lengthy inquiries by Herr Habel the author was able to obtain from Staff Sergeant Hässler, commander of one intercept platoon at the time, about this account of the episode:

At about 4 A.M. on this day, heavy artillery fire awoke us. We were sited hard by the sea, north-west of the Tell-el-Eisa railway station. Soon the artillery began laying down smoke shells; behind this smokescreen enemy tanks advanced westwards along the coast road. Later they encircled the company. The Australian infantry came first, carrying their Bren guns at the slope. As soon as the light machine guns of our company opened fire however they took up aiming positions. Now the mortars began to shoot up our position, tracking their fire forward yard by yard and causing heavy casualties. When the tanks came up from the rear that was that. The rest of the company, except the motor transport which had escaped previously, was captured. The company commander Captain Seebohm had been badly wounded. He was sent to the military hospital at Alexandria.

Hässler later asked a British officer about Seebohm's health. 'He has lost the will to live,' replied the officer. Seebohm died soon after.

The British quickly moved in bringing field ambulances, stretcher-bearers and even a parson for the dying! Their treatment of the prisoners was very *korrekt*. The preliminary interrogations were conducted at Heluan, but they were not very searching and revealing nothing the enemy did not already know from captured documents. Later the prisoners were transferred to the Faid camp on the Suez Canal; on the journey a British lieutenant withdrew the water rations from his Indian escort soldiers on the way and gave them to us German prisoners, as the Indians were better accustomed to the heat and could stand thirst better!

Hässler was able to shed further light on the question as to why Seebohm had sited the bulk of his company so near to the front.

Again it went back to the withdrawal by Seebohm of his intercept company when the enemy threat at Mersa Matruh at the end of June. A colonel – according to Hässler, he was powerfully built and tall in stature – accused him of cowardice before the enemy and threatened him with court-martial, regardless of the fact that this company had totally different duties. Seebohm had called his officers and NCO's together and declared that from now on there would be no retreat. He personally chose the position at Tell-el-Eisa and refused to budge even when his subordinates warned of the conspicuously frequent reconnaissance flights by enemy planes.

The Australian War Memorial elicited the addresses of three participants in the fighting of 10th and 11th July.

Lieutenant-Colonel S.H. Good was at the time a captain and intelligence officer with HQ 9th Australian Division. The intercept company, he writes, was almost certainly at Tell-el-Eisa railway station, a few hundred metres east of the hill of that name. That was the only area that German troops were captured in on 10th July in this sector. Seebohm's No.3 Company was, according to this officer, sited among field artillery, mortars and machine guns of 7th Bersaglieri Regiment, in front of which, north of the railway, were elements of Sabratha Division. The El Alamein box in front of it was held by 3rd South African Brigade, only about 6,000 metres to the east of Tell-el-Eisa. For the attack on the 10th, the South African units came under Australian command.

On 4th July, Good continues, orders were given to 26th Australian Infantry Brigade to attack the coastal sector and capture the coastal ridge, with Point 26, Point 23, Point 33 (Hill 33, Tell-el-Eisa) and Tell-el-Eisa station. The hill had two high points, known to the British as East 24 and West 24. The brigade plan called for the capture of Hill 33 and then East 24 on 10th July. The battalion captured Hill 33, but its supporting tanks and machine guns bogged down in the salt marshes north of the railway. The battalion did not capture 24 until about 5 A.M. on the 11th. This capture was made without any Australian casualties, comments this source, and 500 more prisoners were taken, so there were evidently no German troops in the area at the time.

Point 26 was overrun in a silent attack before 5 A.M. on the 10th. At daybreak Point 23, two thousand yards further west, was captured after artillery bombardment. At 7.15 A.M. two Australian companies captured the Tell-el-Eisa station. C Company, under Captain D. Bryant, came under point-blank fire from field guns near the station; its reserve platoon silenced the guns and captured their crews. The crews were described as German, writes Colonel Good, but he now thinks it likely that the crews were Italian and that the Germans captured were from the German company and may possibly have been helping the Italian crews. According to Colonel Good Seebohm's company probably had no knowledge of what was happening further north.

Lieutenant-Colonel Bryant recalled the incident as follows:

> As you are aware the South African Division was in a defensive position facing the Italian/German position and our attack was launched using this defence as our firm base. The main aim was to capture the high ground between the Tell-el-Eisa station and the sea and to use this as a basis for further operations.
>
> We attacked at approximately one hour before first light with two rifle companies and two in reserve. My company was one of the reserve companies for the first phase. On the success of Phase I my company and 'A' Company – the other reserve company – were to attack in a southerly direction to the railway line and Tell-el-Eisa station. Phase I was completed by approximately 0800 hrs and Phase II then commenced. The distance to traverse was approximately 3,000 yards over flat sandy terrain. The axis of the attack was to the rear of the main defensive positions of the Italians but in front of their artillery emplacements. We had the support of some of our armour but basically it was an infantry unsupported attack.
>
> We reached the railway line after a series of very sharp and determined encounters with the crews of the Italian guns. In all these encounters I did not see at any stage any tents, buses or antennae suggesting a headquarters or some other installation. . . .

The war diary of the Australian unit concerned, 2/48th Battalion, mentioned only that on 10th July about 106 German prisoners were taken. One veteran of that unit remembers well the tents, vehicles and antennae because his mortar platoon attached to C Company mortared this position; he saw Captain Seebohm severely wounded, particularly in the legs.*

The prisoners were taken to the Australian brigade headquarters. Murray Farquhar, who was attached to brigade intelligence at the time, recalls the surprise engendered by a headquarters camp being so far forward, and that some prisoners were sent on with great rapidity. There was powerful conjecture as to their precise role. He

* Communicated to the author by Jack W. Hanley, chairman of the 2/48th Battalion club.

recalls a later intelligence report referring to the capture of a significant 'monitoring' organisation.

Mr Everard Baillieu of Melbourne, Australia, who in 1942 was company commander of 2/24th Battalion, 26th Australian Infantry Brigade, has recently gathered additional evidence that 2/24th Battalion captured 621 Radio Intercept Company. He received a letter from the then brigade major of 26th Australian Infantry Brigade, now Major-General C.F. Finlay, CB, CBE, which reads in part:

> *Re Capture of German Wireless Intelligence Communications Coy 621.*
> I was Brigade Major of 26th Brigade at that time and my clear recollection is that it was captured in the sand dunes immediately by the sea north-east of the main ridge of the Tell-el-Eisa feature. I cannot recall which company of the 2/24 Bn captured it, but I remember clearly about 10 days after the attack a very commendatory message being received at Brigade Headquarters from Eighth Army (through Corps and Division) on the great value of the documents and other material captured.
> I immediately phoned that message to the Adjutant of the 2/24 Bn. There is no ground whatsoever for any other unit claiming to have made the capture; as the attack by the 2/48 Bn did not take them anywhere near the site of the capture, that claim cannot be sustained.

This statement ties in with Intelligence Summary No 8 of the 2/24th Bn, 24th/25th July, which contained a special note: 'Appreciation has been expressed concerning captured material and documents sent back, much valuable information has been gained.'

The following extract from 9th Australian Division War Diary is also significant:

> July 11, 2/24 Bn. captured the Tell-el-Eisa station before dawn and then moved forward to capture and consolidate the main feature nearby . . . .
> During the past two days a large number of enemy documents and equipment was captured and forwarded through I-Channels to Main HQ 30 Corps.

It is indisputable that the capture of the 621 Company was an irreparable loss for the Germans, though it was not the cause of their final defeat in North Africa.

British Report on the Activity of 621 Radio Intercept Company

The author tried to obtain more data on the 10th July attack at the Public Record Office in London. Restrictions on several files of XXX Corps will not be lifted until the year 2043, but with advice of the archivist, Mr Cox, the files on Middle East Forces disgorged one detailed and interesting account of the episode, in a report headed 'Captured Enemy Documents April 1942 – March 1943.' This states under 'German Wireless Intercept Organisation' for 30th July:

> Capture of German intercept personnel with documents. At 0600 hrs on 10th July 1942, two officers and 71 men belonging to the NFAKp 621 were captured west of Alamein. The unit was surprised by an attack by the Australians; but resisted for one and a half hours, during which some of the transport managed to get away.

A large quantity of documents was captured, the report adds. 'From these it appears that NFA 621 was renamed and renumbered with effect from 17th April 1942', possibly for security reasons. Among the captured documents was a file of company orders including the instructions and tasks of the company for the German attack which took place at the end of May.

> The company was arbitrarily divided into two Staffeln, comprising in all five sections. The first Staffel (Company HQ and No 3 Section) was at Army HQ; the second Staffel contained two sections and was captured.

A description of the regular daily and monthly reports issued by the Company is included in this British report. Also included were translations of the report for 7th July 1942, the monthly report dated 24th June 1941, covering the British Battleaxe offensive of 14th June 1941, and the report dated 5th February 1942 covering the period prior to the British attack of November 1941 and the battle itself.

> A captured code list used especially by this unit enabled us to decode messages which had been intercepted for 9th July 1942 from HQ of the Intercept Company to General Rommel. No previous or subsequent messages in this code have been found. Translations of these messages for 9th July are attached.

Also captured by the Australians, according to this report, was an analysis of the row number and call signs from the British call sign book used in the Middle East, with identifications of the units using

---

* Captured Enemy Documents, April 1942 – March 1943, GSI(S) GHQ MEF: Public Record Office WO 201/2150.

the row numbers and particular frequencies. A report found by the Security Officer XXX Corps contained a forecast of the call signs and frequencies expected to be used by various units on 9th July.

> The OC Company [Seebohm] is reported to have been wounded and captured. So far CSDIC [Combined Services Detailed Interrogation Centre] have not succeeded in locating his whereabouts. Lieutenant Herz and numerous other ranks of the company have been interrogated . . .

Also found were German translations of instructions dated 9th and 19th September 1941 giving particulars of the British Map Reference Code. After this there followed a section on 'Consideration of our own Signals and Cypher Security, based on the examination of the documents.'

> Staffel 2 was captured. Staffel 1 was apparently responsible for final decoding and interpretation of all traffic. It was Staffel 1 from whom messages to Rommel were intercepted and decoded. The contents of these messages show a higher degree of success than would have been expected from the messages intercepted and worked on by Staffel 2.
>
> Not all the documents of Staffel 2 were captured. Lieutenant Herz, under interrogation, has referred to a black tin box. No actual copies of captured call sign books or Codes other than R/T codes were found . . . .
>
> Statements by prisoners under interrogation that they were unable to deal with our codes or cyphers must necessarily be taken with reserve, in view of their high security. It is probable that all of them were warned to admit no success in case of capture.

It appeared probable to the British that some of the documents belonged to Lieutenant Seebohm, 'Who was visiting the section at the time of its capture.' Among them was his personal file, includes certificates for awards and medals like the Good Service badge, the War Service Cross with Swords, the Iron Cross (both classes) and the Italian War Cross for Bravery. One of the other folders was marked '*Chef*'. Some of the files, such as the Monthly Reports, have given us more information than would ordinarily have been available, and presumably belonged to Oberleutnant Seebohm.

> *Call Signs*. The Monthly Reports and other documents previously captured show that the Wave Code Call Sign system was thoroughly well understood. The enemy concluded that our plan of attack of 14th June 1941 was based on superiority in numbers and on surprise. Surprise was only successful in relation to the numbers of Armoured Units employed, but *not* in relation to time and direction of attack.
>
> *Introduction of the new Signal Procedure and our Attack of November 1941.*

They were unaware as to whether our preparations were offensive or defensive, of the time of the attack, or the strength of the forces employed at the commencement. This is in sharp contrast to their knowledge before our attack on 14th June, 1941.

The new Signal Procedure eliminated all the bases of former Intelligence work and prevented them from obtaining important identifications of units taking part, even after the commencement of the battle. The excellent wireless discipline of 7th Armoured Division is mentioned.

The analysis of call sign rows and serials of April and May 1942 shows that the security of the call sign book is destroyed to some extent once a copy has been captured.

The fact that they were making a forecast of the call signs to be used by identified units on 9th July seems strange unless they had captured serials, or unless the same serials were used for two successive months. There were numerous unidentified rows however. It is understood that the construction of our serials is not of a systematical nature, so that they can be reconstructed after a few days.

Reference to our free use of clear text is contained in their Monthly Reports. Intercepted messages referring to November 1941 show that no attempt was made to take down clear text Urdu or Africaans. They still seem to rely on intercepted clear text and R/T.

R/T Codes A large number of R/T codes and code name lists were recaptured. These were in folders and very unsystematically arranged. Some amateur work had been done in attempting to crack unknown R/T codes on messages. In one case an attempt had been made on the 7th Armoured Division code by reference to the vocabulary of XIII Corps code; although the two vocabularies were not the same. It must not be forgotten that this was done by Staffel 2 and may have been unauthorised and uncontrolled. The contents of the messages sent by Staffel 1 to General Rommel are evidence of much greater success in decoding our messages.

Syllabic Codes A certain number of syllabic messages were found. Most of these were incomplete, but the absence of any working paper would seem to indicate that they were done by means of captured codes. No captured syllabic codes, however, were recaptured. They are probably kept at Staffel 1.

As for Map Reference Codes, the major who signed the report noted that the daily reports and messages to Rommel included a large number of map references. Since some were described as 'according to D/F', the others had presumably been obtained from the clear text or decodes. Since an examination of the captured intercepts showed that not all map references had been decoded, the British now concluded that the security of their present map reference system was good. 'On the other hand,' the report remarked, 'our practice of giving co-ordinates of enemy positions in *clear* has been of great value to the enemy.' It told the Germans the locations of their own and British troops, since a report of the position of enemy forces by visual observation necessarily revealed the approximate location of the reporting unit. Further, if the British reported the location of unidentified columns in clear it might also give away the position of British troops if the enemy knew that his own troops were not in that area.

In mobile or desert warfare the likelihood of compromising the Map Reference Code because the enemy is aware of the positions of his own units, is small. The difficulty in ascertaining the precise location of a forward unit at a given time has always made it difficult for us to get compromises of German map references. Furthermore, the enemy has again repeated that our habit of giving locations of their troops in clear very often assists them.

From the 'very large number of captured codes and documents' found in Seebohm's files, the British drew the necessary conclusions: 'The practice of forwarding a code name or list to all units in a division and showing the complete distribution list has evidently proved of great value to them in determining our exact Battle Order, and assists in identifying units using wireless.' The report pointed out that some code name lists were *comprehensive*, 'although supplied to units to whom complete particulars were not necessary.' Major A. Toger, the intelligence officer who signed the report, concluded:

High Grade Cyphers No copies of intercepted High Grade Cyphers were captured.* The distribution lists of their own station reports show that documents are regularly sent to the Main Interception Exploitation Bureau in Berlin. The absence of any High Grade Cypher material makes it seem a reasonable assumption that all traffic of this nature is thus sent to Berlin for examination and exploitation. This assumption is borne out by the statements of interrogated prisoners that they rely

* Among the captured documents of Seebohm's intercept company was a printed War Establishment dated March 1st, 1942, showing that its headquarters, communications, compilation, decoding, intercepting, D/F and transport units were staffed by ten officers, sixty-three NCO's and 259 other ranks – with only five machine pistols and six light machine guns between them.

mainly on clear text and do no cryptography in Africa, and by a reference in a message.

Describing the regular daily wireless situation report (*Funklagemeldung*) (produced by Seebohm's company for the use of staffs in Africa, the British observed that it was repeated in a slightly abbreviated form as an inter-station report (*Zwischenmeldung*), distributed to addresses including the Intercept Exploitation Centre in Berlin (HAS), the Commander of Intercept Troops Southeast in Athens, and the Panzerarmee's chief signals officer. The daily report was restricted to intelligence on the organisation and location of enemy units. A typical daily report was that for 7th July 1942:

> *Tagesmeldung 7. Juli 1942*
> Organisation and Employment
> x CORPS *[should read XXX Corps]* Apparently the following are at present under command the Corps: 1st South African Infantry Division; 50th (Infantry) Division; 1st Armoured Division; 10th Indian Motor Brigade (10th Armoured Division?).
> Corps Staff according to D/F is in Region S of Burg el Arab. *[This was not accurate, the British noted; the other HQ positions were accurate.]*
> XIII CORPS commands 7th Armoured Division; New Zealand Division; 5th Indian Infantry Division. Tactical HQ is at 866.264.
> *1st Armoured Division:* Staff 4th Armoured Brigade is at 891.280; Royals are reconnoitring on the right wing up to the area of El Alamein.
> *7th Armoured Division:* 5th Lancers maintained contact with 4th Armoured Brigade at 890.277; 4th South Africa Armoured Car Regiment is employed in front of 5th Indian Infantry Division and reports also to them.
> *5th Indian Infantry Division* Division HQ at 850.269.
> *10th Indian Motor Brigade* belongs apparently to Divisional force (10th Armoured Division?)
> *Special Identifications:* 50th (Infantry) Division made a recce in force after strong artillery preparation; 11th KRRC captured a 15 cm-Inf. - Geschütz.

A file of Composite Monthly Reports called *Funklagebericht* had also been captured by the British. This provided a summary of the successes achieved by the German Intercept Service and offered comments on the British organisation and methods. 'The main body of some of the reports', noted Major Toger, 'contains some extremely interesting remarks about our general methods as well as about our Signal Security.'

He selected extracts from the composite monthly report dated 24th June 1941 covering the period June 15th-17th as particularly revealing. Extracts dealt with German wireless interception during *Sommernachtstraum*, Rommel's September 1941 sortie; the British Signal Communications, and their remarkable carelessness in using plain language, and speaking openly about command problems and intentions – which were discussed with a candour seldom encountered before; and alterations in battle groups even below brigade level.

In a special extract the report examined Seebohm's notes, dated 5th February 1942, on new British procedures and their attack in November 1941. In summary, these recalled that on 16th October a complete change of wireless procedure had been effected. The new procedure proved considerably more secure than its predecessors as it eliminated practically all the bases of the former German wireless intelligence operation. The change had probably been occasioned by the experience of the Battle of Sollum coupled with information about the success of German interception. At the time it could not be determined whether this was connected with preparations for an imminent attack, but in retrospect this possibility cannot be ruled out. The subsequent impediment of wireless intelligence operations resulted in diminishing results; later even more measures were adopted to increase security, notably the reduction of traffic sent in clear.

The results of the German wireless intelligence effort during the British November 1941 offensive could be assessed as follows, after examination of the numerous captured documents and enemy orders of battle: every British formations down to brigade level had been identified through wireless traffic as being in the Western Desert, with the exception of XXX Corps headquarters, 22nd Armoured Brigade and 4th Infantry Brigade. After 18th November no unit entered the battle which had not first been detected through wireless intelligence. No special supply measures were identified except for 1st South African Infantry Division.

This was a dramatic contrast to the Sollum battle, where precise determination of this nature from the wireless traffic yielded the most vital information of an impending attack. The prior movement of the combat units concerned into their concentration areas was not noted, apart from the 1st South African Division.

In conclusion, the British Intelligence report remarked that the German Y-service detected the reinforcement and the forward movement of enemy forces during October and early November, but that as no obvious preparations for attack were seen these measures were dismissed as being equally of either a defensive *or* an offensive character. The distinction in this case could only be made by taking the general military situation into consideration. Neither the timing of the British attack nor the strength of their forces employed at the commencement was known, thanks to the enforcement of strict wireless silence, the other measures introduced to preserve wireless security and the new procedure that had been adopted. On the other, no tactical surprise was achieved in the course of this battle by the arrival of units not previously identified, except for 22nd Armoured and 5th Indian Infantry Brigades.

A typical day's message pad of signals made by the Intercept Group to General Rommel, 9th July 1942, read:

> *0700 hrs* commence
> *1220 hrs* New Zealand Division reported as probably between 1st and 7th Armoured Divisions.
> *urgent*
> *1700 hrs* XIII Corps orders 5th Indian Division to withdraw at 1900 hrs, etc.

Of special significance among the captured documents of *3./N56* was Seebohm's report dated 10th February 1942 on the security of German ciphers as shown by intercepted enemy signals: he concluded that the British Y-service enjoyed certain successes for two reasons: many signals were in clear even at Army command level; and the British were decoding enciphered messages both simultaneously and retroactively, using the quantities of captured signals and by means of captured keys and cryptanalysis. In particular Seebohm suspected (correctly) that the British were breaking and reading Italian ciphers: he referred to one particular case on 20th January 1942, when they detected the move by Panzergruppe Afrika to west of Agheila. Probably the Italian liaison-staff with Rommel sent a signal to the Italian Supercomando along these lines.

The interrogation of one lieutenant and sixteen other ranks of Seebohm's company yielded further insights. Their average age was twenty-six. They were all of high calibre – well trained, intelligent and *very* security-conscious. The majority were of pronounced Nazi convictions and brimming with German propaganda clichés as the result of repeated political indoctrination. Most of the information was obtained from the higher ranks, the least uncommunicative of all the prisoners being Lieutenant Herz, who had been Seebohm's second-in-command.

'Herz admits', stated the report, 'that for Rommel's attack on 26th May 1942 the company was divided into two groups (*Staffel*).' One was attached to Rommel's Panzerarmee headquarters, the other was located south of Tmimi.

Personalities. The pivot on which the whole company turned was obviously the CO – Captain Seebohm – (wounded and POW) who was a staff officer in Panzerarmee HQ. He has been in command of the unit since 1940 and, by concentration and initiative, built up a specialised Army Intercept Organisation with a very high standard of efficiency. Lieutenant Herz admits that this specialisation has the disadvantage that having been deprived of its two best officers and most of its senior NCOs this unit cannot easily be replaced or made to function with the capability exhibited heretofore. The Second-in-Command was Lieutenant Herz. The two remaining officers – Lieutenants Habel and Kröplin – were not with Second Group at the time of its capture. Herz is of the opinion that they do not possess sufficient technical knowledge to reorganise the remainder of the company, even if skilled personnel were to be replaced at once.

It was the Second Group of the company which had been captured, Platoons 1 and 2 and some of the supply transport; the 3rd Platoon (D/F) was not in the immediate vicinity. The group had been in position west of Alamein for four or five days before it was over-run and had carried out limited intercept activities.

Fässy admits that he was engaged on intercept of R/T in the forward area and in direct interrogation has revealed that the Imperial units upon which they were concentrating were the South African, 5th Armoured Division and an Indian Division. The group had been brought well forward on the assumption that it would be quite safe situated as it was behind an Italian infantry division. The sole responsibility for this seems to rest with Captain Seebohm, whose presence with Second Group at the time of capture was purely coincidental. (Herz is extremely worried about this point, as he fears that both Captain Seebohm and he will be courtmartialled and made to bear the responsibility for the loss of the best part of this specialised unit).

For W/T traffic the unit had at its disposal two 100 watt

transreceivers. It used the seemingly impregnable Enigma machine cipher on all the main links and the *Doppel-Rastenschlüssel* on the subsidiary links within the unit. Lieutenant Herz himself took the responsibility for the selecting and allotting of frequencies to his unit. He conceded that the main operating frequency between the two 100-watt transreceivers was 1057 kcs: this was what he styled a 'clean' frequency.

> *Decoding*. The decoding of intercepted messages is carried out on the basis of captured British codes, some of which are believed to have extorted from captured British Signal personnel. The company formed a decoding section under a cipher specialist, thought to be Auswerte-Offizier Wischmann – Sonderführer with 2/Lt rank. (These people had a better life, which annoyed the others.)

The personnel of Seebohm's company were found to have been specially selected, highly skilled wireless operators; a high percentage had a good command of the English language. Given the nature of their activities, they were subject to frequent and intensive indoctrination in security, 'which fact is evident from their stubborn resistance to interrogation.'

However, apart from Lieutenant Herz's disclosures some information on the company's activities was obtained, chiefly by indirect interrogation. This filled in some of the gaps in the captured documentary evidence. Among Seebohm's successes were:

a) The interception of W/T traffic at the battle of Sollum on 15.6.41 which resulted in a quick redisposition of the German forces and consequent reverses for the British.

b) Interception of a ship's W/T call to Tobruk advising arrival time and asking for prompt unloading facilities with consequent employment of Stuka dive-bombers and the reported sinking of the ship.

c) Overhearing of an W/T message passed back by a British reconnaissance aircraft calling for bomber support against a large concentration of German MT between Gazala and Tobruk with subsequent immediate dispersal of the concentration and failure of our bombing attack.

d) Pinpointing of British unit positions through overhearing of R/T conversation between senior officers of the Imperial Forces by Fässy; at least Fässy admits that his task was rendered the more easy by an officer asking for another officer to call him at a certain time.

When the connection was established, Fässy had told his interrogators, it was 'an easy matter' for the interceptor to establish identity of the unit or units, owing to the almost complete lack of security in the conversation.

Reactivation of 621 Radio Intercept Company.
Contrary to the rather superficial judgment of Lieutenant Herz on his brother officers Lieutenants Habel and Kröplin and on the remnants of Seebohm's company, when interrogated by the British, the new 621 company that was reactivated in Germany in September 1942 rendered good service. Lieutenant Habel was the CO. Of course nothing that either the old or the new personnel of the company could do would prevent the British from adopting the most rigorous wireless discipline and security. The author remembers that the entire enemy wireless traffic kept silence for one whole week. Nevertheless, the company did succeed in extracting further data on enemy intentions by breaking a divisional supply code in December 1942 as a result of which the German high command received vital indications. According to Habel the wireless intercept harvest improved again in Tunisia, thanks to the American carelessness in wireless traffic; but now the Company lacked the personnel to make the fullest use of the intercepts.

What kind of success did the company enjoy immediately after that fateful 10th July 1942? The documentation on these intelligence operations is sparse; the Panzerarmee's G-2 reports are only available from 27th July onwards. From then until 31st August they refer usually only to normal reconnaissance and artillery activities. After the sanguinary attacks and counter-attacks by both sides something of a respite set in.

Intelligence harvesting now resumed as usual: thus, prisoners of 69th and 151st Infantry Brigades confirmed the presence of the British 50th (Infantry) Division. At the beginning of August the reinforcement of the coastal sector by elements of the British 1st Armoured Division and heavy artillery was noted.

Enemy Intelligence was equally active in the same sector, which seemed significant.

Our own air reconnaissance confirmed powerful enemy forces in the middle and northern sectors: on the whole front as far as Burg-el-Arab on 8th August about 12,000 vehicles were stated detected, of which more than 10,000 were in the middle and northern sectors.

As for the shipping tonnage docked in the port of Suez – an unerring barometer of enemy reinforcements of personnel, weapons and equipment – this was observed by reconnaissance flights of 13th August to have increased by 150,000 tons. This meant that the anticipated transports of troops and matériel had probably arrived.

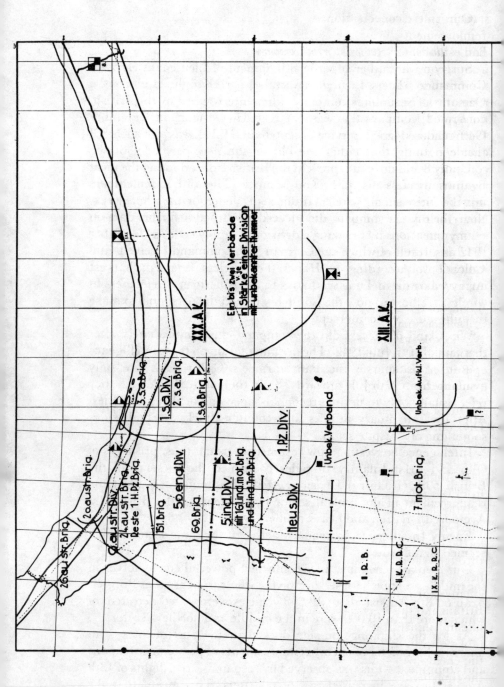

XXX. A.K.

Ein bis zwei Verbände
in Stärke einer Division
mit unbekannter Nummer

XIII. A.K.

3.s.a.brig.

1.s.a.Div.

2.s.a.brig.

1.s.a.Brig.

1.Pz.Div.

Unbek. Verband

Unbek. Aufkl. Verb.

2.a.ustr. Brig.

2.a.ustr. Brig.

50.engl.Div.

5.ind. Div.

mit 16.ind.mot.brig.
und 5.ind.Inf.brig.

neus.Div.

7.mot.brig.

2.austr.Div.

2.a.ustr. Brig.

Reste 1.H.Pz.Brig.

151.brig.

69.brig.

26.au.Str.Brig.

I.R.B.

II.K.R.P.C.

IX.K.R.P.C.

Our Y-service located a new formation in the southern sector and reinforcements in middle and northern sectors; air reconnaissance had established that two or three brigades had arrived there.

Surgeon-Captain von Lutterotti who had been captured by a Commando unit – probably the Special Air Services – south of the Qattara Depression but had escaped at the beginning of August, confirmed that British, New Zealanders, Free French and 'Free' Germans were operating under the command of a Major Stirling in the deep south.

Under 8th August the files register an important product obtained by the remnants of 621 Company. The Scots Greys, a reconnaissance unit of the British 10th Armoured Division, was detected by them for the first time in North Africa; so it was probable that the entire division had been brought to this theatre.

In his Intelligence Summary of 22nd August 1942 Lieutenant-Colonel Zolling, the Panzerarmee's G-2, suggested that Eighth Army was organised as follows: (see plan opposite):

XIII CORPS, commanding 7th Armoured Division, and New Zealand Division; and

   XXX CORPS, commanding 1st South African Division, 9th Australian Division, 50th (Infantry) Division, and the remnants of 1st Army Tank Brigade, as well as one or two formations of division strength of unknown number.

Out of all the enemy divisions, it was noted that the 9th Australian Division could be considered the best – a not undeserved accolade in view of our experiences with the Australians.

The transfer of Eighth Army forward HQ was detected by D/F: on 24th August from El Hammam to Burg-el-Arab, and on 26th August from Burg-el-Arab to Amiriya.

After losing the middle and south boxes, between El Alamein and the Qattara Depression, the British had constructed a system of fortications extending from Alamein and its vicinity south-east through Alam Halfa down to a point east of Imayid. In spite of the heavy losses during the fighting in July, the number of serviceable enemy tanks had increased considerably with new transfusions from Britain and the USA as well as from the repair shops. It was assumed late in August that the tank units at the front disposed of 350 or 400 tanks. 'It can therefore be assumed' wrote Zolling nevertheless, 'that the enemy will remain on the defensive in his Alamein position for the time being.' This was to prove correct for the next two months.

An innovation for the Y-service was the frequency with which stations on command links were ordered to use other means of communication when they indicated their intention of transmitting tactical messages. This precaution was very probably a direct consequence of their study of the documents captured by the Australians on 10th July from 621 Company.

At the end of August 1942 replacements arrived for the remainder of 621 Company from Signals Intelligence Replacement Battalion at Frankfurt-on-Main. Our Y-service was thus in a position to resume its attack on the enemy wireless traffic. It is noteworthy that the reactivated 621 Company under the command of Lieutenant Habel – despite the loss of its most vital working papers on 10th July – was able so quickly to identify new formations like the Scots Greys of the 10th Armoured Division, and to conclude, despite a frequency change, from the organisation and structure of the new wireless nets that the strength of newly arrived formations was of at least one division. Although the precision attained hitherto in identifying enemy formations was as yet beyond their grasp, the signals intelligence results during August 1942 were still astonishing. We shall see later how the enemy began to adopt wireless deception tactics. The surveillance of W/T traffic and decoding of wireless intercepts offered of course vastly reduced chances of success, in view of the greater security precautions taken by the enemy after 10th July.

The Last Chance of Invading Egypt

Rommel made preparations for invading Egypt, and not without reason. He hoped to resume the advance to the Nile Delta and the Suez Canal after a period of rest and reinforcement. In his opinion the end of August offered the last chance of success; after then the British, despite the extended supply route round the Cape of Good Hope, could strengthen their forces more rapidly with American help than the Panzerarmee.

He ordered the attack to begin on the night of 30th August, 1942. According to Winterbotham, Bletchley Park – Britain's deciphering establishment – had revealed in Ultra intercepts by mid-August where *and when* the German attack would take place; evidently German signals on the attack plans had been intercepted. But this is perhaps claiming too much, as the start of the attack was postponed several times, and messages with precise information were not sent in August.* †

In any case we can assume that Montgomery, Commander-in-Chief of Eighth Army since 15th August, was warned via Ultra. At a conference of his commanders he spoke of his 'intuition' as to where and in which direction the German attack would come. He seemingly also mentioned a date.

In this connection a curious remark by a British prisoner, under interrogation weeks later, on 22nd September, is worth mentioning. According to him the British were not surprised by Rommel's attack and were waiting for it; a high Italian officer had declared that the German and Italian forces would attack the Alamein position on the night of 25th/26th August, and that the attack would be made with only a feint attack in the middle sector and the main attack in the south. On the morning of 30th August their commander had declared that to the Italian officer's great surprise the attack had not taken place. It is now evident that the so-called statement of an Italian officer was invented to protect the security of the real source, Ultra. At the same time, the story generated considerable discontent inside the German-Italian alliance at the time.

In the war diary of XXX Corps is proof that at least the approximate date of the German attack was known. A wireless message arrived there on 24th August at 1:17 P.M.:

> All units XXX Corps will be prepared in all respects to offer battle as from 23.59 hrs tonight . . . 'stand to' every morning from 05.45-6.15 hrs and evenings 19.45-20.15 hrs . . . LEAVE STOPPED.

Montgomery's chief of staff, de Guingand, later claimed that a false 'going map' was played into German hands and studied by Panzerarmee's G-2 at the time. It was *no decisive* factor at all! Rommel's original plan to proceed south of El Hammam for some considerable distance eastwards and only then to turn to the north could not be realised owing to the time it would have taken to clear the minefields, and the danger of enemy flank attacks. Thus the turn to the north had to be effected at a more westerly point, i.e. to Alam Halfa.

* The German Federal Military archives have a file of Rommel's signals at this time, RH 19 VIII/26, including messages to General Rintelen, the Liaison in Rome, dated August 22nd, 27th and 29th – the latter referring to 'a limited operation'; on the 30th he signalled briefly, 'Re Panzerarmee signal of 29th: *August 30th, evening.*'

† However, Ronald Lewin in *Ultra Goes to War* refers to Montgomery possessing via Ultra ' . . . a sufficiently accurate knowledge of the date'. *Editor.*

The rapid thrust to the east and turn to the north were made with all the easy mobility to which German command and troops were accustomed; it did not fail because of a faked map, but because of the minefields, because of the stubborn defence put up by the British, and ultimately – and *this* really was decisive – because of the lack of fuel.

At the time of the attack, at the end of August 1942, the enemy order of battle was unchanged according to wireless and air reconnaissance. Prisoners confirmed the presence of the New Zealand Division in the centre sector.

The transfer of Eighth Army forward HQ from Burg el Arab back to Amiriya had been detected by signals intelligence and D/F on 24th August; this withdrawal might have been taken as an indication that a German attack was expected.

A wireless intercept unit was attached to Rommel's forward HQ and this immediately put to him every intercepted enemy signal.

On the night of 30th to 31st August the Panzerarmee began its attack on the southern part of the Alamein position. Delayed by mine clearing, the attacking force initially gained ground but was bombed incessantly. There was a cockiness about the enemy's reactions that augured ill for us. When he now learned that a tanker with 8,000 tons of fuel for which he had been waiting had been sunk before Tobruk, Field-Marshal Rommel realized that the fuel situation would rule out far-reaching operations and decided at his forward headquarters on 2nd September to call off the attack. An intercept on 3rd September revealed that 7th Armoured Division had been ordered to remain in contact with our withdrawing columns but to avoid combat. The enemy ground troops followed at a tender distance, but the RAF harried us mercilessly inflicting heavy losses. By day and night savage bombing attacks were flown against the German formations.

In unsuccessful attacks at Alam Nayil the New Zealand Division had several hundred taken prisoner including the commander of 6th Brigade, Brigadier George Clifton. We learned that General Auchinleck had been nominated Supreme Commander in India and that General Gott was shot down by a Me109 and killed.

During the rest of September the fighting reverted to the routine reconnaissance and artillery exchanges, the latter being more vivid in the southern sector. The Luftwaffe flew daily reconnaissances behind the enemy lines east of Alamein, and special sorties over the tracks around Siwa, along the road and railway from Cairo to Suez, the supply dumps around Cairo, the road from Cairo to Fayum and

Inside Rommel's tent.

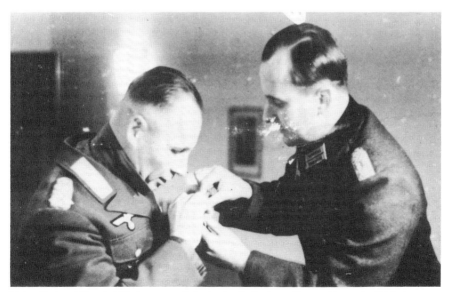

Major Gerhard Engel, Hitler's army adjutant, pins insignia on Rommel in early 1942 at Hitler's HQ. From a damaged negative from Heinrich Hoffmann's album.

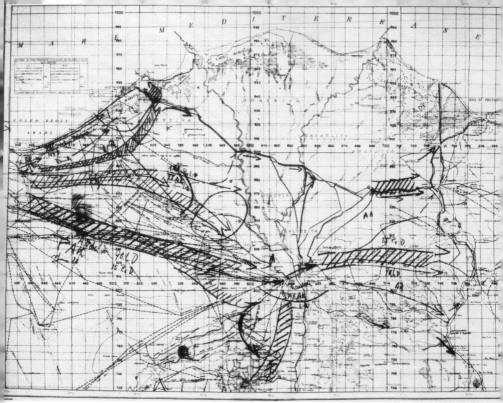

The map on which Rommel marked his plans for the capture of Cairo and Alexandria. It also shows the crossing points on the Nile and the Suez canal which he would have used had he succeeded in breaking through at El Alamein. It was only when he was marking this map that the Germans realised they had no bridging equipment in Africa.

Only 560 kilometres to Alexandria.

farther to the south-west as far as the Baharia oasis. In particular the ports of Alexandria and Suez were kept under constant surveillance. Aerial photos showed at Suez on 1st September forty-three freighters totalling 214,000t and five tankers totalling 35,000t; and at Alexandria on the 27th sixteen freighters totalling 72,500t; and four tankers totalling 31,500t, as well as a troop transporter of 12,500t.

According to this infallible barometer, the British build-up was accelerating.

The Reinforcement of Eighth Army

On 30th September 1942 four air reconnaissance sorties located upwards of 12,000 vehicles behind enemy lines between the Qattara Depression and the coast. While our Y-service now less frequently decoded British radio signals which revealed the enemy's tactical intentions, the remainder of 621 Company was still able to produce results of significance in assessing the enemy. Thus during September it identified for the first time: 131st Infantry Brigade of 44th (Infantry) Division; 4th Hussars, probably under 4th Armoured Brigade; and 10th Indian Motor Brigade.

The organisation of the formations under the command of Eighth Army was now assumed to be:

XXX CORPS:	9th Australian Division;
	1st South African Division;
	50th Infantry Division;
	5th Indian Division.
XIII CORPS:	1st Armoured Division;
	10th Armoured Division;
	7th Armoured Division.
X CORPS:	New Zealand Division;
	44th Infantry Division.

While the positive identification of these units was handicapped by numerous frequency changes by the enemy, the Germans were fairly sure of one thing – the Eighth Army was steadily increasing. Reflecting on this, Field-Marshal Rommel remarked casually to the author in September: 'If I were Montgomery, *we* would not be here any more.' The difference between the two commanders could not be more pungently displayed.

On 24th September Lieutenant Habel returned from his mission to Germany to obtain replacements of personnel and equipment, and reassumed command of the new 621 Company. During October the investigation of the Eighth Army's order of battle continued, relying on signals intelligence and POW interrogations. Accurately identified were three Army Corps – X, XIII and XXX Corps, three armoured divisions – the 1st, 7th and 10th, and the 23rd Armoured Brigade; four Dominion divisions – 9th Australian, 2nd New Zealand, 1st South African and 5th Indian (later corrected to 4th Indian Division). The following formations were identified under their command:

XXX CORPS: 51st Infantry Division (organisation still undetermined);
          1st South African Division with 1st, 2nd, 5th Brigades;
          4th Indian Division with 5th, 10th, 11th Brigades;
          9th Australian Division with 20th, 24th, 26th
             Brigades; and
          23rd Armoured Brigade with 46th and 50th RTR.

XIII CORPS: 7th Armoured Division with 4th Light Armoured
             Brigade and 7th Motor Brigade;
          10th Armoured Division with 22nd Armoured Brigade
             and Reconnaissance Unit; and
          (not absolutely certain:) 1st Armoured Division.

X CORPS: Deployment not clarified:
          2nd New Zealand Division;
          44th Division with 131st, 132nd, 133rd Infantry
             Brigades; and
          50th Infantry Division with 151st Infantry, 69th
             Infantry Brigades (whereabouts unknown.)

On 12th October 621 Company analysed all the known tactical observations made since 10th July; these consisted mainly of intercepted unit identifications from decoded signals, with some information from distribution lists. An increase in wireless traffic had become apparent during the more recent surveillance of the supply networks. With the exception of reconnaissance reports, tactical messages were now rarely transmitted over the command nets. All in all, the enemy wireless traffic in the Western Desert could be classified as well camouflaged and well disciplined, with a daily call sign system, frequency changes every three or four days, and only very rarely signals being sent in clear.

At the beginning of October signals exercises were carried out with putative units in the rear army region in an attempt at wireless deception, but 621 Company was on the alert and not to be deceived. At the same time six new RASC detachments were detected, which was further evidence that Eighth Army's motor transport capacity was being expanded and that the supplying of Eighth Army was being given priority.

Our G-2, Major Zolling, had to leave Africa on 8th October after nine months of successful activity, owing to a serious illness (amoebic dysentery); the author, Lieutenant Behrendt, took over as G-2 on a temporary basis. Since Lieutenant Haeusgen had returned to Germany on the 4th and Lieutenant von Braumüller had been captured north of Kufra Oasis while on a reconnaissance flight, the G-2's staff was significantly below strength until 19th October, when Lieutenant Knapp returned from Germany and could help out as Staff Officer O6.

In addition to signals intelligence which had for example confirmed 51st (Infantry) Division on 4th October, POW interrogations also gave valuable indications of the enemy's organisation simply by revealing which unit prisoners belonged to. Thus a prisoner was captured from 4/5th Seaforth Highlanders of 152nd Infantry Brigade on 5th October, and one from the Household Cavalry Regiment, the reconnaissance unit of 10th Armoured Division on the 8th. Later prisoners were brought in from the 5th/7th Gordon Highlanders, belonging to 153rd Infantry Brigade, which had been shipped to North Africa in the same convoy as 51st Infantry Division.

Aerial reconnaissance on 13th October had detected an increase in the number of military transport vehicles by about 3,000 since 17th September bringing the total up to about 13,400. Our Panzerarmee G-2 pointed out that the enemy might well have succeeded in effecting a much larger build-up behind a screen of good camouflage. On the 16th and 17th violent sandstorms prevented air reconnaissance. By then it had however revealed increased activity behind the enemy's central and southern sectors.

On 20th October heavy bomber and fighter-bomber attacks began against troops and advanced airfields. These lasted until the 23rd, the day that the battle of El Alamein began.

A Panzerarmee intelligence summary was issued on 10th October, still largely based on Major Zolling's work.

Its order of battle information on the command situation under the three British corps was incorrect, as the knowledge developed during the battle and postwar British sources would show,* but it did show that every single enemy formation had been identified. There was no surprise appearance of unknown units.

A comparison shows the German appreciation of the enemy organisation with the reality:

Intelligence Summary of Panzerarmee	*Enemy organisation†*
XIII CORPS	XIII CORPS
7th Armoured Division	7th Armoured Division
44th Infantry Division	44th Infantry Division
1st Greek Brigade	1st Free French Brigade
2nd New Zealand Division	50th Infantry Division
	Greek Brigade
XXX CORPS	XXX CORPS
5th Indian Division	4th Indian Division
(wrong number)	
1st South African Division	1st South African Division
51st Infantry Division	51st Infantry Division
9th Australian Division	9th Australian Division
23rd Armoured Brigade	23rd Armoured Brigade
	2nd New Zealand Division
X CORPS (in rear area)	X CORPS
50th Infantry Division	1st Armoured Division
10th Indian Division	10th Armoured Division
(still not ready)	
133rd Brigade of 44th Infantry Division	
1st Free French Brigade	

There was no doubt as to the enemy's strength. In a consolidated report on possible reinforcements to the British forces in the Middle East during the summer of 1942, G-2 assessed on 20th October that the Eighth Army losses since the end of May of about 85,000 men (if British news reports were to be believed) could have been largely compensated for by the end of November by replacement transports. Prisoners revealed under interrogation that on about 21st July, 44th Infantry Division had arrived at Suez followed by 51st Infantry Division on about 3rd August. Further to these arrivals, air reconnaissance detected shipping movements at Suez in August and

* Francis de Guingand, *Operation Victory*, p.195 f.
† As given in de Guingand, *Operation Victory*.

September totalling about 250,000 tons; a further division, 53rd Infantry Division, was noted as a 'possible' but did not in the event appear on the operational scene.

Our intelligence suggested that it could be safely assumed that 1st Armoured Division was ready for action on 1st July, 7th Armoured Division by 30th August and 10th Armoured Division by 30th September. This estimate was borne out in the Battle of Alamein.

As of 30th September the number of tanks was estimated according to OKH documents on 20th October as being a maximum of 800 tanks at the front and in the Delta area; this total was taken to be increasing at the rate of 200 tanks per month. This meant that 1,000 tanks had to be assumed for the end of October.

This assessment was reasonably accurate. British figures show that in fact Eighth Army disposed on 23rd October 1942 of 1,114 tanks made up of 267 Sherman, 128 Grant, 128 Stewart tanks, all these being American; and 105 Crusader (5 cm gun), 255 Crusader (3.7 cm gun), thirty-five Crusader Support and 196 Valentine (Infantry) tanks.

Montgomery would also have 832 25-pounder, thirty-two 4.5-inch and twenty 5.5-inch guns, making a total of 884 guns.

The British Attack on the El Alamein Position

On 21st October, 1942 Colonel Ulrich Liss, Chief of Foreign Armies West (the Intelligence section of the OKH) visited Panzerarmee Afrika. In the war conferences he expressed the opinion that the decisive British attack would not start before the beginning of November. He had in mind various items of information he had received about an operation by the Americans and the British scheduled for the beginning of November; this turned out to be the major Allied landings in French North Africa.

G-2, on the other hand, was convinced that an all-out attack by Eighth Army was imminent. An important indication bearing this out was that before previous operations of this kind in the Western Desert, stretcher-bearers had been called for by a wireless link with the Nile Valley (Heluan) on each occasion eight days before the attack. As just such a demand had been transmitted over the same link on 15th October it could be assumed – in view of the administrative handling of these requests hitherto – that the most probable date of attack would be 23rd October. G-2 supplemented this with a briefing report on 16th October, for the Panzerarmee chief of staff, Colonel Westphal. The draft actually stated, if memory serves, 'The start of the attack can be expected on 23rd October.' But Colonel Westphal changed this precise date to read 'from 20th-25th October' because – as he told the author – an over-precise date might diminish confidence in headquarters and G-2 if the prediction did not come true. The cannonade which erupted on 23rd October at 9:40 P.M. dissipated any doubts that this was the expected all-out attack by Eighth Army.

The Intelligence Summary of 10th October had concluded: 'Various pieces of contradictory information exist as to the timing of the offensive. As assembly of the attacking troops and artillery will take at least one or two days, our own troops cannot be taken by surprise provided they keep their eyes open and make use of every means of observation.'

Among these means was signals intelligence. Several times during October Eighth Army had ordered wireless silence, for example on the 4th and 14th. It occurred again from 9 A.M. on the 22nd to 5 P.M. on the evening of the 23rd. This was confirmed through a decoded cipher signal. The protracted wireless silence was reported to Panzerarmee who regarded it as an additional alarm bell.

The main reason supporting the view that the British offensive took the Germans by surprise was the fact that Field-Marshal Rommel was in Germany at the beginning of the offensive, taking an urgently needed cure. He later wrote himself that his deputy General Stumme was not exactly enthusiastic when he told him that he would break off his cure and return if the British opened a full scale offensive.

But in view of what has been stated above, the thesis sometimes advanced, by German critics too, that the Panzerarmee was completely in the dark about the strength and timing of the British offensive, does not hold water. An all-out attack by Eighth Army had been widely expected any day. Air reconnaissance showed the army getting stronger by the week. The exact date was guessed fairly accurately; on the other hand, the axis of thrust and the sectors of attack were unknown.

The course of the battle is so well known that the only events that need be dealt with here are those connected with our enemy intelligence reports. On 24th October, the second day of the battle, we noticed an increase in enemy wireless activity. A large number of new nets was established: 'D/F indications of intensive enemy concentrations in the *northern* sector of the front' – a first sign of the possible direction of the main attack. By 28th October much light had been thrown on the enemy order of battle by prisoners and captured documents. In the south was XIII Corps with 1st Free French Brigade, 7th Armoured, 44th Infantry, 50th Infantry, 5th Indian Divisions (still the leader identified). In the northern sector, XXX Corps was operating with 1st South African Division, 2nd New Zealand Division, 9th Armoured Brigade, 51st Division and 9th Australian Division. Spearheading the attack by then had been 2nd New Zealand Division, thrusting west-south-west, and 51st Division, thrusting west. X Corps was supporting the two attacking divisions with 10th Armoured and 1st Armoured Divisions. According to captured documents the battle order of X Corps was: Royals (Armoured Reconnaissance Regiment); 8th Armoured Brigade Group, with 3rd RTR, Notts. Yeomanry, Staffs. Yeomanry, 1st Buffs, 1st RHA (Artillery); 24th Armoured Brigade Group, with 41st, 45th, 47th RTR, 9th KRRC, 5th RHA (Artillery); and 133rd Infantry Brigade (Motorised), with 2nd, 4th, 5th Royal Sussex with 104th RHA (Artillery) and 104th RHA (Artillery).

Interrogations of prisoners at the Daba collecting centre yielded valuable results. Especially noteworthy was the previously mentioned revelation by a British soldier that this time the main thrust would not be conducted as a 'left hook' (in the south) but in the northern sector. This reinforced the C-in-C's intention of transferring 21st Panzer Division to the north; he issued the order for the transfer on 26th October at 10:20 P.M. The soldier had given the impression of being well-informed, and this was borne out by the fact that his statement proved to be correct.

Comando Supremo in Rome felt differently. They even warned that at 6 P.M. on 29th October, according to their wireless intelligence two British divisions were on the march across the Qattara Depression, were already at a position sixty miles south of Mersa Matruh, and were turning north to Matruh. The Panzerarmee could not have defended itself against this threat. G-2 regarded it as improbable since the Qattara Depression was impassable for heavy vehicles and tanks unless they were like ducks; the crust on the top of the salt swamp was too thin. Rommel's comment, in spite of G-2's reassurance, was: 'That's all we need right now.' The next morning two Ju88s flew reconnaissance sorties and reported that the region south of Matruh was absolutely clear of the enemy. Only now was he reassured. The message from Rome was a rather bowdlerized indication of future enemy plans; only some days later, on 5th November, would 1st and 7th Armoured Divisions be employed in blocking the coastal road west of Mersa Matruh. However, just when the fate of Rommel and his army seemed sealed, a heavy rainstorm flooded this flat region and converted it into a morass. By the time the enemy could resume pursuit, the German-Italian Panzerarmee had escaped.

Some days later 7th Armoured Division had the same experience when they blocked the escarpment at the Halfaya Pass and Sollum, the most dangerous bottleneck on the road of retreat. The British supply columns were again delayed by heavy rains and this plan also failed.

The enemy breaches in the German-Italian positions from the start of the battle to 1st November were patched up again and again by our counter-attacks, even if some ground was lost. But casualties were heavy because of the enemy artillery superiority and the constant bombing by the RAF. Intercepted enemy signals indicated that most of the German soldiers taken prisoner by the British were wounded.

On 2nd November 'Supercharge', the decisive major push, began. It was to force a definite breakthrough through the German-Italian front. Since Eighth Army learned on 1st November, probably as a result of the German counter-attack near the coast,* that 21st Panzer Division had been shifted north, Montgomery did not adhere to his original plan of attacking as far north as possible but decided to launch his main thrust somewhat farther south, with the Sidi Abd el Rahman track and Tell el Aqqaquir (six miles south of Sidi Abd el Rahman) as objectives.

The 51st (Highland) Division and 2nd New Zealand Division broke through here in order to secure a starting position for the armoured push by 1st and 10th Armoured Divisions. But despite its superiority Eighth Army had still not succeeded in gaining open ground by 3rd November. This was finally achieved in an attack carried out on the following night by 51st Infantry Division and 4th Indian Division.

On 2nd November Comando Supremo advised the Panzerarmee at 8:40 A.M. by radio that according to a reliable source a new British attack on the Egyptian front was imminent on the 2nd and 3rd.

---

* More probably through Ultra. – *Editor's Note.*

Moreover, a full scale landing was to be attempted to the rear of the Panzerarmee. This message was evaluated in the light of the intelligence of 29th October which had proven to be erroneous or at least open to misinterpretation. Besides it had been overtaken by events anyway as Supercharge had been in progress since 1 A.M. on the 2nd.

Rommel, whose Panzerarmee Afrika had been known as the 'German-Italian Panzer Army' since 25th October, reported on 2nd November that he intended to make a fighting retreat to the Fuka position beginning on 3rd November to avoid encirclement and annihilation; in fact the infantry divisions began pulling out that night. At 1:30 P.M. on the 3rd a wireless message arrived from Hitler ordering him not to cede one inch. It ended with the sentence: 'To your troops you can show no other way than Victory or Death'. This message did not comment on Rommel's signal about his intended withdrawal; nonetheless Rommel stopped his retreat. Only after asking again on the evening of the 4th for approval did he learn that the withdrawal was now approved by Hitler. By then he had again ordered the retreat, in a signal issued at 3:30 P.M.. Thus two precious days had elapsed unused, during which however the enemy had also shown little initiative.

On 4th November a wireless message from a British unit was intercepted, which read roughly as follows: 'We have captured a *Herren*; his name is von Thoma. He says he is the Commanding General of the Afrika Korps.'

De Guingand has described how General Montgomery invited General von Thoma to dine with him. They discussed on this occasion the most recent fighting and Montgomery sketched the current situation on the tablecloth. British armoured cars, he claimed, had just raced round to Fuka. Von Thoma admitted that if this was so it would put the German forces in a difficult position; this was very true, but hardly new.

Perhaps we can here comment on the role of Ultra during Alamein. Winterbotham in *The Ultra Secret* claims that Panzerarmee asked for Hitler's 'victory or death' message to be repeated, and that therefore Rommel received it later than Bletchley Park. Ultra, he says, had also previously decoded Rommel's request for approval of his intended retreat. The surviving German wireless messages do not show this, but on 4th November Ultra did decode a message by Rommel admitting defeat even before Montgomery's victory signal reached Churchill – probably Rommel's signal No. 135/42* which in Hitler's reply was referred to as dated 4th November: in this, Rommel openly admitted that there was a six mile wide breach in the northern sector of the main battle front to a depth of ten miles and that since a coherent front no longer existed, the only possibility of inflicting damage on the enemy was by mobile fighting. This intercept lay before Montgomery, when he reported that the objective of the battle had been attained, namely to smash the German-Italian front and to gain open ground for pursuit.

* For full text, see page 231.

CHAPTER FIVE

The Difficulties of gaining Intelligence during the Retreat

Surveillance of a pursuing enemy.

The belated retreat by the Panzerarmee after losing the battle began on 4th November. During this long retreat all the intelligence sources continued to shed light on enemy organisation and strength, but they provided little help as to the enemy's tactical intentions. It was no longer possible to guess at these, quite apart from the fact that given the enemy superiority in tanks and artillery and their huge expenditure of ammunition and aircraft, tactical intelligence was not much use anyway. We were just too weak. We realised this again and again during the further course of the retreat, but fortunately Montgomery was very cautious in pursuing and attacking us.

Of no less importance for the overall situation of the Germans and the Italians in North Africa was that at the same time American and British troops had landed in Morocco and Algiers. We now had to take an advance of these forces to the east into account, even if over the following months, our main fighting front was against the east. On 7th November Colonel Mainwaring, the G-1 (operations officer) of Eighth Army, was taken prisoner at Mersa Matruh after being ordered to reconnoitre a position there for a forward army headquarters. Montgomery had ordered this against the advice of his chief of staff; the place was still held by a rearguard of our 90th Light Division. We hardly needed to interrogate the colonel about Eighth Army intentions; these were clear enough. Late that same afternoon, 90th Light Division repulsed three enemy attacks against Mersa Matruh and took a number of prisoners. But the command of our troops was now hampered not only by the lack of means of communication but also by the appearance of enemy jamming stations.

On 8th November the enemy reached Mersa Matruh. On the 10th Buqbuq fell to 1st Armoured Division, and the area east of Sidi Omar on the Egyptian-Libyan frontier to 7th Armoured Division. We had now identified as these British commanders: XIII Corps, Lt-General Horrocks; XXX Corps, Lt-General Leese; 50th Infantry Division, Major-General Nichols; 1st Armoured Division, Major-General Briggs; 10th Armoured Division, Major-General Gatehouse.

On 11th November the enemy attacked via Capuzzo-Sollum in considerable strength – about one armoured division – then turned north-west and followed the German troops withdrawing to El Adem. From there the enemy continued the attack the next day towards Acroma and re-took the Tobruk stronghold.

Our air reconnaissance reported 6,000 vehicles at Sidi Barrani and Sollum moving west on 13th November; but only smaller enemy forces were reported on the 15th on the south flank at Mechili. But then bad weather stopped further air reconnaissance – rain would impede friend and foe alike frequently during the days that followed. Enemy reconnaissance forces advanced westward from Msus and bore down on our holding troops near Sceleidima in force. Owing to the chronic fuel shortage we could now fly only tactical reconnaissance: this reported on the 22nd heavy traffic heading south from Benghazi and confirmed details of the enemy build up around Agedabia. On the following days the enemy moved south-west through Agedabia, established contact with our rearguards and pushed them back on the 25th.

From signals intelligence we recognised that the enemy movements along the Via Balbia were being badly delayed by our mines. The rear enemy formations followed slowly across Cyrenaica, echeloned in depth as far as air reconnaissance could observe. On 26th November our air reconnaissance reported much traffic from the north-east and east to Agedabia (possibly the 2nd New Zealand Division), and long range air reconnaissance on the following day established that the British were bringing up further forces on the southern road through Barce and Tocra to Benghazi. According to signals intelligence an entire transport brigade was employed on this road alone with twelve companies of 180 tons capacity each. Long range air reconnaissance again confirmed on the 28th that strong enemy forces were approaching southwards through Benghazi. (The 2nd New Zealand Division might have reached Agedabia).

Thus we could expect the enemy would have one armoured and one motorised division in position from about 30th November to attack our Mersa el Brega position: given the rate of movement hitherto observed we could assume it would take two weeks to line up and assemble the mass of the enemy forces. According to wireless reconnaissance the enemy was having difficulty supplying fuel, water and rations. The slow bringing up of the rearward formations might be taken as confirmation of one report according to which the enemy wanted to wait for the restoration of Benghazi's port facilities before starting the build-up against Rommel's Army.

The performance of the German troops during the necessarily rapid withdrawal of the Panzerarmee is vividly mirrored by the report by 621 Company on its own movements:

29th October,	2.45 A.M.:	Company departs for ten miles west of Daba.
3rd November,	4.30 P.M.:	Company departs, new locality six miles south-east of airfield El Qasaba.
4th November,	12 noon:	Receiving station resumes service.
	3.30 P.M.:	Departure of company for ten miles south-west of Mersa Matruh.
5th November,		Company commander ordered to assemble company at Upper Sollum.

During this retreat the company lost two cars and two lorries on the 4th; on the 5th, one lorry east of Matruh, one lorry west of Matruh, three captured lorries at Matruh, and one lorry and one captured lorry west of Daba.

6th November:		Company en route to Upper Sollum.
7th November:		Arrival at new command post eight miles west of Bardia; east of Sidi Barrani the evaluation car was so badly damaged by bombs that it had to be set on fire after the documents were salvaged.
8th November:		Rest of transport arrived.
	10 A.M.:	Receiving service resumed.

During this time No.4 D/F Troop was able to escape from British captivity, as did two men of D/F Troop 2 who were cut off by English armoured cars.

9th November:		After setting up one Y-platoon the rest of the company was despatched to Gambut. D/F Troop 4 arrived at Y-platoon intact.
10th November:		Y-platoon shifted position to Gambut.
11th November:		Baggage train ordered to Signals Equipment Depot at Tobruk, and then to assemble at Martuba. Y-platoon took up new position at 'White House' west of Tobruk.
12th November:		Y-platoon ordered to Tmimi.
	2 P.M.	Resumed operations there.

13th November,	7 A.M.:	Y-platoon departed.
	3 P.M.:	Y-platoon ready to receive two miles west of Martuba crossroads.
14th November,	7 A.M.:	Y-platoon departed for new position at Maraua.
15th November,	5 A.M.:	March continued to Tocra.
16th November,	6.30 A.M.:	Arrival at Benghazi, and
	2 P.M.:	Agedabia. Baggage train sent ahead, reached new position forty miles west of El Agheila.
17th November:		Rest of company arrived there; receiving operations resumed.

It was evident from our intercepts that our mines and demolitions had badly delayed the enemy. On 20th November an unknown unit was heard signalling at 12.31 P.M.: 'If Tocra pass blown up, repair must be finished in one day at most.' An hour later we heard on the command net of 7th Armoured Division: 'Is Tocra also blown up?' At 1:25 P.M. the headquarters of 7th Armoured Division signalled 4th Light Armoured Brigade: 'Road northward from Benghazi is mined.' On the 23rd it was the same story: 7.28 A.M. 'They [the mines] are ingeniously laid and difficult to find. Some are on the road, some beside it. They have been laid in twos, threes and fours. That's why we are advancing rather slowly.' On the 25th at 10.20 A.M.: 'So you'll have to be prepared for considerable delays with us, as we are not advancing at the moment.'

10.35 A.M.: We're moving again but only dead slow.
10.35 A.M.: We advise you to give us as wide a berth as possible. Someone's just blown up again after advancing two yards. Seems we've got into the midst of them.
Yes, stay right where you are! Was that someone blowing up again?
Answer: Not from our lot!

During the retreat, naturally, as is explained by the narrative of 621 Company's transfer, only a few signals revealing the enemy strength and intentions could be intercepted and deciphered. Nevertheless the company recognised that 4th Queen's Own Hussars and 8th King's Royal Irish Hussars had been consolidated into the '4/8th Hussars' and were not two separate armoured regiments as had been hitherto assumed. Moreover our Y-service revealed that the 7th Armoured Division and 4th Light Armoured Brigade were in the

Tocra-Benghazi region on 20th November. Intercepts deciphered and decoded by us made mention of the 7th Armoured Division, 2nd New Zealand Division, 51st Infantry Division, 4th, 8th and 22nd Armoured Brigades, the Royals, 11th Hussars, King's Dragoon Guards and others. These were therefore the formations pursuing the German-Italian Panzerarmee. Yet we were still in the dark about their tactical intentions, while their overall plan to expel the Army slowly but surely by sheer superior strength from North Africa was obvious enough. This changed somewhat at the beginning of December 1942 when, according to the recollection of this author and of Lieutenant Habel, a soldier of 621 Company succeeded in breaking the supply code of 4th Indian Division. Thereafter some of the context of individual signals became clearer and occasionally tactical intentions could be perceived.

On 23rd November, 1942 Major Leibl was appointed G-2 – chief intelligence officer – and took over from the author Lieutenant Behrendt who had filled the post in the interim since 8th October.

On the same day a situation report on the enemy and a survey of his strength after the retreat. This put the following units in the *east*, i.e., facing our army: 7th Armoured Division; 1st and 10th Armoured Divisions under X Corps; New Zealand Division, 9th Australian Division, 1st South African Division and 51st Division under XXX Corps; and 44th and 50th Divisions, and 5th Indian Division, under XIII Corps.

In the *west* there were supposed to be these units: the American 1st Armoured Division, 1st Infantry Division and a further division, the British 65th in Algeria; the American 2nd Armoured Division and 3rd and 4th Infantry Divisions in Morocco. The enemy's aim, our G-2 further indicated, was the annihilation of the Axis forces in North Africa by attacking them on both fronts. At about the end of the month they would attack our Mersa el Brega position using limited forces at first developing into an all-out attack which could be expected in mid-December.

The British Attack on the Mersa el Brega Position

During December 1942 the enemy remained initially quiet but they were continuously reinforcing as our tactical air reconnaissance showed. Longer range air reconnaissance revealed a continued flow of enemy troops and supplies along the Via Balbia through Barce, Tocra and Benghazi; in the latter's harbour two small merchant ships were sighted for the first time on 1st December. Vehicles sighted by tactical air reconnaissance on 4th December at Haseiat, Ghemines, Agedabia and Brega totalled 2,500; this was a marked increase. The assumption that the bulk of 7th Armoured Division and 51st Infantry Division had arrived was confirmed by the interrogation of prisoners of the latter division.

G-2 gained the impression that if Eighth Army launched an early attack it would have 7th Armoured Division, units of 51st Infantry Division and some elements of 9th Australian Division at its disposal. The disengagement of 9th Australian Division after the battle of Alamein had not yet been detected.

The number of vehicles and tanks increased to 7,000 on 7th December. Right up to the 11th we were registering increased patrol activity by the enemy and continuous preparations for an attack. From signals intelligence we knew that the New Zealand Division, 4th Indian Division and the Greek Brigade had passed El Adem on 6th and 7th December – the same day as 152nd and 153rd Infantry Brigade (of 51st Division) had been mentioned in decoded messages.

Long range air reconnaissance reported on 11th December that Benghazi harbour was occupied by eight freighters totalling some 11,000t; so the harbour had apparently been fully restored. Only about three weeks had elapsed since we demolished the harbour, so the short interval had evidently been well utilised by the British Navy. Further long range reconnaissance missions could not be flown because of lack of fuel but also because no serviceable Ju88 aircraft were available.

The anticipated enemy attack on our Mersa el Brega position began on 12th December; thrusts by enemy patrols up to fifteen miles south-south-east of Arco dei Fileni indicated that the enemy intended to force the outcome by an outflanking attack. The employment of 51st (Highland) Division was confirmed by POW statements of the 153rd Infantry Brigade, and signals intelligence established that large parts of 7th Armoured Division were in action against the German front, which was pulled back in the course of the evening.

On 13th December the enemy followed, albeit hesitantly. Our mining of our road of retreat delayed their movements, but wireless and air reconnaissance made it clear that their rearward formations were rapidly closing up. According to wireless reconnaissance, XIII Corps led the assault, with 51st Infantry Division and 7th Armoured Division attacking north-west of Maaten Giofer; an assault from

(*right*) Generalleutnant Ludwig
Crüwell, Rommel's successor as
Commander of the Deutsches
Afrika Korps. From Heinrich
Hoffmann's album.

(*below*) Rommel inspects his
troops with General Gariboldi,
February 1941. The beginning of
a campaign . . .

. . . The end of a campaign: (*above*) the wounded are taken away, and (*below*) an Italian gun graveyard.

further to the south reached the area thirty miles west of that during the afternoon.

On 15th December the enemy tried again to annihilate the bulk of the German-Italian motorised formations, by attacking our front and flanks but they were repulsed. Attempts by the southern encircling group to cut our line of retreat at Merduma also failed after heavy fighting. Parts of 7th Armoured Division and of 2nd New Zealand Division were identified in this group. The enemy hesitantly followed us to south-east of Nofilia. Signals intelligence confirmed that XIII Corps was in command and identified units of 4th Indian Division as well as 44th and 50th Divisions in the second wave that was closely following.

Further outflanking attacks by the enemy north-west of Nofilia on 17th December were thwarted with heavy losses; a thrust by them to the north misfired, as the Africa Korps had withdrawn.

Essential long range reconnaissance could not be flown on 18th December, again owing to the lack of aircraft. But over the following days signals intelligence uncovered revealed frantic supply activities; and subsequent long range reconnaissance observed major enemy concentrations at Nofilia and intense convoy traffic between Agheila and Arco. It was deduced from captured documents that a new outflanking movement, beginning far to the south of Sirte, was being prepared against the flank of our Buerat position. This impression grew stronger when intercepted signals exchanged on the RAF nets confirmed that the enemy was conducting photo reconnaissance of Gheddahiat and Bu Ngem. Eighth Army headquarters was reported by our signals intelligence on 22nd December to be located at Agedabia; on 18th December X Corps had been located at Tmimi, north of Gazala on the Gulf of Bomba).

No significant fighting occurred until 23rd December, and not until 24th December did Eighth Army's advance begin, starting from Nofilia to the south-west and west, and finally reaching the area south of Sirte. On both the 17th and the 18th no long range air reconnaissance could be flown owing to the shortage of aircraft. But on the basis of the available evidence our G-2 appreciated that we were being pursued by 2nd New Zealand Division, with 5th and 6th Infantry Brigades and 1st Armoured Brigade; 51st Infantry Division; 7th Armoured Division with 4th Light Armoured Brigade and 7th Motor Brigade; and 10th Armoured Division with 8th (?)

Armoured Brigade and 131st Motor Brigade. The 22nd Armoured Brigade and 131st Infantry Brigade were also supposed to be near the front. The Eighth Army had moved its command post forward, and we located it on 26th December, north-west of Arco dei Fileni; by that day the enemy had reached Wadi Tamet, twenty miles south of the coastal road, or in other words about thirty miles south-west of Sirte. Once again long rough air reconnaissance proved almost impossible, this time because of cloudy weather; but on the basis of the number of vehicles detected it could be assumed that the four divisions reported were already west of the Arco.

During the night of 27th/28th December the Panzerarmee retreated to the Buerat position. The enemy advanced, now on a broad front, against our rearguards. By the 30th Eighth Army had advanced to the road from Gheddahiat to Bu Ngem, throwing out reconnaissance forces ahead, until we forced them to withdraw by launching an attack which outflanked them to the south. Air reconnaissance confirmed strong enemy forces south-east of Buerat; in fact aerial photos showed more than 6,000 vehicles between Nofilia and Buerat. On the basis of signals intelligence and this photographic cover the following enemy situation was deduced on 29th December: 7th Armoured Division, was believed to be at Bir el Zidan, south of Tmed Hassan, on the coastal road; 2nd New Zealand Division with 8th Armoured Brigade was fifteen miles west of Buerat; 10th Armoured Division was behind 7th Armoured Division east of Wadi Tamet, thirty miles south of the coastal road; and 51st Infantry Division with three infantry brigades and 23rd Armoured Brigade were advancing astride the coastal road between Sirte and Nofilia. The arrival of 23rd Armoured Brigade (equipped with I-tanks) which had been presaged by signals intelligence was confirmed by aerial photos which showed the disembarkation of tanks and tank transporters at Sirte.

Heavy traffic was observed on 30th December by long range air reconnaissance at Arco and Agheila. Coupled with signals intelligence this was taken to mean the transfer of strong elements of Army and Corps artillery which had until then been reported at Mersa el Brega. Intense enemy supply activity was also reported by signals intelligence.

During early January 1943 signals intelligence provided some good material. Between the 1st and 10th it detected the following tanks passing through British traffic control points in the rear: eighteen

American M 3s Stewarts, sixteen I-tanks Mk II Matildas, forty-eight American medium M 3s Grants, fifty-five American medium M 4s Shermans, and 142 cruiser tanks (Crusaders). Altogether they identified 279 tanks and 54 armoured cars. Whilst the location of these control points remained unclear, according to these decoded messages 104 vehicles of 1st Armoured Division passed through Agedabia at 11 A.M. on, 1st January heading west. The records show that between 1st and 6th January we broke two number codes, 1 Codes cipher and 6 Shestex ciphers.

On 7th January we pinpointed the headquarters of 7th Armoured Division at a location eighteen miles south-east of Buerat; on the eighth we identified Eighth Army headquarters ten miles west of Sirte, and the headquarters of XXX Corps fifteen miles south-east of Buerat near the coastal road; this showed that these enemy headquarters were moving forward, which usually heralded a forthcoming attack.

The work of 621 Company was hindered by having to change position – on 15th/16th January via Tarhuna to south of Castel Benito, three miles south of Tripoli, and then on the 20th/21st via Bianchi to Agelat six miles west of Sabratha. Before January was over the company had had to move twice more, finally coming to rest west of Ben Gardane on Tunisian territory.

Earlier that month there had been largely normal enemy artillery and patrol activity. Our air reconnaissance detected continual reinforcement of the enemy and a greater level of activity at airfields near to the front; for instance, 130 aircraft were counted on one airfield near Nofilia. Long range air reconnaissance increasingly furnished the basis of intelligence appreciations – these would have been virtually impossible without it.

Since failure of their last attempt to cut off and annihilate the Panzerarmee 17th December 1942 by outflanking attack, the enemy now began a methodical strategic build-up preparatory to a new attack. This time he would be attacking our Buerat position, and carefully felt his way forwards while establishing lines of supply.

Our G-2 assumed fairly accurately the organisation of Eighth Army to be: In the southern sector 7th Armoured Division (with 4th Light and 22nd Armoured Brigades, and 7th Motor Brigade); 2nd New Zealand Division (with 5th and 6th Brigades and 8th Armoured Brigade). The 133rd Motor Brigade was not deployed.

In the northern sector he located 51st Infantry Division, with 152nd, 153rd and 154th Brigades, 44th Infantry Division (though it had not been noted in wireless traffic for some time). In addition to these the following were thought to be moving forward as of January 8th: X Corps with 1st Armoured Division, 50th Infantry Division and 4th Indian Division. A few days later, however, on January 10th and 19th it was realised that X Corps was still back at Benghazi. G-2 thought that the new enemy offensive could be expected from 11th January onwards.

As for estimating the number of weapons in these enemy formations, after crosschecking the establishments against POW statements, the following picture emerged: 352 guns, 624 anti-tank guns and 580 tanks, in comparison with which on the Panzerarmee side there were 72 German and 98 Italian guns, 111 German and 66 Italian anti-tank guns, and 36 German and 57 Italian tanks.

Even more overwhelming was the enemy superiority in armoured cars, which could be employed in the desert in many ways: opposed to some 200 British armoured cars there were 17 German and 16 Italian.

While light Free French forces advanced against the Italian holding forces at Fezzan, but did not seriously threaten the southern flank of the Panzerarmee, the Army now had to take increasing account of the Tunisian front which had existed since the Allied landings in French North Africa.

On 12th January an important enemy signal was intercepted – Eighth Army intended to shift its forward command post (located by D/F west of Sirte on the 8th) to Tamet, whilst the headquarters of its operations staff was to be transferred to Sirte on the 14th and the Quartermaster Section to Arco dei Fileni.

This suggested that the attack would be shortly resumed. The increase in enemy air activity at night and bombing attacks on troops and headquarters were an additional indication that the attack was imminent. G-2 anticipated that the attack would begin in the middle of the month as the moon would then also be favourable.

The British Attack on the Buerat Position
Early on 15th January 1943 the enemy began his anticipated all-out attack on our Buerat position. The aim of this well prepared British attack was not only to obtain Tripolitania but, more importantly, to destroy the German-Italian Panzerarmee. The main assault was on

our southern front; here, two thrusts were deflected. On the remaining front the enemy completed his preparations. Owing to sandstorms only small scale air reconnaissance operations could be flown, and only during the morning; but these detected intense enemy activity between the front and Sirte. RAF operations were also greatly impeded by the weather.

The next day Eighth Army continued the attacks in the south and north. As Panzerarmee was too weak to withstand the thrust in the north it retired to the general line of Beni Ulid-Bir Dufan-Tauorga. The Eighth Army tried repeatedly to outflank and cut off the Panzerarmee with its strong southern force, but in vain.

The Eighth Army order of battle established during this attack confirmed everything predicted by our G-2, as captured documents showed in detail: the northern group (following the coastal road) consisted of the 51st and 50th (not 44th) Infantry Divisions, and the 23rd Armoured Brigade (with two battalions on transporters); the southern (outflanking) group between Beni Ulid and Tarhuna were the 7th Armoured and 2nd New Zealand divisions and the 8th Armoured Brigade. Not deployed were the 1st Armoured and 44th Infantry Divisions. The British who were making their main effort in the south vigorously pursued the German rearguards and these withdrew after scotching some over-impetuous attacks.

After executing several initially unsuccessful attacks and taking on further stores, the enemy moved forward in strength against our Tarhuna-Homs position on 19th January, committing strong tank forces to a wide outflanking movement towards Garian, with the objective (as captured documents showed) of reaching the town of Zauia and thereby cutting off and destroying the Panzerarmee.

In order to thwart this plan the Tarhuna-Homs position was evacuated.

Meanwhile, the northern force (51st Infantry Division with two tank battalions on transporters) pursued our rearguards which warded off several attacks.

The enemy offensive was continued along the entire front on the 21st. Their southern outflanking force (probably 7th Armoured Division) wheeled to the north and north-west. The units making for Garian ran into bad going – according to the author's recollection our radio monitors intercepted some pretty choice language in which the swear-words flowed quite freely.

Air reconnaissance on 22nd January revealed that the enemy formations had closed up on the area from north-west of Garian to

Tarhuna and that further powerful forces had followed through into the area south and south-west of Tarhuna, where 6,000 vehicles could now be observed. From this it seemed that a further division had arrived, in addition to the two divisions already recognised at the southern end of our front, 7th Armoured and 2nd New Zealand Divisions.

On 23rd January Eighth Army occupied Tripoli. After that it began a cautious pursuit, with a strong northern force on the coastal road and a mobile southern force. The enemy plan continued to be to cut off the Panzerarmee by wide outflanking movements. But it failed again, this time because we counter-attacked against the southern force. Signals intelligence confirmed at this time that X Corps was deployed not at the front but in the rear; its Quartermaster HQ was detected at Um er Rzem, which was north of El Gazala. The same source also detected that 8th and 23rd Armoured Brigades were deployed on the coastal road, and that 4th Light Armoured Brigade was operating thirty miles south of Zauia. Counting and listing all these enemy brigades may seem singularly boring, but for our G-2 it was vitally important to locate all probable formations without missing any, in order to avoid being taken by surprise.

On 28th January the enemy closed up further to our positions. Our air reconnaissance was hindered by overcast, but so were the enemy fighter-bombers as our Y-service intercepted RAF messages reporting them returning with their bombs owing to their inability to find their targets.

It was at this time that Colonel David Stirling, Commander of 1st Special Air Service Regiment, was captured. His task had probably been to reconnoitre the region south of the Mareth Line. The Long Range Desert Group (LRDG) was also very active in South Tunisia.

At the end of January our air reconnaissance observed considerable reinforcement of the Eighth Army's forces in the Sabratha-Zuara area. After seeming extremely cautious at the beginning of February the enemy advanced from the 3rd to 5th with stronger reconnaissance forces along the coastal road.

We learned from captured documents that the 'reconstructed' 4th Light Armoured Brigade consisted of 4/8th Hussars (Stewart Tanks), Greys (Grant tanks), 2nd Derbyshire Yeomanry (with fifty-four armoured cars), and 3rd Royal Horse Artillery with 8.76 cm gun howitzers. This brigade was always employed if quick movements were expected.

Over the next week air reconnaissance was again restricted by bad weather – heavy rain alternating with sandstorms. For this reason no significant enemy thrusts occurred until 12th February. Given our changed circumstances, G-2 now included the situation on the western front the Gafsa-Tozeur area in his appreciation, as well as the existing south-east front against Eighth Army. South-east of Gafsa there was increasing enemy patrol activity although Tozeur and the area to the north of it were occupied only by light enemy forces. A strong Eighth Army thrust towards Ben Gardane pushed our holding forces back, but an enveloping movement failed. On 15th February tactical air reconnaissance detected strong enemy forces just south-east of Ben Gardane and thirty miles south of it.

Greater attention now had to be directed to the western front. The greatest danger was that an American advance might come between the two armies, the German-Italian Panzerarmee and the Fifth Panzerarmee that had been brought over rapidly to defend the Tunisian bridgehead. Our Y-service reported indications that Gafsa had been provisioned by the enemy. Therefore as a prelude to the planned operations against the Americans on the orders of Fifth Panzerarmee 21st Panzer Division had occupied the Faid Pass (sixty miles north of the Gabes Narrows) as early as 1st February and Sidi Bou Zid on 14th February. 21st Panzer Division had been under the command of 5th Panzerarmee since 13th January 1943. We learned from an order intercepted on the 16th that the enemy had orders to avoid contact with the Germans. Therefore we ordered both Panzer divisions (the 10th and the 21st) to take Sbeitla that night; they had succeeded by the evening of the 17th.

In the meantime the Americans had to evacuate Gafsa. It was occupied by our troops on the 15th. From our Y-service we also knew that units of the British 6th Armoured Division were dug in near Sbiba. At Gafsa there was believed to have been only American units – one Combat Command of the 1st Armoured Division; our signals intelligence confirmed the 133rd and 168th Regiments of the 34th Infantry Division and the 81st Armoured Reconnaissance Battalion as well as the 68th Armoured Artillery Battalion of the 1st Armoured Division.

The Battle of Kasserine

During this fighting that began on 19th February, signals intelligence repeatedly yielded valuable troop identifications, but only rarely details of tactical decisions by the enemy of the kind that

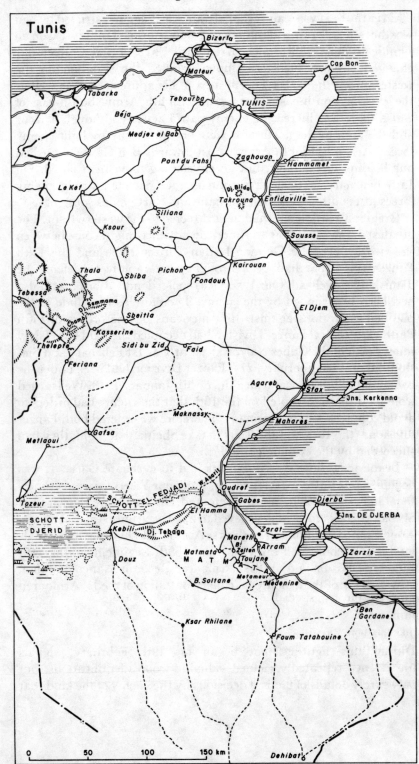

it had provided prior to the summer of 1942. For instance it stated that according to British reports elements of the 1st Guards Brigade could be assumed to be located near Sbiba. As Mark VI Crusader tanks armed with a 3-inch gun were employed there for close support, units of 6th Armoured Division were probably also present there. In addition the remnants of the Combat Commands of the American 1st Armoured Division were again detected, this time south-east of Tebessa.

After heavy fighting the enemy had to evacuate the pass north of Kasserine at 5 P.M. on 20th February, but they continued to reinforce Sbiba and north of Kasserine. By order of the Italian Comando Supremo on 19th February 19th the German offensive was switched to Le Kef about sixty miles north of Kasserine instead of the more north-westerly axis, towards Tebessa-Bône, that Rommel had in mind. There he would not have encountered the enemy reserves and he would have had a better chance of forcing the enemy west and south-west of Tunis to withdraw into Algeria and perhaps of cutting them off altogether. Thus G-2's summary on 21st February reported mounting enemy resistance to our thrusts north-west of Kasserine. After an initial success nine miles north-west of Kasserine the enemy resistance at Sbiba, Thala and west of Kasserine stiffened so much so that orders were given during the night of 22nd-23rd to call off the attack and pull back the attacking troops.

On 23rd February the enemy kept in touch with our retreat only with reconnaissance forces. According to intercepts he was badly hampered by our mines. During the last days of February strong enemy forces approached Sbeitla from the north, but their attacks were halted twenty miles north-east of this town.

Rommel had requested that the Italian General Messe, who had been transferred from Russia to Africa, take command on the Mareth front opposite the Eighth Army, in order to make sure that this front was not deprived of command during his own battles at Kasserine. Messe had been nominated Commander-in-Chief of the German-Italian Panzerarmee on 25th January; he had arrived in Africa on 1st February. At first he declined the position proposed by Rommel, but by special order of Comando Supremo he took command of the First Italian Army – the former German-Italian Panzerarmee – on 20th February.

At that time Rommel was directing the offensive at Kasserine with the 'North Group'. According to the Duce's desire he was to retain command of 'Group Rommel' – the First Italian Army and 'North

Group' – until the Mareth position was reached. But now the First Italian Army took over all the German and Italian troops that had previously been under the German-Italian Panzerarmee.

On 23rd February our order came from Comando Supremo that to provide for the unified command of the forthcoming battles in Tunisia, a headquarters, Army Group Africa, should immediately be activated by the hitherto headquarters of the German-Italian Panzerarmee. Field-Marshal Rommel was to take over this Supreme Command at once – which he confirmed at 6 P.M. – and he was thereupon to report the time and date when Army Group Africa would be taken over by Colonel-General von Arnim, presently commanding the Fifth Panzer Army.

The End of the Rommel Campaign

This development shows that Rommel no longer had such absolute command as before; the Comando Supremo would henceforth intervene increasingly. No special powers of discernment were needed to recognize that this was the end of the Rommel era. That the Comando Supremo had decided on 19th February against Rommel's 'major solution', the thrust to Tebessa, showed very clearly the 'competence' of this command.

In the meantime Eighth Army, following hard on the Axis troops on the south-eastern front, had occupied Foum Tatahouine on 17th February. Air and wireless reconnaissance showed that the bulk of the enemy formations had closed up halfway between Ben Gardane and Medenine. They pressed our holding troops into falling back to the north on the 19th. On the 20th Eighth Army tried to cut off 15th Panzer Division, which was holding a rearguard line, from the south in order to relieve the Allied western front in Tunisia. This attack was repulsed and the Panzer division was then pulled back behind the forward positions on our Mareth Line. Eighth Army followed and settled down in front of the Mareth Line at Medenine.

The counter-attack suggested on the 23rd by Rommel by two or three Panzer divisions against Eighth Army should have resulted in a proper counter-offensive immediately after the end of our attacks at Sbeitla and Kasserine. The preparations for a counter-attack against Eighth Army were not completed as rapidly as desired, since an attack by our Fifth Panzerarmee in northern Tunisia, using 10th and 21st Panzer Divisions, engaged both these divisions Thus they arrived too late at the Mareth front, and Montgomery gained enough time to strengthen his line and build up his anti-tank defences.

Rommel's attempt to turn the tide was finally made on 6th March. His three weak Panzer divisions encountered such stiff resistance that Rommel was forced to decide at 5 P.M. to halt the operation. On the same day several positions which had been evacuated by the British prior to the German attack – the British having received adequate warning from Ultra – were reoccupied by Eighth Army troops.

Rommel decided to fly again to the Führer's Headquarters to report on the untenable situation. He handed over command of Army Group Africa to Colonel-General von Arnim and left Africa on 9th March. He attempted to persuade Hitler to transfer to Italy the troops hitherto employed in Africa in order to repulse Allied invasion attempts, but he did not succeed.

He was not returned to Africa, but obliged to take a cure. How little Hitler had grasped the realities of the situation was demonstrated by his assurance on this occasion that when the time came he would give Rommel command of operations against Casablanca. To Rommel this must have seemed macabre vapourings. He told the author during his cure at Wiener Neustadt that he suffered immensely from the feeling that he had deserted his 'Africans'.

But the Rommel Campaign was at an end when he left Africa. What happened thereafter was a slow, brave finale that ended with Arnim's capitulation on 13th May 1943.

On 8th March Major General Fritz Bayerlein had been nominated chief of staff of First Italian Army. The author, Captain Behrendt, became G-2 but was transferred home on 27th March and departed on the 30th; his successor was Lieutenant Hiltmann, who remained G-2 until the capitulation. Intelligence on the enemy order of battle was, to judge from the G-2 summary of 26th March, fairly comprehensive during the fighting at Mareth. Though the prisoners taken were almost without exception very security-conscious, they often had instructive documents on them. Repeatedly important lists, codes and maps were found on officers. Captured maps often contained the latest air and other reconnaissance data. They showed that German positions and above all the locations of our heavy weapons were reconnoitred very carefully. The grid over-printed on some of these captured maps facilitated the deciphering of the code numbers and letters used to denote pinpoints in enemy signals. Signals intelligence was badly hampered by blanket security measures such as the enciphering of all wireless traffic. But our air reconnaissance often provided timely warning of the displacement of enemy forces. During the fighting retreat from 18th March to 12th April, reconnaissance results were naturally fragmentary. The air reconnaissance suffered at the hands of the superior fighter resistance and prisoners were few and far between. Therefore the detailed enemy picture remained obscure until the final days before Montgomery's offensive on the front of our First Army.

Wireless reconnaissance continued to intercept a multitude of messages but the majority were unproductive. Once in a while an Eighth Army signal might be decoded, like this one on 13th March:

> *T.O.O. 12th March, 1904 hrs:* Still no vehicles back from Dehibat. An officer is to be sent for who reports on the chaotic situation at 'Geisha' (Nalut) pass. Vehicles are without fuel(?).

But even then our forces were in no position to exploit such enemy misfortunes, as was shown by the handwritten remark of the Ic: 'Air command can't get at them!' (Nalut was 100 miles south-west of Zuara on the Libyan-Tunisian frontier.)

With many of the intercepts it was a case of quantity, but seldom quality. Our own command was unable to make use of them anyway, both because of the overwhelming enemy superiority and because of our own impotence which became increasingly evident.

Intelligence from 10th March to early May 1943 produced the following picture: After 12th March the enemy had continued supplying the Mareth front but was also preparing for a possible thrust west of the Matmata mountain to take Gabes from the south. Air reconnaissance detected heavy traffic and reinforcements at Ksar Rhilane. Captured documents revealed that XXX Corps was employed with 51st Infantry Division on the right wing and 7th Armoured Division on the left; the 51st consisted of the 152nd, 153rd and 154th Brigades. Prisoners stated that the 201st Guards Brigade (formerly 22nd or 200th Guards Brigade) was composed of 2nd Scots Guards, 3rd Coldstream Guards, and 6th Grenadier Guards. Air reconnaissance revealed vehicle movements on the deep southern flank, which might be connected with the approach of XXX Corps which was in command there. Signals intelligence reported an unusual silence on all wireless nets on the Mareth front. This suggested that Eighth Army had largely finished their preparations here. Similar signs had been observed before all large scale attacks by Eighth Army.

The target date for the different supply fields mentioned most often was 17th March. Furthermore call sign and frequency changes were ordered over the entire Eighth Army sector for the 17th. This seemed to indicate that 18th March would see the opening of the offensive; after that date the Eighth Army attack might start any day.

In the southern region air reconnaissance observed 800 vehicles thirty miles south-west of Foum Tatahouine, from which it could be assumed that XXX Corps was beginning to bring up reinforcements.

Our assessment of the enemy (as of 15th March) was as follows: The build-up of his main forces under XXX Corps opposite the Mareth front was evidently finished. From captured documents and POW interrogations the following battle array were deduced. In the front-line were, on the right 51st Infantry Division, on the left 7th Armoured Division; and in the second line were, on the right 50th Division, on the left 2nd New Zealand Division. Behind them probably waited the 1st Armoured Division which had reappeared for the first time in the wireless traffic on the 15th. The build-up in the southern sector (X Corps) was still continuing; in the absence of supporting documents about the structure of this Corps our G-2 believed that besides the Free French formations under Leclerc and Koenig, the 10th Armoured Division and perhaps the 4th Light Armoured Brigade came under this Corps' orders.

The enemy attack on the Mareth front started on 16th March at 8:30 P.M. after strong artillery fire. It was parried by a counter-attack by 90th Light Division. According to air reconnaissance the southern enemy group (thirty miles south-west of Foum Tatahouine) had swollen to 3,000 vehicles. Here too signals intelligence detected a significant wireless silence and supply traffic activity at X Corps so that a further attack by the enemy could be expected at any time, the more so as the headquarters of XXX Corps had changed its position.

This all-out attack began on 20th March at 9:45 P.M. with very heavy artillery support, and gained some ground before the leading troops of the southern group, 10th Armoured Division, were held. It had advanced south of the Matmata mountain first to north-west, and now urgently requested – according to our signals intelligence – ammunition and fuel as such strong resistance had apparently not been expected.

Eighth Army executed several lesser attacks in the next few days, and the resulting prisoners gave us a clearer picture of the enemy formations employed. The movement of troops from the rear area and transfers from the Mareth to the southern front made it likely that the decisive attack would be made in the southern sector.

Whilst the Mareth front showed only little activity, the decisive attack began on 26th March at 6 P.M. after a heavy artillery prelude. The X Corps formations attacking on the left flank, supported by artillery and the RAF, succeeded in breaking through south-west of El Hamma on the 27th. They advanced with their forward troops to the level of El Hamma.

Wireless reconnaissance reported that at 2:42 P.M. the enemy had detected considerable Axis vehicle traffic from Gabes to El Hamma and infantry advancing from the north-east to El Hamma; this infantry was to prevent any breakthrough and thus its movements were kept under close surveillance by the enemy. On the 28th our G-2 reported shelling, heavy tank attacks and attempts to break through from the south-west to Gabes; these could be warded off. But the enemy made no attempt to disrupt our withdrawal from the now untenable Mareth front. Italian interrogations of some of the prisoners captured on the Mareth front gave some indication of the toughness of the fighting there. They claimed that the 2nd battalion Scots Guards had been nearly wiped out in the fighting and that the 151st Brigade of 50th Infantry Division had also suffered heavy casualties.

In the first days of April the enemy approached our new position strung across the narrows between Schott el Djerid and the sea; meanwhile attacks by the American Second Corps near Maknassy failed in their bid to cut off the Italian First Army from the Fifth Panzerarmee operating in the north. Early on 6th April after a swift build-up the enemy launched what they hoped would be their decisive attack, and forced our troops to fall back to the north. An unidentified wireless net was heard to transmit at 4:50 P.M. on 7th April, 'We have now made contact with Eighth Army on other side'. And at 9:11 A.M., 'Considerable transport movements during night from Wadi Akarit [Schott position]. It is now reported to be empty.'

Under heavy enemy attack the Italian First Army retreated on 12th April into the Enfidaville position. The enemy attempts to destroy units of the Africa Korps and the Italian First Army which were withdrawing separately failed; the enemy attack was halted at Kairouan and the road to the north remained open.

Early in April the enemy situation seemed to be that X Corps was spearheading the offensive, with the 1st and 10th Armoured

Divisions, 2nd New Zealand Division and parts of 4th Indian Division; behind it followed XXX Corps with 7th Armoured, 50th and 51st Infantry Divisions.

By 13th April the enemy had reached our main line of resistance four miles south of Enfidaville. On the western front the Italians identified prisoners from 6th Armoured Division, including 1st Derbyshire Yeomanry, one of this division's tank units. The presence in line of 4th Indian Division was also confirmed by prisoners of the Royal Sussex Regiment of 7th Indian Brigade taken thirty miles south of Kairouan.

After a five hour artillery barrage on April 20th an offensive was launched against four sectors of our defensive line and breached it in some places. On the 21st the enemy reached Takrouna and occupied Gebel Blida (four miles to the west) after killing or incapacitating the German defenders. The enemy line largely confirmed by prisoners saw the 2nd New Zealand Division on the coast with 4th Indian Division to its left and 7th Armoured Division to the left of that. There was yet no independent confirmation that 50th Infantry Division was at Enfidaville.

On the following days several minor attacks were beaten off but the artillery harassing fire was becoming noticeably more troublesome. On the 27th artillery spotters were able to fly for an hour over the artillery positions of 90th Light and 164th Divisions at 11 A.M., 1 and 4 P.M. because they had not the slightest fighter defence.

In one of the last intelligence summaries issued by the German chief of staff attached to the Italian First Army on 26th April, the following enemy assessment was given:

> Current enemy reinforcements and closing up of forces on the road from Béja to Mateur indicate an imminent attack with newly deployed tank forces 1st US Armoured Division) in the direction of Mateur.
>
> Since despite three days of attacks the enemy has failed to achieve a breakthrough north-east of Bou Arada with his superior tank forces, the impression today is that the enemy is regrouping again in this sector and winding up for an attack further south towards the narrows of Pont du Fahs.
>
> In addition, further displacement of some Eighth Army units to the south-west and west of Pont du Fahs has been detected by both air and ground reconnaissance. Thus a new powerful British attacking force is standing by north-west and south-west of Pont du Fahs. This group probably consists of three armoured divisions and two to three infantry

divisions. At Enfidaville and to the north heavy movements northwards, i.e. a new tank attack is imminent on both sides of the coastal road.

May 6th was the day that marked the beginning of the end for the Fifth Panzerarmee, the Africa Korps and the Italian First Army: the enemy broke through on the road from Mateur to Tunis with powerful tank forces, and in a second thrust at Medjez el Bab destroyed the 15th Panzer Division and opened way into Tunis.

On all fronts there was strong enemy air supremacy. This facilitated the breakthroughs and made it impossible for us to supply our troops. During the days that followed the enemy overwhelmed the forces of Fifth Panzerarmee and Africa Korps piecemeal. They ceased fire after having destroyed their weapons and equipment on 12th May. The Italian First Army reported that it had opened capitulation negotiations on the same day, but after this there was just silence. The final resistance by German and Italian troops in Tunisia must have ended on 13th May 1943. The silence about North Africa in the German High Command war diary after 12th May is very eloquent even after forty years. How optimistic those first OKW reports about Africa had been! But now they passed over the end of Army Group Africa with as little publicity as possible.

The fate of German and Italian prisoners of war was to bear the consequences and march towards Casablanca. More than 100,000 German and 90,000 Italian soldiers went into captivity. An English surgeon a major general, related to the author in 1948 one most unforgettable experience of the campaign. Two columns of Africa veterans passed each other in those days following the capitulation – Montgomery's 7th Armoured Division marching to the victory parade, and Rommel's 90th Light Division marching in the same direction, into captivity. Both columns were in good array, and both were singing the same song, 'Lili Marlene'. Perhaps it was the only success that German radio propaganda ever scored in Africa. From their tank turrets the British officers saluted our men of the 90th Light, or so the author was told by Lieutenant Hiltmann who was marching with his old division. It was a scene of symbolic reconciliation, and a fitting conclusion for any study of a campaign which had been fought with chivalry on both sides.

CHAPTER SIX

Conclusions

Looking back over the whole field of intelligence operations in North Africa, we find some unanswered questions that still need examination. How effective was our intelligence in North Africa during the different phases of the campaign? What influence did it have on the overall direction of operations in the North African theatre and in the war as a whole? What was its role in relation to Rommel himself, the supreme dynamo on the German side?

While from May 1941 onwards the German command had been well briefed on the enemy's plans by signals intelligence, this all but dried up with the twin events at the end of June and early July 1942. These can be considered a turning point. Colonel Bonner Fellers' telegrams ceased late in June and the greater part of 621 Company was annihilated on 10th July and its documents captured by the enemy. This had the further consequence that the British introduced strict wireless security procedures on the German model. This occurred at the very time when Rommel most needed a clear insight into the enemy plans. A third source of intelligence mentioned by Mr Anthony Cave Brown in *Bodyguard of Lies* – the two German agents in Cairo – never produced anything for Rommel, so their arrest late in July was hardly any loss.

During the decisive weeks of July and August 1942, prior to our final attack at Alam Halfa, order of battle information on the enemy was gleaned virtually entirely from POW interrogations; enemy positions were known only from air reconnaissance; but as for the enemy's intentions we were virtually in the dark. In intelligence terms Rommel could be compared to a man accustomed to going around at will and in broad daylight but suddenly forced to grope around in the pitch dark.

But the enemy knew just where and roughly when the German attack at Alam Halfa would be made late in August, thanks to Ultra. This was a further handicap for Rommel.

Although the opening date of Alamein was detected by our signals intelligence, after that our air reconnaissance provided the most reliable intelligence. Signals intercepts certainly recovered some of their former value during our long retreat. But given such overwhelming enemy superiority his intentions could no longer be thwarted, even if they were detected. Since our supplies were usually totally insufficient, especially fuel, the Panzerarmee lacked the necessary mobility to advance offensively against the pursuing forces, a cruel fate for such an active commander as Rommel.

It goes without saying that even the most brilliant intelligence about the enemy cannot replace either soldiers or weapons, equipment, ammunition and fuel, or compensate in the long run for inferiority in the air. This lesson was learned again and again during the Battle of Alamein and the ensuing retreat by the German-Italian Panzerarmee and during the fighting in Tunisia until the capitulation in May 1943.

As for how far intelligence influenced Rommel in his planning the author would go along with the late Ronald Lewin who wrote in *Rommel as Military Commander* that this was by no means clear and that in this respect the Rommel Papers provided little guidance. 'Experience,' wrote Lewin, 'tends to suggest that this may have been less than might be supposed.' During the whole campaign Rommel certainly studied all the most important intelligence carefully and made use of it with imagination and an intuitive insight into the enemy's intentions. His truly extraordinary grasp of the terrain concerned merely by looking at maps helped him particularly in this respect. Intercepted messages about the relief of commanders which therefore highlighted enemy difficulties (as in 1941) may have prompted his counter-attack in January 1942. Equally the titbits from Colonel Fellers about the 'flap' in Cairo may have been instrumental in his decision to pursue the battered Eighth Army that June. The frantic determination of the British to defend their position in Egypt and the Middle East showed clearly how vital both were for the Empire, and how vulnerable Britain was here. Under these circumstances, the Supreme Command in Germany should perhaps have taken a firm decision to defeat Britain in the Middle East. The Axis powers would then have controlled the Iraq oilfields. With their own oilfields at Baku only 500 miles away, the Russians would have had to face facts and take notice of such a menace in the south. The Africa Korps would probably have been strong enough to realise these plans, once Malta had been captured. As it was, the North African theatre, was entered half-heartedly, supplied inadequately and treated as only a secondary theatre of war.

Clausewitz once wrote that war is the domain of the unknown.

Three-quarters of the matters upon which any action in war is built lie more or less shrouded in the fog of uncertainty; a great part of intelligence received in war is contradictory, a still greater part false and by far the greatest is subject to a high degree of uncertainty.

All the more highly Rommel's successes must therefore be rated. They give him a place of honour among the great military commanders in history. He excelled not only in his sheer abundance of ideas and energy, but also in his determination to dispel the uncertainty of war by making use of every source of intelligence. He was always pondering the strength, and still more the intentions, of his opponent. He tried to frustrate them by putting himself in the shoes of the enemy commander. Deception certainly played its part, and Rommel applied it with a wealth of inventiveness. To ascertain what the enemy was up to he was constantly at the front. When the opposing forces clashed he exploited in superior style the intelligence provided by his staff on the basis of air, ground and especially wireless reconnaissance. The Afrika Korps soldiers sensed instinctively that he knew his business as a leader; he was never indecisive and above all, he was often right up there with them, at the front facing the enemy. There he often issued orders that asked a lot of his troops and more, but thanks to their efficiency and devotion they resulted in victories in the 'good times' and were faithfully executed without grumbling during the retreat. Never did his men feel they were being led by an incompetent. Rommel was merciless even with senior officers who could not keep up the pace or meet his requirements. Finding one general still shaving outside his tent at 6:30 A.M. he sent him home immediately. The scene was unpleasant; but his only comment was 'At this time of day the war is half over!' On the other side he appreciated congenial leaders like Crüwell or Westphal, who shared his sorrows with him even if they were not always his kind of man. Those who acted according to Napoleon's dictum '*activité, vitesse*' enjoyed most approval and favour with Rommel. Restless and energetic, he felt responsible to the highest degree for everything going on in his area of command. 'I would like to be here one thousandfold,' he told the author on a desert ride to an Italian division, 'I could take care of everything'.

Of course, Rommel did make mistakes, as von Taysen has described in *Tobruk 1941*. But he grew with his task and, independent thinking as he was, finally paid with his life. This, besides his fame as general, has won him high esteem all over the world.

Finally, a special tribute to Rommel might be mentioned which came from Mr Winston Churchill in 1942. Speaking in the House of Commons in January 1942, he could not resist paying tribute to Rommel: 'We have a very daring and skilful opponent against us,' he declared. 'And, may I say across the havoc of war, a great general.'

He continues in his memoirs: 'My reference to Rommel passed off quite well at the moment. Later on I heard that some people had been offended. They could not feel that any virtue should be recognised in an enemy leader. This churlishness is a well-known streak in human nature, but contrary to the spirit in which a war is won, or a lasting peace established.'

With that tribute to Rommel made in the midst of war and the reference to the spirit that establishes a lasting peace, Churchill has clearly testified to the spirit which could bring subsequent union and finally created a lasting peace between the nations that were at war with one another from 1940 until 1943 in North Africa.

APPENDICES

Text of Signal from Rommel to Hitler admitting defeat at Alamein

To the Führer and Supreme Commander of the Wehrmacht, Führer's Headquarters.

Re your 1130 of 3rd November, I report: In the north sector the enemy has breached the main battle front with 4-500 tanks and strong infantry forces during the last few days on a front six miles wide and up to ten miles deep. The former front line troops have been virtually wiped out. We are doing our utmost to hold the field. But the losses are so high that there is no longer a coherent front.

Reinforcement by fresh German troops is out of the question. Moreover the Italian troops have no fighting strength left in view of enemy superiority on the ground and in the air. Part of the Italian infantry is abandoning previously secure positions without orders.

I am fully aware of the necessity of holding the line to the utmost and not to yield one inch. But I believe that the tactics employed by the British in destroying one formation after the other by rigorous fire concentration and constant air attack is turning the tide against us and increasingly exhausting our troops.

Therefore, as I see it at present the only possibility of doing further damage to the enemy and preventing the loss of North African lies in mobile warfare, and contending with the enemy for every foot of ground. I ask for approval for this.

If this is granted I intend without delay to pull the fighting troops back to a new position running from Fuka to the south. That front is about forty-five miles long and about twenty miles of its southern sector are virtually impassable by large tank formations

ROMMEL, Field Marshal

No. 135/42, Most Secret.

Examples of Colonel's Fellers' signals to Washington from Cairo

June 1st, 1942. 7.11 am.

Report of battle for period May 27 to May 30, obtained from personal observation and conversation with participating British Officers:

May 27: Due to lack of proper security German Armored attacks completely surprised the British resulting in complete break through of the 7th Armored Division on the left. The 3rd India Brigade was nearly destroyed and half of tanks of 4th Armored Brigade were lost. All this happened in first hour of attack. Less than 30 minutes warning was given according to officers. Long supply route was great handicap. Splendid holding of position by Free French forces was the largest factor contributing to the German failure. Approximately 3,000 vehicles withdrew in wild panic, these being remnants of 4th Armored Brigade, 3rd India Motor Brigade, 7th Armored Division and Free French Forces. Germans were obviously materially hurt and British Tank forces were widely scattered and suffered heavy losses. No German air attack developed which was most fortunate.

May 28: Hard attacks on German supply lines were continued by miscellaneous British units and Free French. I saw the British 4th Armored Brigade, supported by artillery, attack, however, they were bombed by their own aircraft. Field was left to the Germans at night when the tanks withdrew to Leaguer since no Infantry was available.

May 29: Heavy dust storms prohibited any attacks.

May 30: Withdrawal through mine field gaps started by Germans. Main tank units on the field were 30 light, 30 medium, and 30 cruisers of the reinforced Armored Brigade. In uncoordinated attacks without artillery or Infantry support, they attacked the German right. I saw the Germans withdraw through mine fields and except for artillery and medium tank fire the British were too weak to attack.

June 1st, 1942 4.43 pm.

Personnel losses of the British are fairly light but loss in materiel heavy. It is estimated that 70% of British tanks engaged were put out of action and at least 50% permanently destroyed. The air ground liaison was poor and the RAF repeatedly bombed own forces. The ground units of the armored divisions were never present to occupy the ground captured by the tanks. The German losses were believed to be only about half that of the British but their ignorance of the situation, their inability to dislodge the front line units, and difficulty of supply caused withdrawal. Although the main action occurred on May 27 replacements had not reached the front on evening of 30th. The bulk of the German tanks could have been destroyed if 2 fresh battalions of American tanks had been available on the morning of May 30. The British will undoubtedly attack as they have adequate replacements in men and materiel and if properly planned will be successful and should go as far as Benghasi. Their supply problem is considerably relieved by railhead in vicinity of El Adem.

Recommendations: Repeated bombings and anti-tank action against friendly tanks was evident during the entire battle and it is essential that American troops have means of definitely identifying ground and air troops. Indications are that medium tanks burned too easily when pierced but most of them were lost because of surprise action at close range. Crews were loud in their praise in spite of this fault. I talked with tank commanders who claimed 8 German tanks to their credit whose tanks had been hit by 88 mm, and as high as twelve times with 50 mm.

June 2nd, 1942 4.42 am.
30 tanks were placed into combat units yesterday of 130 which the British claim were recovered. In the north activities have been slow. Hacheim is still held by the Free French, who claim to have destroyed two work shops of the 21st and 15th Armored Divisions. Axis lines of communication are believed by the British to be very unstable and General Ritchie is planning to push pursuits. Picture may be changed however, by necessity of using units of 1st Armored Brigade as replacements.

Disposition as of June 1:

Axis forces–Well covered by artillery and anti-tank guns in the general areas 36-40 and 36-39. Future moves are not apparent. 300 German tanks have been lost according to British.

British forces–It is believed that the Southern Brigade of the 50th Division has been completely destroyed. 1st and 7th Armored Divisions are being reinforced by units of the 1st Armored Brigade. In square 37-42 is the 4th Armored Brigade with one regiment of the 1st Armored Brigade. Balance of 2nd and 22nd Brigades, totalling approximately one brigade, are in square 37-40. In square 38-40 is the 200th Guard Motor Brigade. Exact position of 7th Motor Brigade is not known but they moved south and west of Bir Hacheim and its car regiment of KDG's was in square U6-5 yesterday.

June 4th 1942 7.49 am.
On night of June 2-3 Germans evacuated Eleut Ettamar, which position was then occupied by British Infantry Battalion, supported from the east by remnant of 4th Armored Brigade. This position has again been attacked from the North by German 70th Armored Tanks with unknown results. The maine German position in mine fields is unchanged.

At Bir Hacheim Free French withstood Italian attack of June 2. RAF assisted with adequate air support. The 7th Motor Brigade is in a position west and slightly north of Free French. Night Flank is being covered by 29th Indian Brigade of 5th Indian Division.

Axis lines of communication are being raided from south by 4th Armored and from the north by 50th Division and 3rd South African Brigade.

The 11th Indian Brigade from 4th Indian Division is now at Tobruk and the 10th Indian Division is moving up in rear of South African Division.

Guide to map symbols*

Army Group Command

Army Command

GHQ of an armoured corps

GHQ of a motor corps

GHQ semi-mobile corps

Command, armoured division

Command, infantry division

Command, motorised infantry division

Command, semi-mobile infantry division

Infantry brigade staff

Armoured regiment staff

Infantry regiment staff

Staff of motorised infantry regiment

Staff of semi-mobile infantry regiment

Rifle regiment staff

Staff of motorised Rifle regiment

Staff of motorised artillery regiment

Staff of armoured regiment

Staff of infantry battalion

Staff of motorised infantry battalion

Staff of motorised artillery regiment

Staff of motorised reconnaissance unit

Commander of armoured squadron

Motorised Rifle company

Anti-tank squadron

Armoured reconnaissance squadron

Battery of light field howitzers in position

Battery of field guns in position

* Units are translated literally from the designations used by German Intelligence of Allied units during the campaign.

Sources and Bibliography

Unpublished Sources

Bundesarchiv-Militärarchiv, Freiburg

RH 19 VIII/	Panzergruppe Afrika, Panzerarmee Afrika, Deutsch-Italienische Panzerarmee, Heeresgruppe Afrika
5	Chefsachen, (Juni) August bis Dezember 1941
6	Pz.Gr. Afrika/Ia, KTB, 15. 8.-18. 11. 1941
7	Pz.Gr. Afrika/Ia, Anlagen zum KTB, 6. 8.-16. 11. 1941
10	Schlachtbericht Pz.Armee Afrika, 18. 11. 1941-6. 2. 1942
13	Pz.Gr. Afrika/Ia, KTB, 7. 2.-25. 5. 1942
14	Pz.Gr. Afrika/Ia, Anlagen zum KTB, 7. 2.-25. 5. 1942
15	Pz.Armee Afrika, Armeebefehl vom 20. 5. 1942
20	Schlachtbericht Pz.Armee Afrika, 26. 5.-27. 7. 1942
25	Pz.Armee Afrika/Ia, KTB, 28. 7.-23. 10. 1942
26	Pz.Armee Afrika/Ia, Anlagen zum KTB, Bd 1, 28. 7.-19. 9. 1942
31	Pz.Armee Afrika/Ia, Schlachtbericht, Bd 1, 23. 10. 1942-15. 1. 1943
32	Pz.Armee Afrika/Ia, Schlachtbericht, Bd 2, 16. 1. 1943-23. 2. 1932
33-46	Anlagebände zu Schlachtberichten, 23. 10. 1942-23. 2. 1943
47	Pz.Gr.Afrika/Ic, Tätigkeitsbericht, 15. 8.-17. 11. 1941 (30. 11. 1941)
48	Pz.Gr.Afrika/Ic, Anlagen zum Tätigkeitsbericht, 15.-31. 8. 1941
49	Pz.Gr.Afrika/Ic, Anlagen zum Tätigkeitsbericht, 1.-30. 9. 1941
50	Pz.Gr.Afrika/Ic, Anlagen zum Tätigkeitsbericht, 1.-31. 10. 1941
51	Pz.Gr.Afrika/Ic, Anlagen zum Tätigkeitsbericht, 1.-17. 11. 1941
52	Pz.Gr.Afrika/Ic, Tätigkeitsberchit, 18. 1. 1941-6. 2. 1942
53	Pz.Gr.Africa/Ic, Anlagen zum Tätigkeitsbericht, 18.-30. 11. 1941
54	Pz.Gr.Afrika/Ic, Anlagen zum Tätigkeitsbericht, 1.-15. 12. 1941
55	Pz.Gr.Afrika/Ic, Anlagen zum Tätigkeitsbericht, 16.-31. 12. 1941

56 Pz.Gr.Afrika/Ic, Anlagen zum Tätigkeitsbericht,
    1.-15. 1. 1942
57 Pz.Gr.Afrika/Ic, Anlagen zum Tätigkeitsbericht,
    16.-31. 1. 1942
58 Pz.Gr.Afrika/Ic, Anlagen zum Tätigkeitsbericht,
    1.-6. 2. 1942
65 Pz.Armee Afrika/Ic, Tätigkeitsbericht, 7.-28. 2. 1942
66 Pz.Armee Afrika/Ic, Anlage A zum Tätigkeitsbericht,
    7.-28. 2. 1942
68 Pz.Armee Afrika/Ic, Tätigkeitsbericht, 1.-31. 3. 1942
69 Pz.Armee Afrika/Ic, Anlage A zum Tätigkeitsbericht,
    1.-31. 3. 1942
71 Pz.Armee Afrika/Ic, Tätigkeitsbericht, 1.30. 4. 1942
72 Pz.Armee Afrika/Ic, Anlagen zum Tätigkeitsbericht,
    Bd 1, 29. 3.-30. 4. 1942
74 Pz.Armee Afrika/Ic, Tätigkeitsbericht, 1.-25. 5. 1942
75 Pz.Armee Afrika/Ic, Anlage A zum Tätigkeitsbericht,
    1.-25. 5. 1942, Teil 1
76 Pz.Armee Afrika/Ic, Anlage A zum Tätigkeitsbericht,
    1.-25. 5. 1942, Teil 2
78 Pz.Armee Afrika/Ic, Anlagen C-E zum Tätigkeitsbericht,
    1.-25. 5. 1942
79 Pz.Armee Afrika/Ia Nr. 50/42 g.Kdos.Chefs. vom
    20. 5. 1942, Anlage 1, Feindnachrichtenblatt
80 Pz.Armee Afrika/Ic, Anlagen G-K zum Tätigkeitsbericht,
    1.-25. 5. 1942
81 Pz.Armee Afrika/Ic, Tätigkeitsbericht, 28. 7.-31. 8. 1942
82 Pz.Armee Afrika/Ic, Anlage A zum Tätigkeitsbericht,
    28. 7.-31. 8. 1942, Teil I
83 Pz.Armee Afrika/Ic, Anlage A zum Tätigkeitsbericht,
    28. 7.-31. 8. 1942, Teil II
85-86 Pz.Armee Afrika/Ic, Anlagen zum Tätigkeitsbericht,
    28. 7.-31. 8. 1942
87 Pz.Armee Afrika/Ic, Tätigkeitsbericht, 1.-30. 9. 1942
88 Pz.Armee Afrika/Ic, Anlage A zum Tätigkeitsbericht,
    1.-30. 9. 1942, Teil I
89 Pz.Armee Afrika/Ic, Anlage A zum Tätigkeitsbericht,
    1.-30. 9. 1942, Teil II
91 Pz.Armee Afrika/Ic, Anlagen C-E zum Tätigkeitsbericht,
    1.-30. 9. 1942
92 Pz.Armee Afrika/Ic, Anlagen F-H zum Tätigkeitsbericht,
    1.-30. 9. 1942
93 Pz.Armee Afrika/Ic, Tätigkeitsbericht, 1.-31. 10. 1942
94 Pz.Armee Afrika/Ic, Anlagen zum Tätigkeitsbericht,
    1.-31. 10. 1942

96 Obkdo. Deutsch-Italienische Pz.Armee/Ic,
    Tätigkeitsbericht, 1.-30. 11. 1942
97 Pz.Armee Afrika/Ic, Anlagen zum Tätigkeitsbericht,
    1.-30. 11. 1942, Bs 1
99 Pz.Armee Afrika/Ic, Anlage zum Tätigkeitsbericht,
    Dezember 1942
100 Pz.Armee Afrika/Ic, Anlagen zum Tätigkeitsbericht,
    Januar 1943
101 Pz.Armee Afrika/Ic, Anlagen zum Tätigkeitsbericht,
    Februar 1943
105 Pz.Gruppe Afrika, Offizier-Stellenbesetzung 19. 10. 1941
106 Pz.Armee Afrika, Stab, Geburtstagsliste
133 Pz.Armee Afrika, Armee-Pionier-Führer, Planung nach
    Ägypten hinein (Nilakte)
322 Handakte Gen. Fdm. Rommel, Dezember 1940-April 1943

RH 31 VIII Deutscher Chef des Generalstabes der italienischen 1. Armee
4   Deutscher Chef GenSt ital. 1. Armee/Ic,
    Tätigkeitsbericht, 8. 3.-27. 4. 1943
5   Deutscher Chef GenSt ital. 1. Armee/Ic, Anlagen zum
    Tätigkeitsbericht, 8. 3.-27. 4. 1943
6-10 Funkmeldungen April 1943, März 1943

RH 24-200 Deutsches Afrikakorps
1   D
    DAK/Ia, KTB Nr. 1, 6. 2. 1941-14. 8. 1941 (Abschrift)
2   DAK/Ia, Gedanken des DAK über die Fortführung der
    Offensive gegen Ägypten. Planstudie des DAK vom
    27. 7. 1941, mit Stellungnahme OKH/GenStdH/Gen.
    Qu. vom 27. 8. 1941
3   DAK/Ia, KTB nr. 2, 15. 8.-17. 10. 1941
87 DAK/IIa, Geschäftsverteilungsplan vom 4. 6. 1941
89 DAK/III, KTB, 5. 4.-26. 8. 1941
91 DAK/III, Wasserversorgung der deutschen Truppen in
    Nordafrika
117 HQ U.S.Army, Logistical Reasons Germans Lost in
    North Africa

Public Record Office, London

W.O.201/2150 GSI (S) GHQ MEF, Captured Enemy Documents April
              1942-March 1943, German Wireless Intercept
              Organization
        2154 HQ Eighth Army, Intelligence Summaries 255, 257, 278
    169/4042 30 Corps Signals, War Diary, 20. 5.-27. 10. 1942 (Auszüge)

Military History Research Office: Freiburg

Typewritten manuscripts:
B-495 Rintelen, Enno, v., Die deutsch-italienische Zusammenarbeit im II.
    Weltkrieg
P-038 German Radio Intelligence, S. 51-64

Privately owned:
Baillieu, Everard, Melbourne, Documents about the attack of 10 July 1942
    by 2/24th Aust Inf Bn.
Bryant, D., Colonel (RL) MBE MC, report on the attack of 10 July 1942,
    as Commander 'C'-Company 2/48 Aust Inf Bn, dated 7.1.1975
Finlay, C.H., Major-General, CB, CBE. Letter about 10 July 1942, as then
    Brigade-Major 2/26th Aust Brig.
Good, S.H., Lt.-Col. Record of his impressions of 10 July 1942 as Staff
    Captain 9 Aust Div dated 4.11.1974.
Habel, Heinrich, Hauptmann; Note on the Radio Intercept Service,
    2.10.1974.
Hanley, Jack W. Note on his investigations for 10 July 1942 dated
    10.4.1975.
Hässler, Leader Intercept Platoon of 621 Company information of 1.6.1977
    about the end of the company.
Hundt, Werner, Coy-Chief Panzer Pionierbataillon 33, 'Thus began the
    Africa Campaign for me'.
Mainwaring, Hugh S.K., Brigadier: Three Score Years and Ten, Chester 1976.
Neurath, Constantin Frhr. v., Letter dated 17 June 1974 on the beginning
    of the Alamein Battle in October 1942
Ponath, Lt.-Col., Commander MG-Btl.8, Diary extract from 27 Feb-8
    April 1941 (sent by Australian War Memorial, Canberra, as appendix
    of 'Report of Operations in Cyrenaica' of 9 Australian Division
    entitled: 'Translated Extracts of Diary of Oberstleutnant Gustav
    Ponath, Late Commander 8 Machine Gun Battalion (5 Light
    Motorized Division) killed at Tobruk 14 April 1941).'
Rommel, Erwin, Afrika-Diaries, transcribed from shorthand of Lance-
    Corporal Böttcher by David Irving
Wischmann, Berno, Lieutenant in 621 Company. Information on the
    10.7.1942, dated 27.2.1974.

Literature:
Bagnold, Ralph A., Libyan Sands, London 1941
Barnett, Corelli, The Desert Generals, London 1960
Bayerlein, Fritz, El Alamein, in: The Fatal Decisions, New York 1956
Behrendt, Hans-Otto, Ratschläge für Wüstenfahrten in Ägypten, Kairo
    1936
Brown, Anthony Cave, Bodyguard of Lies, 1976

Burdick, Charles B., Unternehmen Sonnenblume. Der Entschluß zum
    Afrika-Feldzug, Neckargemünd 1972 (= Die Wehrmacht im Kampf,
    Bd 48)
Carell, Paul, The Desert Foxes, London 1960
Churchill, Winston S., The Second World War, Vol IV. 1951.
Ders., Weltabenteuer im Dienst, Hamburg 1951
Clausewitz, Carl v., Vom Kriege, Bonn 1952
Connell, John, Auchinleck. A Biography of Field-Marshal Sir Claude
    Auchinleck, London 1959
Cordier, Sherwood Stanley, Erwin Rommel as Commander, High
    Wycombe 1963
Cowles, Virginia, Who dares, wins (The Phantom Major), London 1958
Dixon, Norman F., On the Psychology of Military Incompetence, London
    1976
Dumreicher, André v., Fahrten, Pfadfinder und Beduinen in den Wüsten
    Ägyptens, München 1931
Eppler, John W., Rommel ruft Kairo. Aus dem Tagebuch eines Spions
    (nach Gesprächen, Tagebuchnotizen und zeitgenössischen Berichten
    gestaltet von Heinz Görz), Gütersloh 1960
Gause, Alfred, Der Feldzug in Nordafrika im Jahre 1941/42/43, in:
    Wehrwissenschaftliche Rundschau, 1962, H. 10, S. 594-618, H. 11, S.
    652-680, H. 12, S. 720-728
Geyr v. Schweppenburg, Leo Frhr., Erinnerungen eines Militär-Attachés,
    Stuttgart 1949
Guingand, Sir Francis de, Operation Victory, London 1947
Gunzenhäuser, Max, Geschichte des Geheimen Nachrichtendienstes.
    Literaturbericht und Bibliographie, Frankfurt/M. 1968 (= Schriften
    der Bibliothek für Zeitgeschichte, N.F. H.7)
Hinsley, F.A., British Intelligence in the Second World War, Vol. I,
    London 1979
Irving, David, Hitler and seine Faldherren, Frankfurt/M. 1975
Kahn, David, The Codebreakers. The Story of Secret Writing, London,
    1969
Kriegstagebuch des Oberkommandos der Wehrmacht
    (Wehrmachtführungsstab) 1940-1945, geführt von Helmuth Greiner
    und Percy Ernst Schramm, im Auftrage des Arbeitskreises für
    Wehrforschung herausgegeben von Percy Ernst Schramm in
    Zusammenarbeit mit Hans-Adolf Jacobsen, Andreas Hillgruber und
    Walter Hubatsch, 4 Bde, Frankfurt/M. 1961-1965.
Lewin, Ronald, Rommel as Military Commander, London 1968
Liddell Hart, Basil H., The Other Side of the Hill, 1948.
Liddell Hart, How Hitler missed in the Middle East, in: Marine Corps
    Gazette, November 1956, Nr. 11, S. 50-54

Liss, Ulrich, Was der Truppenoffizier vom Nachrichtendienst wissen soll, in: Truppendienst, 3. Jg (1964), H. 2 and 3, S. 128-130 and 208 f.

Masterman, John C., The Double-Cross System in the War of 1939 to 1945, New Haven 1972

Maughan, Barton, Tobruk and El Alamein, Canberra 1966 (= Australia in the War of 1939-1945, Series 1: Army, Vol. III)

Mellenthin, Friedrich Wilhelm v., Panzer Battles 1939-1945. A Study of the Employment of Armour in the Second World War, London 1952

Montgomery, Bernard L., Memoirs, London 1958

Moorehead, Alan, African Trilogy. Comprising Mediterranean Front, A Year of Battle, The End in Africa (1940/43), London 1944

Murray, G.W., Dare me to the Desert, London 1967

Nalder, R.F.H., The History of British Army Signals in the Second World War, London 1953

Peillard, Léonce, Geschichte des U-Boot-Krieges 1939-1945, Wien 1970

Playfair, J.S.O., The Mediterranean and Middle East, Vol. I-IV, London 1954, 1956, 1960, 1966 (= History of the Second World War.) HMSO Official History. 1948.

Randewig, Kunibert, 50 Jahre deutsche Heeres-Funk-, Nachrichten- und Fernmelde-Aufklärung, in: Wehrwissenschaftliche Rundschau, 14. Jg. (1964), H. 10, S. 615-621, H. 11, S. 685-693

Rintelen, Enno v., Mussolini als Bundesgenosse, Erinnerungen des deutschen Militärattachés in Rom 1936-1943, Tübingen und Stuttgart 1951

Rohlfs, Gerhard, Drei Monate in der Libyschen Wüste, Kassel 1875

Rommel, Erwin, Krieg ohne Haß, Heidenheim 1950

Rommel, The Rommel Papers. Ed. by B. H. Liddell Hart, London 1953

Schramm, Wilhelm v., Der Geheimdienst in Europa 1937-1945, München, Wien 1974

Senger and Etterlin, Ferdinand M. v., Der Kampfpanzer von 1916-1966, München 1966

Shaw, William B.K., Long Range Desert Group – The Story of its Work in Libya 1940-1943, London 1959

Sievers Fonck, Harald, El extrano caso de la compania de Radioexploración del Mariscal Rommel, Memorial del Ejercito de Chile, Ano 1946, Nr. 255 (1953), S. 85-87

Steffens, Hans v., Salaam. Geheimkommando zum Nil – 1942, Neckargemünd 1960 (=Landser am Feind, Bd 6)

Taysen, Adalbert v., Tobruk 1941. Der Kampf in Nordafrika, Freiburg 1976 (= Einzelschriften zur militärischen Geschichte des Zweiten Weltkrieges, Bd 21)

Ufficio Storico,
    In Africa settentrionale. La preparazione al conflitto. L'avanzata su

Sidi El Barrani (ottobre 1935 – settembre 1940), Roma 1955

La prima offensiva britannica in Africa settentrionale (ottobre 1940 – febbraio 1941), Roma 1964

La prima controffensiva italo-tedesca in Africa settetrionale (15 febraio-18 novembre 1941), Roma 1974

Seconda offensiva britannica in Africa settentrionale e ripiegamento italo-tedesco nella Sirtica orientale (18 novembre 1941-17 gennaio 1942), Rome 1949

Seconda controffensiva italo-tedesca in Africa settentrionale da El Agheila a El Alamein (gennaio – settembre 1942), Roma ²1971

Terza offensiva britannica in Africa settentrionale. La Battaglia di El Alamein e il ripiegamento in Tunesia (6 settembre 1942 – 4 febbraio 1943), Roma 1961

Operazioni italo-tedesche in Tunesia (11 novembre 1942 – 13 maggio 1943), Tomo I, La Iᵃ Armata Italiana in Tunesia, Roma 1950

Verney, G.L., The Desert Rats. The History of the 7th Armoured Division 1938 to 1945, London 1954

Walther, Johannes, Das Gesetz der Wüstenbildung in Gegenwart und Vorzeit, Leipzig ⁴1924

Ward, Philip, Touring Libya, London 1969

Warlimont, Walter, Im Hauptquartier der Deutschen Wehrmacht 1939-1945. Grundlagen, Formen, Gestalten, Frankfurt/M. 1962

Warlimont, Walter, Die Entscheidung im Mittelmeer, in: Entscheidungsschlachten des Weltkrieges, hrsg. von Hans Adolf Jacobsen and Jürgen Rohwer, Frankfurt/M. 1960

Westphal, Siegfried, Heer in Fesseln. Aus den Papieren des Stabschefs von Rommel, Kesselring und Rundstedt, Bonn 1952

Westphal, Siegfried, Schicksal Nodafrika, Döffingen Kreis Böblingen 1954

Westphal, Siegfried, Erinnerungen, Mainz 1975

Winterbotham, F.W., The Ultra Secret, London 1974

Young, Desmond, Rommel, London 1950

INDEX